# PIPE FITTINGS

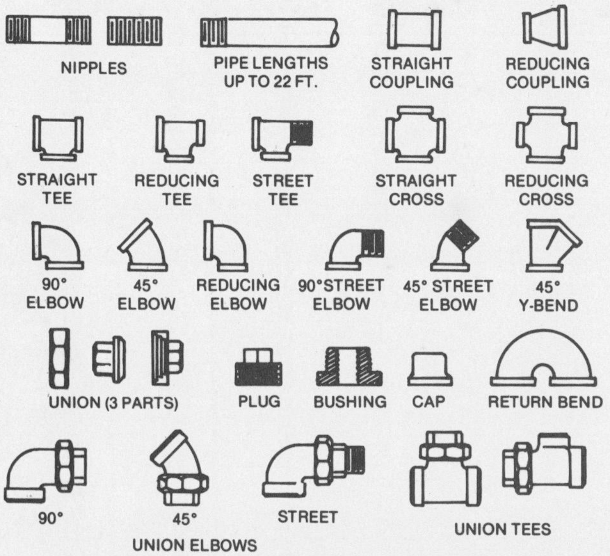


Here are the common steel pipe fittings. Nipples are simply short lengths of pipe threaded on both ends. Reducing fittings join two different sizes of pipe.

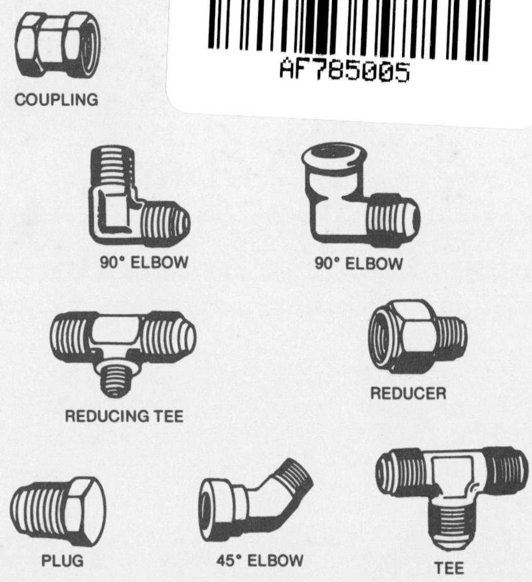


Compression fittings of the flared-tube type are the easiest for the novice to handle when working with copper tubing.

| STANDARD STEEL PIPE (All Dimensions in Inches) | | | | | |
|---|---|---|---|---|---|
| Nominal Size | Outside Diameter | Inside Diameter | Nominal Size | Outside Diameter | Inside Diameter |
| 1/8 | 0.405 | 0.269 | 1 | 1.315 | 1.049 |
| 1/4 | 0.540 | 0.364 | 1 1/4 | 1.660 | 1.380 |
| 3/8 | 0.675 | 0.493 | 1 1/2 | 1.900 | 1.610 |
| 1/2 | 0.840 | 0.622 | 2 | 2.375 | 2.067 |
| 3/4 | 1.050 | 0.824 | 2 1/2 | 2.875 | 2.469 |

## SQUARE MEASURE

144 sq in = 1 sq ft
9 sq ft = 1 sq yd
272.25 sq ft = 1 sq rod
160 sq rods = 1 acre

## VOLUME MEASURE

1728 cu in = 1 cu ft
27 cu ft = 1 cu yd

## MEASURES OF CAPACITY

1 cup = 8 fl oz
2 cups = 1 pint
2 pints = 1 quart
4 quarts = 1 gallon
2 gallons = 1 peck
4 pecks = 1 bushel

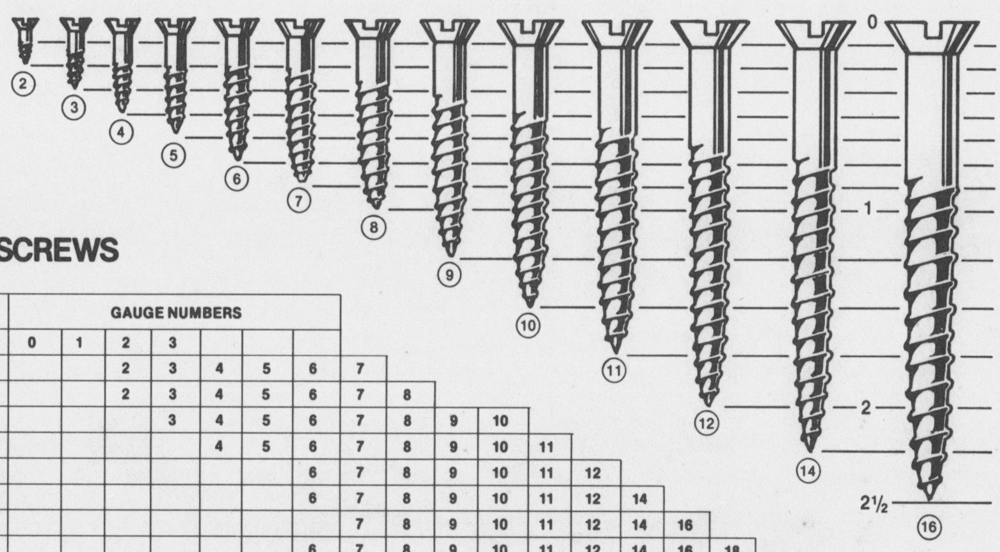


## WOOD SCREWS

| LENGTH | GAUGE NUMBERS | | | | | | | | | | | | | | | | |
|---|---|---|---|---|---|---|---|---|---|---|---|---|---|---|---|---|---|
| 1/4 INCH | 0 | 1 | 2 | 3 | | | | | | | | | | | | | |
| 3/8 INCH | | | 2 | 3 | 4 | 5 | 6 | 7 | | | | | | | | | |
| 1/2 INCH | | | 2 | 3 | 4 | 5 | 6 | 7 | 8 | | | | | | | | |
| 5/8 INCH | | | | 3 | 4 | 5 | 6 | 7 | 8 | 9 | 10 | | | | | | |
| 3/4 INCH | | | | | 4 | 5 | 6 | 7 | 8 | 9 | 10 | 11 | | | | | |
| 7/8 INCH | | | | | | | 6 | 7 | 8 | 9 | 10 | 11 | 12 | | | | |
| 1 INCH | | | | | | | 6 | 7 | 8 | 9 | 10 | 11 | 12 | 14 | | | |
| 1 1/4 INCH | | | | | | | | 7 | 8 | 9 | 10 | 11 | 12 | 14 | 16 | | |
| 1 1/2 INCH | | | | | | | 6 | 7 | 8 | 9 | 10 | 11 | 12 | 14 | 16 | 18 | |
| 1 3/4 INCH | | | | | | | | | 8 | 9 | 10 | 11 | 12 | 14 | 16 | 18 | 20 | |
| 2 INCH | | | | | | | | | 8 | 9 | 10 | 11 | 12 | 14 | 16 | 18 | 20 | |
| 2 1/4 INCH | | | | | | | | | | 9 | 10 | 11 | 12 | 14 | 16 | 18 | 20 | |
| 2 1/2 INCH | | | | | | | | | | | | | 12 | 14 | 16 | 18 | 20 | |
| 2 3/4 INCH | | | | | | | | | | | | | | 14 | 16 | 18 | 20 | |
| 3 INCH | | | | | | | | | | | | | | | 16 | 18 | 20 | |
| 3 1/2 INCH | | | | | | | | | | | | | | | | 18 | 20 | 24 |
| 4 INCH | | | | | | | | | | | | | | | | 18 | 20 | 24 |

WHEN YOU BUY SCREWS, SPECIFY (1) LENGTH, (2) GAUGE NUMBER, (3) TYPE OF HEAD—FLAT, ROUND, OR OVAL, (4) MATERIAL—STEEL, BRASS, BRONZE, ETC., (5) FINISH—BRIGHT, STEEL BLUED, CADMIUM, NICKEL, OR CHROMIUM PLATED.

# In this volume . . .

**BUILD THIS CONTEMPORARY** toolbox and someday it will be an heirloom. Beautifully crafted drawers carry small tools and hardware, and the top serves as a work surface. Because the toolbox is hefty when loaded, we've fitted it with a removable strap for over-the-shoulder carrying. You'll find plans on page 2896.

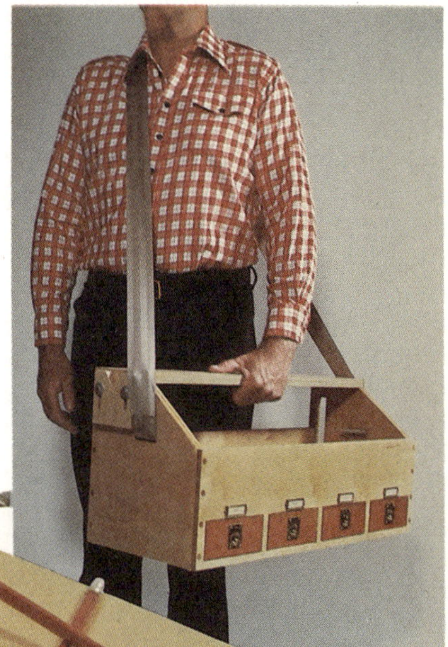

**HERE THEY COME!** Four racing cars roar down the track to an exciting finish. You can make this handsome toy yourself, mostly from scraps you'll find around the house. The plastic cars are available at toy stores. See complete plans on page 2922.

**THESE BEAUTIFULLY DESIGNED** toys not only are fun to play with, they're fun to make. They include a circus-wagon toy box, a giraffe clothes tree, a gobbling whale, a classic wood-block train, and a separate engine that puff-puffs as it's pulled across the floor. We know that *you* know certain children who'd love to have these special toys. Plans start on page 2914.

**HOW DO YOU CHOOSE** the right tree for your yard? It should be handsome in winter as well as summer, clean, and do its job well, whether that job is shading your home, decorating a patio, or providing a privacy screen. Find tips on selecting trees on page 2952.

**THIS ROLLABOUT STACK** of swinging trays offers ingenious storage for the hobbyist or the man with a home office. You'll find complete plans on page 2949.

Popular Mechanics

# do-it-yourself encyclopedia

in 20 volumes

a complete how-to guide for the homeowner, the hobbyist—
and anyone who enjoys working with mind and hands!

All about:

home maintenance
home-improvement projects
wall paneling
burglary and fire protection
furniture projects
finishing and refinishing furniture
outdoor living
home remodeling
solutions to home problems
challenging woodworking projects
hobbies and handicrafts
model making
weekend projects
workshop shortcuts and techniques
hand-tool skills
power-tool know-how
shop-made tools
car repairs
car maintenance
appliance repair
boating
hunting
fishing
camping
photography projects
radio, TV and electronics know-how
clever hints and tips
projects just for fun

volume 19

ISBN 0-87851-084-2
Library of Congress Catalog Number 77 84920



MANUFACTURED IN THE UNITED STATES OF AMERICA

# contents

VOLUME 19

# How to read a tire label

By MORT SCHULTZ

■ CAR OWNERS who need tires should disregard advertisements. Instead, they should learn to read the "gobbledygook" on the tires themselves in order to determine which tire best suits their needs and also gives them the best value. Markings on sidewalls tell you all you need to know about each tire, except its price.

Since the adoption of the U.S. Government Uniform Tire Quality Grading (UTQG) standard, sidewall markings reveal more than ever. The purpose of the UTQG is to allow buyers to judge each tire against others to determine if a less expensive tire has lower, the same or better qualities *for their needs* than more expensive tires.

**three ratings given**

Three ratings are embossed on a tire alongside the terms *tread wear, traction* and *temperature.* The tread-wear rating is a numerical designation.

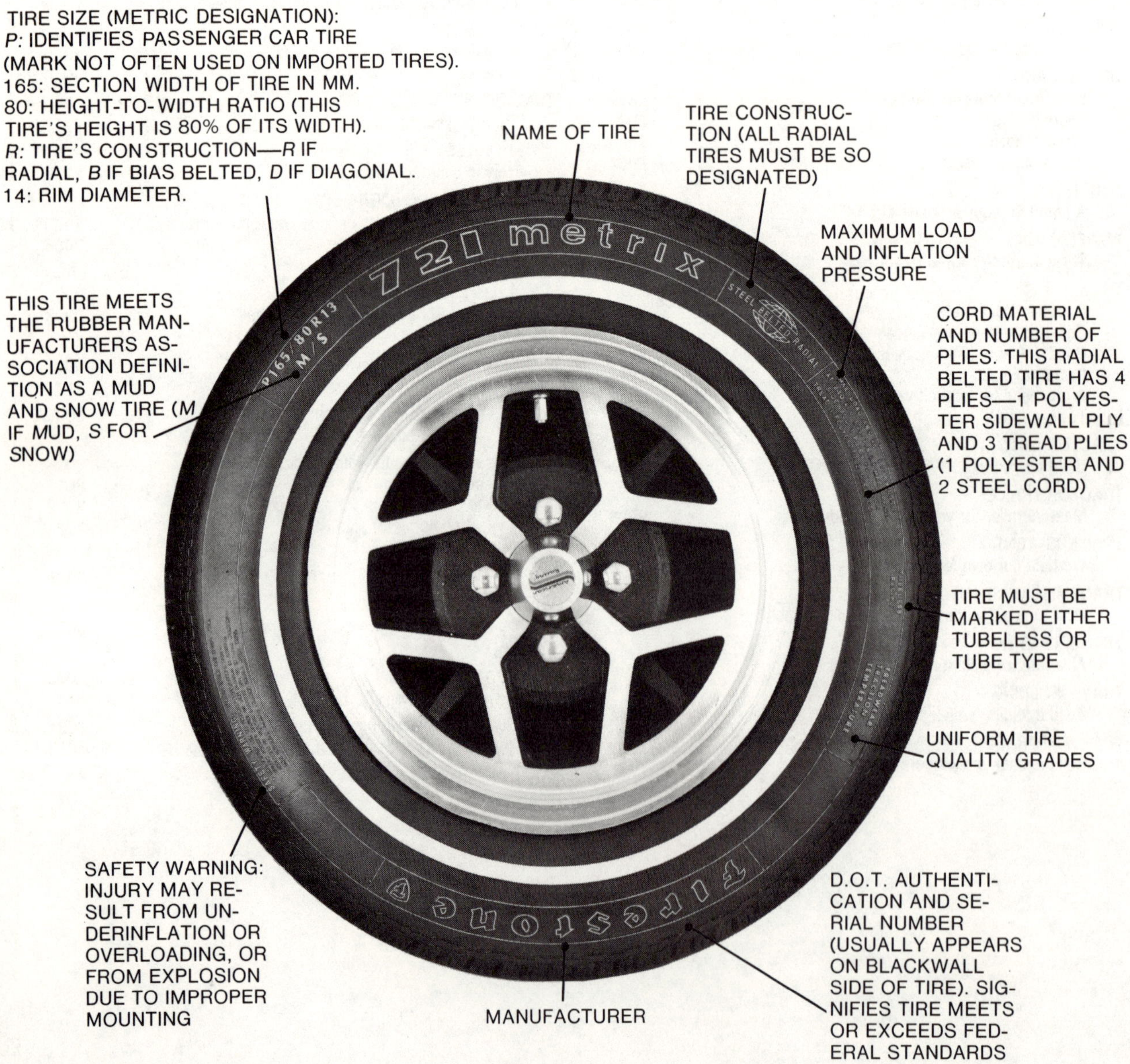

According to government tests that are done to establish grades, a tire with a higher number is likely to give longer tread life than a tire with a lower number when they are used under similar conditions. For example, a tire having a tread-wear rating of 180 should provide longer tread life than a tire with a tread-wear rating of 150.

Comparative government tread-wear ratings signify a 3000-mile difference in tread wear for each 10-point difference in the rating comparison. Thus, all things being equal, government testing suggests that the tire having a rating of 180 should get 9000 more miles of tread wear than the tire having a rating of 150.

Traction and temperature ratings are given as the letters *A, B* or *C. A* is the highest rating, *B* is next and is followed by *C.*

Traction refers to wet traction; that is, the ability of the tire to hold its grip on a wet roadway. Thus, according to the grading system, a tire with a rating of *A* has demonstrated an ability to provide better traction on a wet roadway than tires having ratings of *B* and *C.*

The temperature rating on a sidewall indicates temperature resistance and is a measure of a tire's ability to withstand the higher temperatures generated by high speed, overloading the tire and underinflating. Again, an *A* rating is highest, *B* is next and *C* follows.

**interpreting ratings**

It is important to interpret ratings realistically. Consider tread wear and traction.

The components put into a tire to give it long tread life can reduce its ability to provide the best traction on a wet road. Therefore, if your driving is confined primarily a wet climate, you may want to buy a tire that, according to the government rating system, provides maximum traction in preference to one that affords the best tread wear.

Similarly, if most of your driving is done at sustained high speeds, a tire that is graded as resisting temperature the best may be the one to consider. However, the three factors that make tires run hot—underinflation, overloading and exceeding the speed limit—are within your means to control.

**maximum load and pressure**

The operational characteristics of a tire just mentioned are also printed on the sidewall. They are the maximum load the tire can handle and the recommended maximum inflation pressure. The tire shown, for example, will accommodate a maximum of 1069 lbs. when inflated to a recommended maximum pressure of 35 psi (pounds per square inch).

*Note:* Both English and metric scales are used on most modern tires, since most are sold in the U.S. and overseas.

The recommended maximum inflation pressure is the pressure the tire should be inflated to when it is cold. Sustained highway driving raises the cold-starting pressure by several psi. However, this is allowed for in the tire design and poses no danger.

Quite the contrary. The additional pressure is necessary to permit the tire to resist the higher temperature generated by use. Therefore, never reduce air pressure when tires are hot, and check tire pressure and add air only after the car has been parked for at least three hours.

**markings that you may see**

Another designation that may or may not be printed on a tire (it is not shown on the tire in the photograph) is load range. This is a letter designation that is of little consequence, since the actual maximum load range and maximum inflation pressure are provided. The load range (*A, B, C* or *D*) identifies a given tire with its load and inflation limits. However, a table is needed to interpret the meaning of each letter.

There is another designation that may or may not be provided. It is the Tire Performance Criteria (TPC) number and indicates that the particular tire meets performance specifications established by General Motors.

If you have a GM car and want to replace an original tire with a tire that meets the exact specifications set by GM for the car, read the TPC number off the original tires and find a replacement that has this number embossed on the sidewall.

Consult the illustration for explanation of other sidewall markings.

**MARKINGS MAY CHANGE**

Although most sidewall markings have remained consistent, some have been revised and others have been added or deleted over a period of time. Therefore, some of the information in this article, which was accurate at the time it was written, may no longer apply. For example, as this article is in preparation, the National Highway Traffic Safety Administration is considering suspending the tread-wear grading requirement of the Uniform Tire Quality Grading standard. When buying tires, you may or may not find this rating on sidewalls.

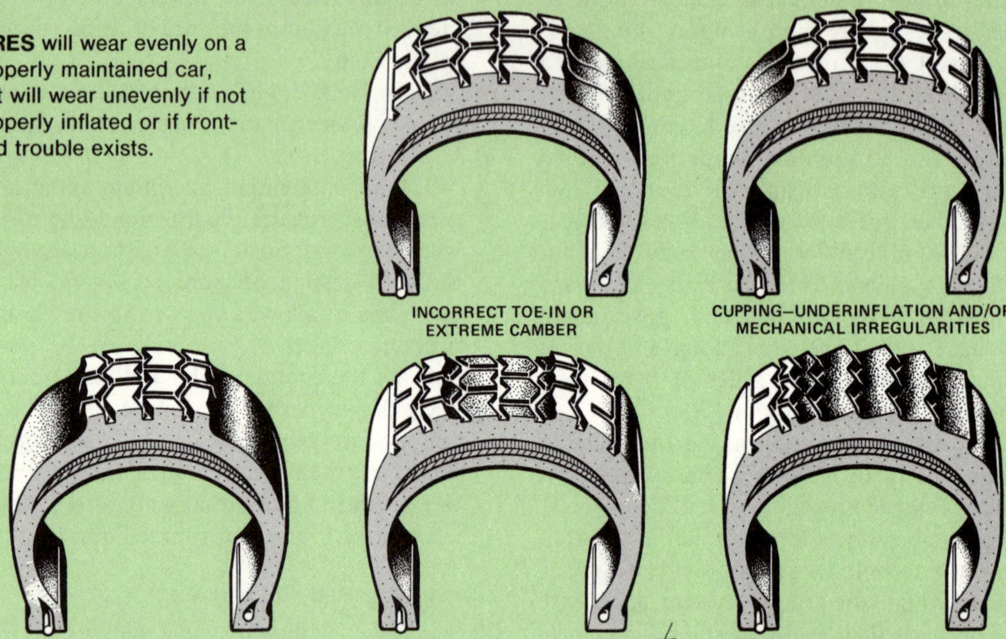


**TIRES** will wear evenly on a properly maintained car, but will wear unevenly if not properly inflated or if front-end trouble exists.

# How to take care of your tires

DID YOU EVER WONDER why your tires are wearing unevenly? Or why your radials have a tendency to shimmy? Perhaps it has to do with unequal inflation pressure or the pattern you used the last time you rotated them.

Unequal inflation pressure between radial tires will hamper vehicle stability. Keep your pressure gauge handy always. You may actually extend the useful life of radials beyond 40,000 miles, and the useful life of bias-type tires many thousands of miles, by checking pressure every day and making certain it is to the recommended level.

Radial tires will exhibit oscillations resulting in shimmy between 50 and 60 mph if tire-wheel assembly balance is the least bit off. The assemblies should be tested, but keep in mind that balancing radials with static-type balancing equipment will probably *not* improve or eliminate the condition.

In a radial situation, tire-wheel assemblies should balanced dynamically. The dynamic balancer may be off-the-car or on-the-car equipment. Both types are effective.

Before we explain the difference between static and dynamic balance, this important point must be made:

Many car owners believe that any equipment which tests balance on the car is dynamic equipment. This is not the case. Static equipment consists of both the familiar off-the-car bubble balancer and on-the-car equipment that spins the assembly, but with insufficient force to cause oscillation if it is present.

SEE ALSO
**Autos, maintenance . . . Brakes, auto . . .**
**Chains, tire . . . Steering and suspension, auto**

**static dynamic forces**

When a wheel-tire assembly is statically out-of-balance, it means that a heavy spot exists at a single point on the assembly. As the assembly rotates, the heavy spot is forced against the pavement with each revolution. This will create a significant vertical vibration—a bouncing effect.

If a tire and wheel assembly that is out-of-balance statically were balanced in midair on a shaft, the assembly would always revolve and come to rest with the unbalanced portion on the bottom, in dead center.

**static or dynamic imbalance?**

If you have a problem deciding whether the condition you feel as you drive is being caused by static or dynamic imbalance, remember that static imbalance creates a vibration at slow speeds. Dynamic imbalance shows up at 50 to 60 mph.

Dynamic imbalance refers to a wheel-tire assembly that has masses which are throwing equalization out of kilter at more than a single point. This creates an oscillating effect—a side-to-side movement. Not only will shimmy result, but if the situation is allowed to continue, the tire may develop flat spots. As the offending assembly oscillates, the tire is scuffed against the pavement.

Let's sum it up with two key points:

**1.** If you are getting a pronounced vibration in a car that's equipped with radial tires and inflation pressure is correct and equal, have the tire-wheel assemblies balanced with dynamic balancing equipment.

**2.** If the condition persists after balancing, switch tires front to rear.

**mugwumping down the road**

Sometimes a car will be unstable towards one side of the road. It doesn't lead straight and has to be oversteered. This can result in a very strenuous driving situation.

The rigid belts in radials when coupled with natural road crown and crosswinds are the factor. Once correct tire pressure is confirmed and it has been established that the power steering gear valve is centered properly and isn't the cause, there is a definite procedure to follow that should eliminate or at least reduce substantially an over-leading condition. Here it is:

Cross-switch the *front* tire and the wheel assemblies only. The car will now lead either in the opposite direction or in the same direction when it's road-tested. If the car should lead in the *opposite* direction, switch the tires as follows: LF to LR, LR to LF, RF to RR, RR to RF. Now:

**1.** If the car still leads, cross-switch *front* tire only. Road-test it once more.

**2.** If the car still leads, replace the right front tire with the spare. Test again.

**3.** If the car still leads, the left front tire is to blame. Replace it.

If the car leads in the *same* direction, the prob-

**FOR LONGER** tread life, it is strongly suggested that you rotate your tires following these patterns.

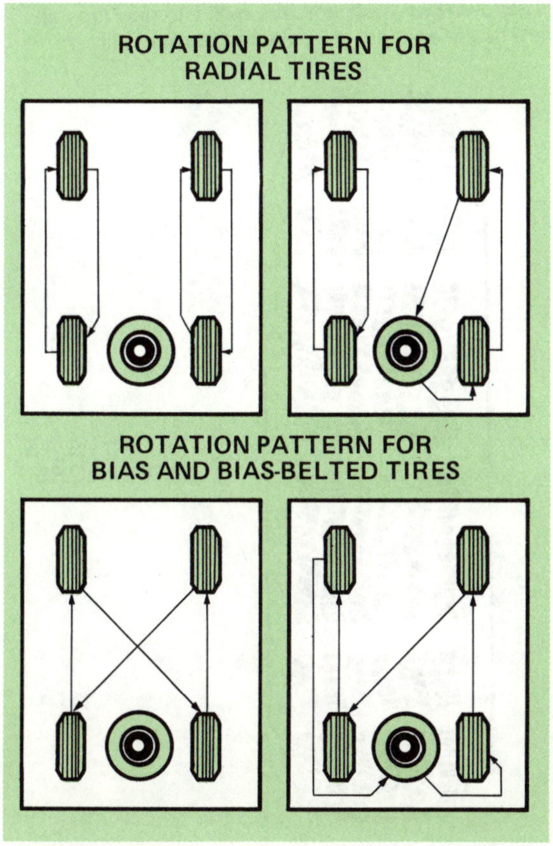


**ACCURATE** tire-pressure gauge should always be used to check each tire for proper inflation.

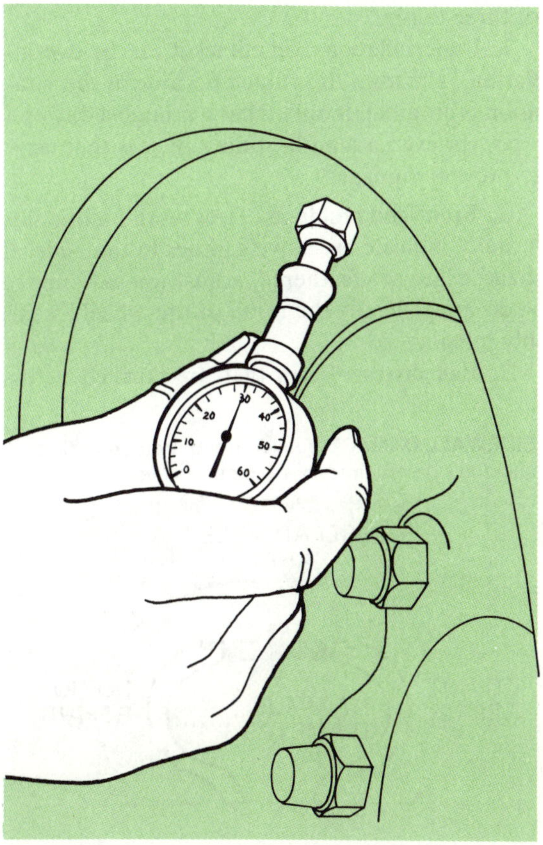

able cause of your trouble is front-end misalignment.

If the car still leads after adjusting the alignment to specification, increase the caster in the direction of lead ½° at a time until the pull is eliminated. In other words, if the lead is to the left, increase the left caster—leave the right alone. If the lead is to the right, try increasing the right caster and leave the left one alone.

**additional radial information**

Two more facts about radials should be mentioned:

■ Never try to eliminate the bulge where the tire contacts the road. It's natural and inflating a radial until the bulge is eliminated will ruin the tire. Inflate to specification only.

■ Radial tires can be repaired if they are punctured. However, the puncture must not be more than ¼ inch in diameter, which gives you a lot of latitude, and it has to be confined to the major tread area, between the outer grooves. If the puncture doesn't meet these conditions, the tire should be replaced.

**tire wear tells story**

One concern among many car owners is tire-wear patterns. As you can see by the illustrations, abnormal tire wear can usually be traced to one of three things:

**1. Underinflation** (sometimes it can be overinflation). Having a tire ruined because of this situation is criminal. It only takes a minute a day or a week (or even a month, if the driver is that lazy) to prevent damage.

**2. Front-end problems.** Tires worn on one side usually indicate excessive camber to that side. If tread edges are feathered, adjust toe-in. Cupped spots are generally the result of tire-wheel assembly imbalanced.

**3. Bad driving.** Tires that are cracked across the tread or that wear out rather quickly although inflation is maintained often indicate that the driver is engaging in a lot of screeching stops and starts, is trying to negotiate corners and curves on two wheels, and/or is hauling excessively heavy loads. Well, it's his money he's wasting—a set of new skins doesn't come cheap.

**give tramp the bum's rap**

The only other significant tire problem that we haven't touched on, but one that shows up from time to time, is an out-of-round tire that creates a tramp or thump at 20 to 30 mph. There is a precise procedure you can follow to find the offending tire:

■ Inflate all tires to 50 pounds pressure and take the car for a test drive. If tramp has vanished, it confirms the presence of an eccentric tire.

■ Now reduce one of the tires to its normal pressure and test drive again. Tramp? If not, then this tire is not the guilty one.

■ Continue in this manner, reducing pressure in one tire at a time and test driving, until the reappearance of tramp uncovers the bad tire.

■ Return the tire to whomever you bought it from to receive an allowance on a new one.

**SIDEWALL DAMAGE** outside tread area on radials shouldn't be repaired, nor punctures over ¼ in.

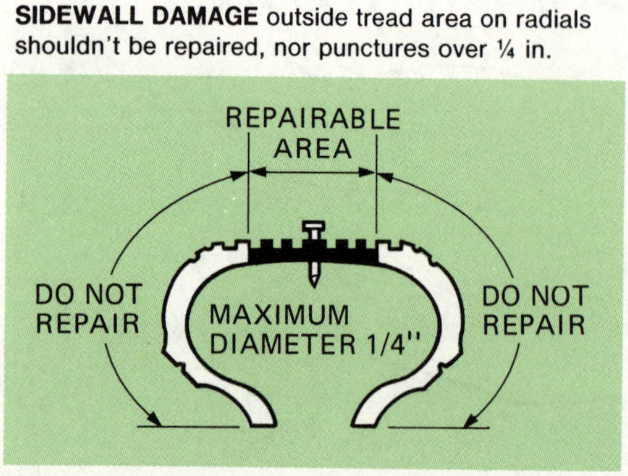


**TREAD-WEAR** indicators are built into new tires and are designed to tell you when to replace a tire.

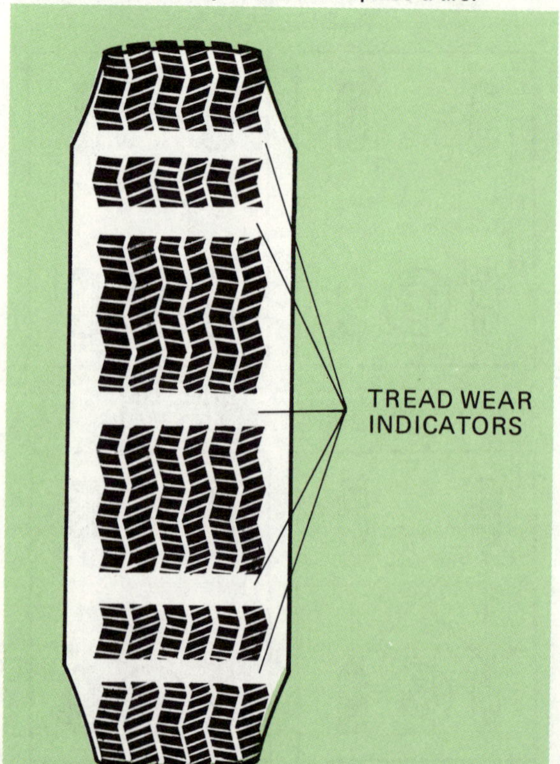

**Painting aluminum siding**

*I'm about to paint my aluminum siding. What preparations must I take? What type paint must I use?—Tom Johnson, Burlington, N.J.*

Aluminum siding has a built-in cleansing action called chalking. According to a spokesman for Reynolds Aluminum, chalking span varies from geographical region to region. The theory is that after the siding has chalked, rains will wash it and the dirt away. Then the cycle repeats.

You can use a good-quality exterior latex paint on aluminum siding. In addition, PPG Industries, 1 Gateway Center, Pittsburgh, Pa. 15222, has recently developed an exterior finish designed expressly for aluminum and steel siding called Metal Siding Refinish.

First wash the aluminum with this solution: ⅓ cup detergent (Tide), ⅔ cup sodium phosphate (Soilax), 1 quart Clorox and 3 quarts water. Apply solution with a sponge and hose off. Don't use abrasives and avoid contact with the solution.

**Tanks for nothing**

*When we converted from oil to gas heat, we were left with a 500 gallon oil tank buried in our front yard. Removing it or filling it with concrete would be too expensive. Filling it with water would only cause it to rust and collapse. Help!—Paul Gustafson, Saginaw, Mich.*

First, I would check with a local heating contractor. Depending on the age of your tank, he may be willing to dig it up and back-fill the hole for salvage value.

I believe the tank will last as is for years. But, if it really bothers you, try this: 500 gallons is only about two and one half cu. yds. of mortar sand. Have it dumped near the filler neck and fill the tank through a large funnel. Sand pours easily and will compact well in the tank. This might be a good time to invite your relatives for a barbecue!

**Furniture marks in carpets**

*I have wall-to-wall carpeting. Whenever I rearrange furniture there are always deep indentations in the carpeting left by the furniture legs. Is there some way of raising the nap to the original level?—C. Mann, Dallas, Tex.*

If you are referring to textured carpeting rather than the shag types, I think I can help. I've used a suede shoe brush for this purpose. It works out well where the pile is deeply textured. Brush lightly and in several directions. On some types of carpeting a few drops of water will do the trick. Plastic leg pads to prevent such indentations are also available. Check your local hardware or floor coverings dealer.

**To seal or not to seal**

*I just had my driveway paved. Two neighbors had theirs paved, too. All of us used different contractors. My contractor said to seal the driveway, but the others said not to seal it, as the driveway had to breathe. Who's right?—W. Zuscin.*

Since you haven't mentioned whether the driveways were paved with asphalt or concrete, here's some food for thought on both. The Asphalt Institute, Asphalt Institute Building, College Park, Md. 20740, says defintely don't seal new driveways. Since asphalt is "cut" and softened by gasoline and oil, some commercial installations—where heavy vehicular traffic can be a problem (for example, gas stations)—are sealed with a coal-tar emulsion. This sealer is applied cold 60 to 90 days after installation. Aside from this application, new asphalt is usually not sealed.

For cosmetic reasons, you may want to seal an asphalt driveway every three to five years. Most hardware stores and home centers, as well as Sears Roebuck and Co., sell coal-tar driveway sealers.

The Portland Cement Assn., 5420 Old Orchard Rd., Skokie, Ill. 60077, says that concrete driveways normally aren't sealed. However, in a very cold climate you might want to seal concrete poured in September with a diluted linseed-oil sealer. This could be brushed on in November to help prevent spalling over the first winter.

In very warm climates, a curing compound is sometimes sprayed on the concrete as soon as it is floated smooth. This retards evaporation and ensures better quality concrete.

A rule of thumb might be: Rarely seal concrete driveways. For aesthetic reasons only, seal asphalt driveways three or more years after installation.

**Damp concrete floors**

*How do we eliminate the cold dampness of the concrete floor at a lake cottage in Northern Michigan? We've heard that putting down plastic topped by hardboard would help solve the problem. Although we read your column, we've never seen this mentioned.—Jim Okuly, Saginaw, Mich.*

Not only would it help, but if you then add carpet and pad, you will have it made. Remove the baseboard and carefully lay a minimum of 4-mil-thick polyethylene plastic on the floor, taping it at least 1 in. up the walls. Set your ¼-in.-thick tempered hardboard so there is a minimum ½-in. gap between it and all walls. Leave a 1/16-in. gap at joints.

# How to repair a pop-up toaster

**It's one of the most intricately designed small appliances in the home, but don't let that fact throw you. It also happens to be one of the most reliable devices and many of its common malfunctions are easy to repair**

THE ELECTRIC POP-UP toaster is not an appliance that is easily repaired if it suffers a major parts failure. How it operates is not difficult to comprehend, but in practice the various mechanisms, levers, elements and switches make this one of the most difficult appliances in the home to salvage if a major breakdown occurs (Figure 1).

Fortunately, there are redeeming factors. First of all, the electric pop-up toaster is probably the most reliable small appliance you own. It probably will last a score of years or more, and the cost of a replacement is not great. Furthermore, if it does develop a malfunction within a relatively short period of time, the cause more often than not is a *minor* one that is easy to fix.

Keep things in perspective. Do not probe for complex answers to simple problems.

**how electric pop-ups work**

An electric pop-up toaster must perform several distinct functions in order to give you your morning toast. It must latch the cradle (carriage) holding bread firmly in place when the lever controlling the cradle is pushed down. It must then turn on electricity so the heating elements that do the actual toasting can begin glowing.

As with room heaters, the heating elements in a toaster are commonly made of a nickel-chromium alloy, called nichrome. Elements are connected in parallel in most toasters, so they are controlled by a common conductor.

Smaller toasters have three elements so two slices of bread may be toasted simultaneously. Larger toasters have more than three elements so that four or more slices of bread can be handled at a time.

SEE ALSO

**Appliance repair . . . Electrical wiring . . . Food mixers . . . Food processors . . . Irons . . . Kitchens . . . Mixers, food . . . Ranges**

*Caution:* A toaster's heating elements are not insulated. Touching one, even if the toaster is not turned on, may result in serious injury since one side of the heater circuit is always "live"—it is in constant touch with the wall outlet. When working on a toaster, make certain that it is disconnected from the wall plug except when taking voltage readings. In this case, keep the toaster disconnected until the voltmeter is connected—then plug it into the outlet, but keep your hands away from "live" elements.

Another function that an automatic toaster must perform is to shut off the current to the elements when the toast is done. At the same time it must trigger a latch that allows the cradle to surface. However, the spring-loaded cradle must have a brake on it to prevent it from snapping up too forcefully, which could cause the toast to fly halfway across the room. (Indeed that happened frequently in the very early models!)

Manufacturers have devised various methods to perform each of these functions. There is no reason to delve into each method that has been used—there are too many. A general discussion of the more common methods probably will cover your model (Figure 2).

Generally speaking, when you push down the cradle-control lever, you cause the cradle to engage a mechanical latch. (In models in which bread lowers itself automatically, a motor is used. When bread is placed in the cradle, it causes a switch to close that starts the motor which lowers the rack by means of gears.)

At the same time that the cradle is lowered, a switch is closed that activates the heater-element circuit, allowing current to flow and elements to glow.

"Light," "medium," or "dark" toast commonly is achieved by a timing mechanism that winds itself up when the cradle is pushed down. A bimetal regulator (or compensator) is used in many toasters so the first slices of toast, which are made with a cold appliance, will be toasted

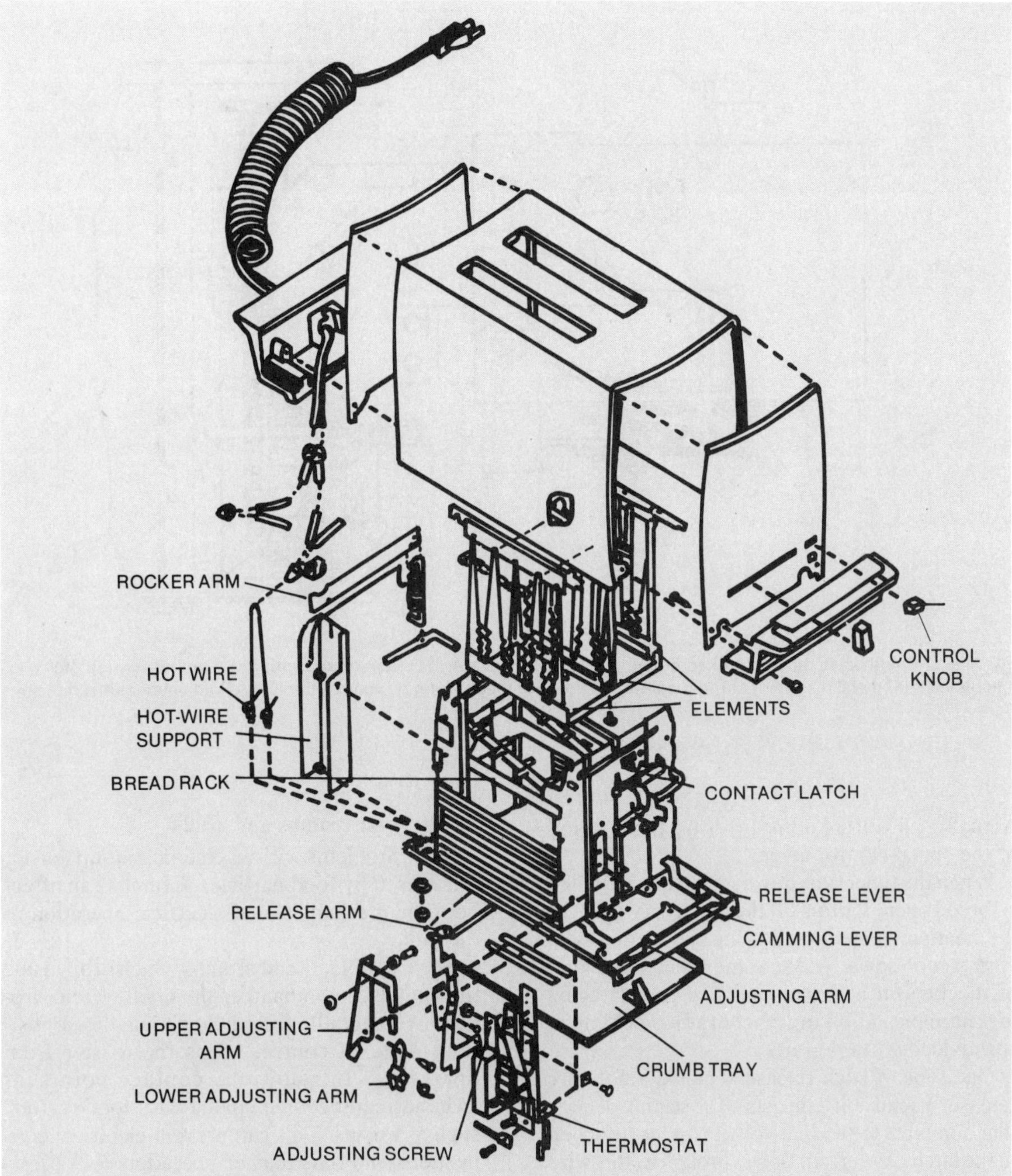


**FIGURE 1.** This drawing of a typical electric pop-up toaster shows what you face when you attempt to repair one. With all of its mechanisms, it is one of the most intricate small appliances.

the same as the second and subsequent slices, which are made with a hot appliance.

When the toaster is cold, the bimetal regulator is straight and does not come into contact with the timing mechanism. The mechanism is allowed to wind down for the longest period of time, giving bread more time to toast.

However, with the toaster hot and subsequent slices of bread placed in it for toasting, less time is needed. Heat affects the bimetal strip, bending it toward a speed-control lever. This lever controls the timing mechanism. When the lever is "pushed" by the bimetal strip, it causes the mechanism to speed up, which in turn results in a shorter period of operation of the timer.

The timing mechanism is set for light or dark toast, or any degree in between, by turning a knob or sliding a lever on the outside of the case.

**FIGURE 2.** Thermostatically controlled cradle mechanism includes: (1) rack-return spring; (2) guide rod; (3) latch mechanism; (4) metal blade; (5) contact points; (6) hooking mechanism; (7) contact points; (8) adjustment mechanism.

Actually, all you are doing is setting the position of the speed-control lever.

When the timer runs down, an auxiliary switch is forced open. It turns off the electricity going to the heating elements, allowing the elements to start a cool-down. At the same time, some kind of mechanism activates and trips the latching mechanism, allowing the cradle, which is spring-loaded, to pop up.

One type of latch release is called a hot-wire release, because it consists of a strand of wire that connects to the line voltage and is attached to the latch. As current flows through it, this wire gets hot and expands. But when current to the elements is shut off, it is also shut off to the hot-wire release. The wire cools down and contracts. As it contracts, it "pulls" the latch release with it, thus releasing the cradle.

Another interesting element in an electric pop-up toaster is a shock absorber, or snubber, that cushions the cradle as it springs up. This device is similar in operation to a pneumatic stop that is employed by storm doors to keep the door from slamming. The snubber puts the brake to the cradle, allowing it to ease up so the toast doesn't fly out.

**the big foes: crumbs and crud**

Most problems with an electric pop-up toaster are caused by food particles. Crumbs can affect both the mechanical and electrical operation of the unit.

For example, bread crumbs which drop inside the appliance can hamper the cradle latch, preventing the cradle from holding in a down position. This, of course, keeps the toaster from operating. In addition, contact points of switches can become coated with food matter, such as raisins. This can prevent electrical connections and thus toaster operation.

You should clean your toaster periodically and thereby avoid foreign-matter problems.

Most toasters have clean-out traps that permit you to reach inside and brush out dirt (Figure 3). First *detach the power cord*. Open the trap door and brush particles from all surfaces you can reach with a one-inch paint brush that is used only for this purpose (Figure 4).

If the toaster doesn't have a trap door, disconnect the power cord and turn the appliance upside down. Shake it vigorously (Figure 5).

If the unit develops a problem and has to be disassembled, make certain that you clean the

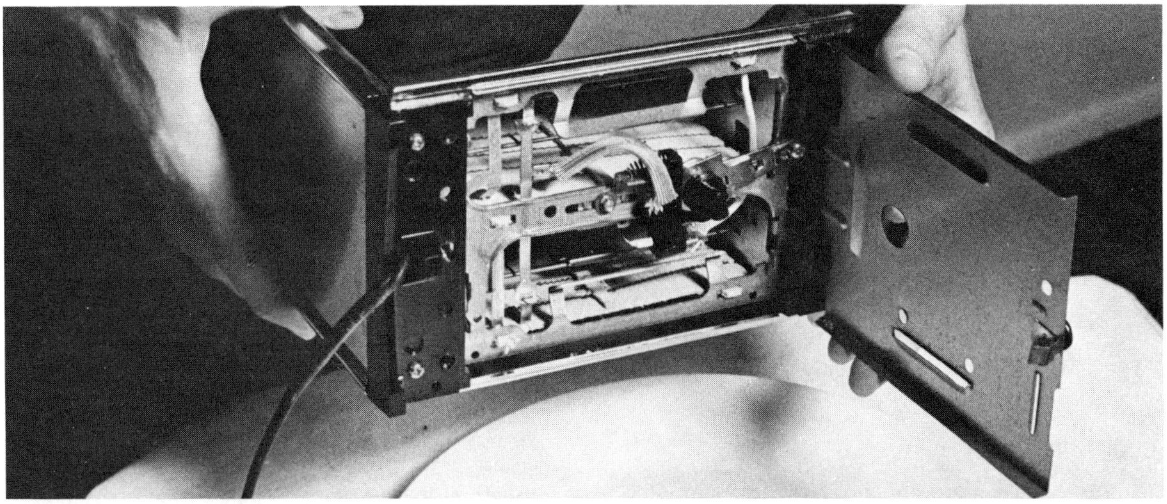

**FIGURE 3.** From time to time, open the trap of toaster and let loose crumbs fall out.

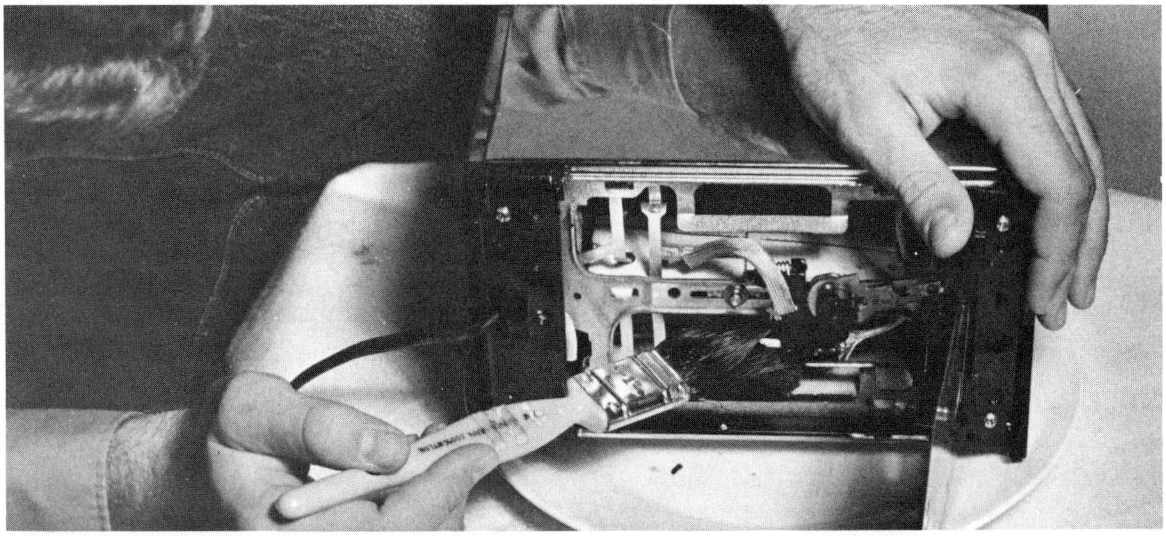

**FIGURE 4.** The insides of the toaster are delicate, so use a 1-inch paint brush to dislodge stubborn crumbs.

**FIGURE 5.** If the toaster doesn't have a clean-out trap, turn the unit upside down and shake it.

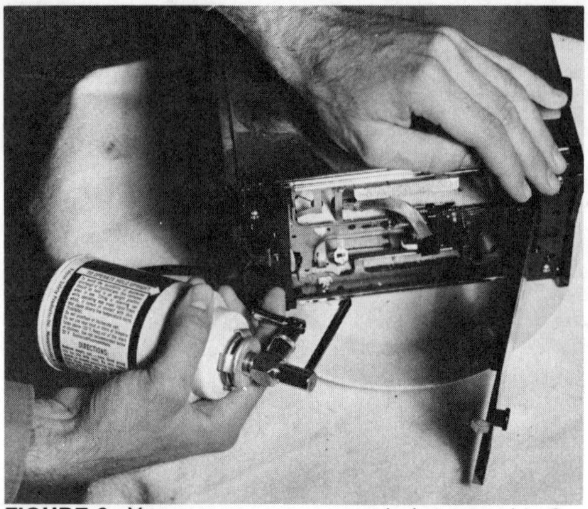

**FIGURE 6.** You can use compressed air to get rid of crumbs that the paint brush can't reach.

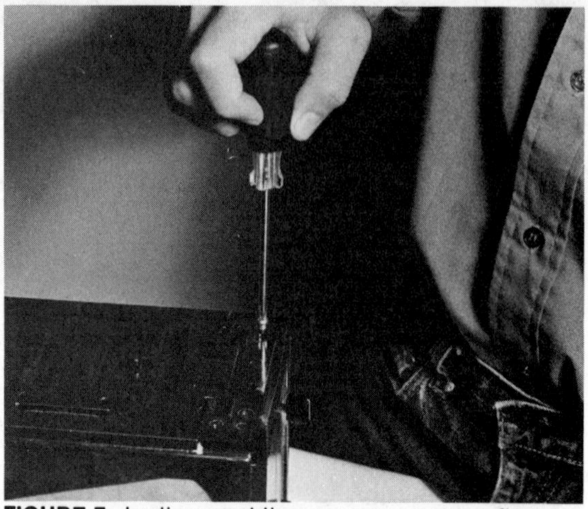

**FIGURE 7.** In disassembling a pop-up toaster, first remove all exposed screws.

parts as thoroughly as you can. It's still possible that crumbs, raisins, or jelly are the cause of the trouble.

The best "tool" to clean toaster parts is compressed air. You can employ it even if you don't have a compressor and air hose (Figure 6).

Visit a photography shop. Most such shops sell compressed air in a can with a nozzle. Photographers use it for cleaning dust from negatives. It is ideal for cleaning out the inside of a toaster.

When you are inside a toaster, examine all contacts and other parts carefully for burned matter which compressed air won't remove. This will have to be scraped off—carefully.

Take pains to make sure that the scraper doesn't slip accidentally and rupture a heating element.

After cleaning mechanical parts—springs, levers, catches and so forth—lubricate them lightly with a heat-resistant grease. This is available from hardware stores, but make sure that the tube stipulates that the lubricant may be used on toasters and other heat-generating appliances.

*Caution:* Do not apply lubricant to electrical components.

**when crumbs aren't the cause**

Essentially there are five problems that can afflict an electric pop-up toaster. They are:

1. The toaster doesn't work at all.
2. The toaster burns the toast.
3. The toast doesn't pop up.
4. The toast is either too light or too dark.
5. The bread doesn't toast evenly.

The easiest repairs, strangely enough, are made if the toaster doesn't work at all, assuming that all elements don't suddenly burn out at once, which isn't likely to happen. Start, of course, by examining the power cord.

Next, to check the innards, make sure that the power cord is pulled from the wall outlet. Remove the light-dark control knob, which is usually only pressed into place (Figures 7, 8, 9).

Now look for a set screw holding the cradle-control lever in place. Remove it and the lever. Unscrew all the screws you can find holding the cover and whatever ornamental trim must come off so the cover can be lifted, revealing the inside of the toaster.

The first thing to do is to give everything a very close look. See if you can spot loose connections or broken wires. Make sure the toaster end of the line cord is okay and is held tightly by its terminals.

Now check voltage, using a voltmeter on both sides of the main switch. Replace a switch if there is a lack of voltage. Other than line-cord problems, a bad switch is the chief reason a toaster will refuse to function.

*Important:* To check voltage, you must depress the cradle to close the switch. Don't forget to connect the power cord to a wall outlet. *Be careful!*

Suppose your problem is uneven toast, which is a common thing. Chances are that one element is burned out or a wire has come loose, disconnecting the element from its conductor. You can buy a new heating element in many cases, but before you do, check the cost of repair against the cost of a new toaster. This should be done in every instance where a repair is a major one.

The best way to discover and correct the most common causes of electric pop-up toaster problems is to use the chart.

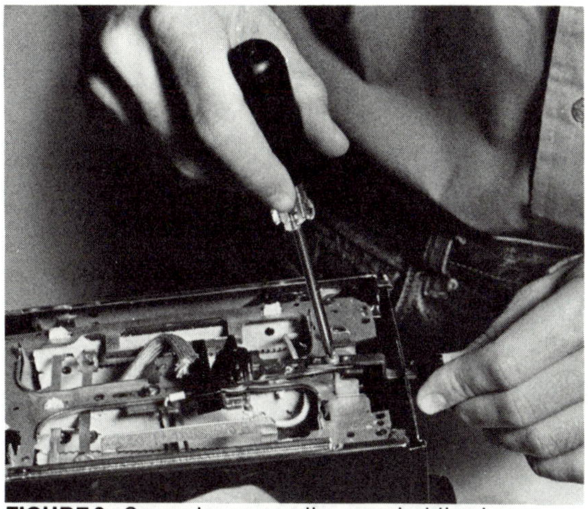

**FIGURE 8.** Second, remove all screws holding levers, so they don't block disassembly.

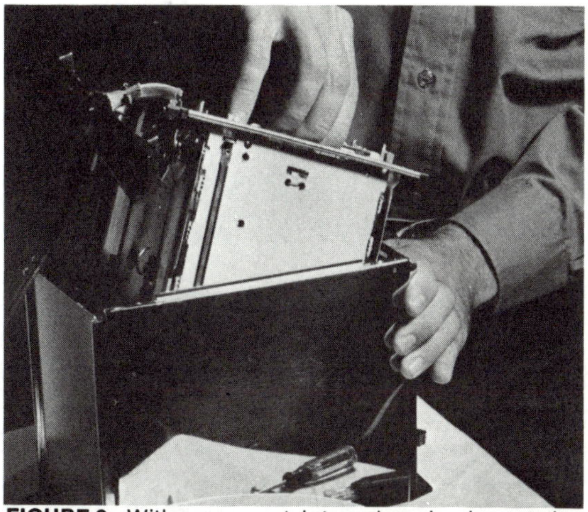

**FIGURE 9.** With screws out, internal mechanism can be removed from the shell.

| TROUBLE | USUAL CAUSES | HOW TO CORRECT |
|---|---|---|
| Toast is either too dark or too light | • Timer setting incorrect | • Check position of timer control knob or lever. |
| | • Timer mechanism has gone awry | • Replace |
| Bread doesn't toast evenly | • Heating element is open | • Check for loose connections; replace element if necessary. |
| | • Reflective surfaces are dirty | • Clean |
| Toaster doesn't work at all | • Damaged power cord | • Replace |
| | • Open switch | • Replace |
| | • Impediment between latch and catch | • Clean away foreign deposits and make sure tension of clutch is sufficient to make effective contact. |
| Toast burns | • Improper timer setting | • Check position of timer control knob or lever. |
| | • Bimetal regulator is distorted | • Replace |
| | • Auxiliary (cool-down) switch stuck closed | • Replace |
| Cradle doesn't pop up | • Bread, raisins or some other foreign matter impeding catch release | • Clean thoroughly and lubricate. |
| | • Bimetal regulator is distorted | • Replace |
| | • Hot-wire or some other catch release mechanism damaged or burned out | • Replace |
| | • Cradle spring broken or lacks tension | • Replace |

# Build a contemporary toolbox

**DRAWERS CARRY** hardware and the like (above); top serves as work surface; handle for short lifts (below).

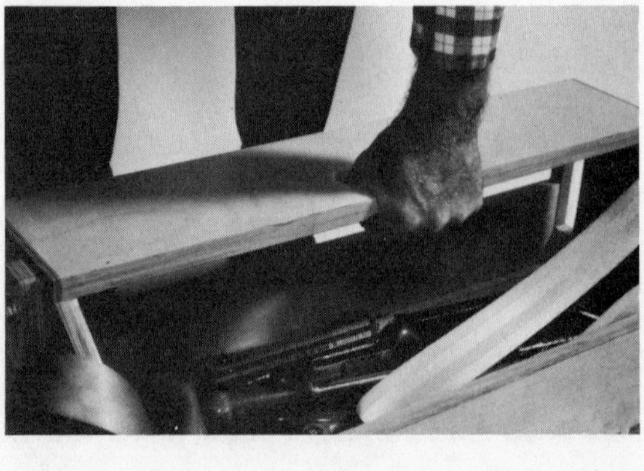

SEE ALSO

**Caddies, tool . . . Calipers . . . Claw hammers . . . Screwdrivers . . . Sharpening, tool . . . Shop tools . . . Tools, hand . . . Workbenches . . . Workshops**

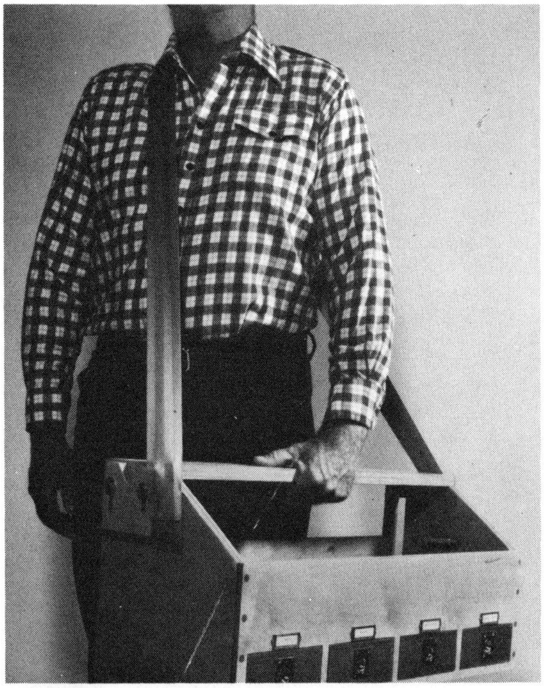

**BECAUSE TOOLBOX** is hefty it is fitted with a removable strap for over-the-shoulder carrying.

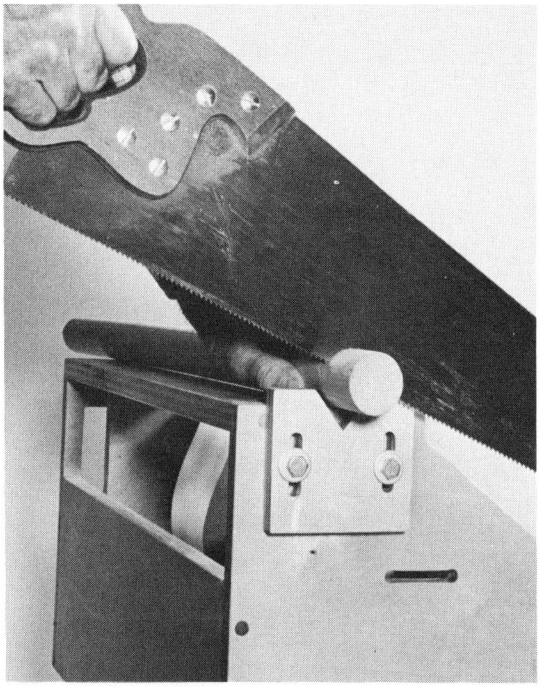

**RETRACTABLE BLOCK** is raised with apex of V flush with top surface when you work a round piece.

A TOOLBOX'S BASIC function is to store tools conveniently for easy job-site usage. But the assignment we gave designer David Stiles was to come up with a contemporary version that would do more, and would appeal to today's craftsman.

We asked Dave to incorporate such features as storage and on-the-job conveniences. He met the challenge by coming up with a toolbox that could aptly be called a "portable workshop." It includes these features:

- A work surface you can use for assembly and sawing, and other carpentry operations.
- Safe storage for your prized 26-in. handsaw.
- A retractable bench stop for planing or sanding wood.
- A helpful shoulder strap that takes some of the weight off your arms when carrying the box from one job to the next.
- Four drawers for the storage of small tools and materials.
- A V-notch in the bench stop which lets it double as a "vise" of sorts. This is handy when you have to cut dowels or pipes on the jobsite.

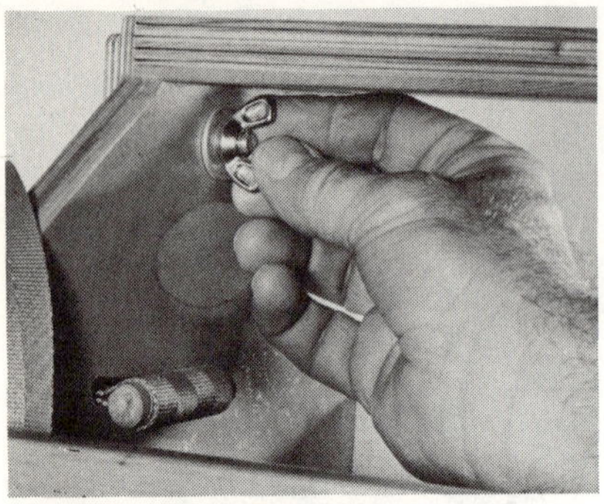

**STOP IS** adjusted up or down by loosening a pair of wingnuts.

**PLANING** or sanding wood is easy with the stop at one end of "workbench."

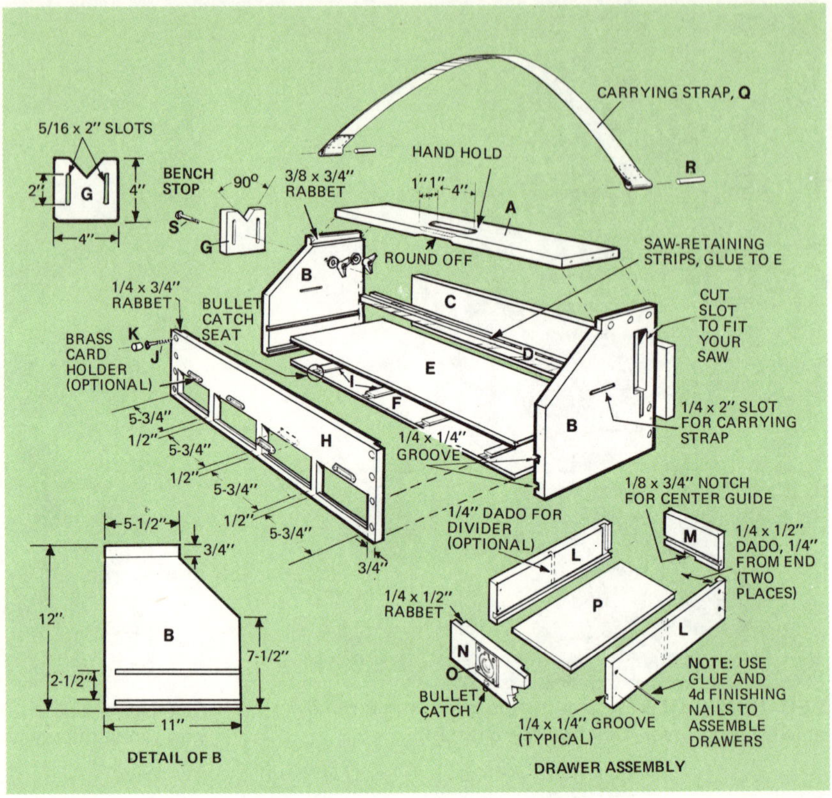


■ A bonus is the fact that the top shelf can double as a short stepladder.

For looks, we built the box of many-layered Baltic Birch plywood (though solid-core plywood could be used). Baltic Birch's multilayers provide an attractive finish and no edge work is required beyond the final sanding with 120-grit sandpaper. Chances are you will have to ask your lumberyard to order the plywood from the same source that provided ours: Allied International, Box 56, Charlestown, MA 02129.

**how to build the box**

**1.** Start by cutting the individual pieces to size. Use a sabre saw to cut out the drawer holes, being extremely careful to make the cuts straight and square.

**2.** Next, cut the rabbet and dado grooves as shown in the drawing. Temporarily assemble all parts without glue to check their fit. Mark any pieces that need refitting. Disassemble and reshape as needed.

**3.** To assemble, glue the false bottom and top into the sidepieces and backpiece; omit the front piece at this time.

**4.** Cut the ⅛x¾-in. center drawer guides from hardwood stock. Mark the center of each drawer opening and, using a square and pencil, mark the center-guide strip locations. Glue them in place.

**5.** Assemble the drawers with nails and glue. Test drawers for fit before the glue dries; leave the drawers in place overnight.

**6.** Using clamps to hold all pieces together temporarily, assemble remaining pieces with glue, screws.

**7.** Install the four drawers. Cut a ⅛x¾-in. notch in the bottom back edge of each drawer to straddle its center guide strip.

**8.** Finish with satin-finish varnish.

**MATERIALS LIST—TOOLBOX**

| Key | No. | Size and description (use) |
|---|---|---|
| A | 1 | ¾ × 5½ × 25¼" Baltic Birch plywood (top) |
| B | 2 | ¾ × 11 × 12" Baltic Birch plywood (sides) |
| C | 1 | ¾ × 7½ × 24½" Baltic Birch plywood (back) |
| D | 2 | ¾ × ¾ × 24½" pine (saw-retaining guides) |
| E | 1 | ¼ × 10 × 25" hardboard (shelf) |
| F | 1 | ¼ × 10 × 25" hardboard (bottom) |
| G | 1 | ¾ × 4 × 4" Baltic Birch plywood (bench stop) |
| H | 1 | ¾ × 7½ × 26" Baltic Birch plywood (front) |
| I | 4 | ⅛ × ¾ × 8½" hardwood (drawer guides) |
| J | 18 | No. 8 × 2" fh screws |
| K | 18 | ⅜" wood plugs |
| L | 8 | ½ × 2⅜ × 10" plywood (drawer sides) |
| M | 4 | ½ × 2⅜ × 5⅛" plywood (drawer backs) |
| N | 4 | ¾ × 2⅜ × 5⅝" hardwood (drawer fronts) |
| O | 4 | Merit flush-ring pulls, Model No. 11510-3 |
| P | 4 | ¼ × 5⅛ × 9½" plywood (drawer bottoms) |
| Q | 1 | 2" × length to suit, nylon webbing |
| R | 2 | ⅜-dia. × 2" dowels |
| S | 2 | ¼ × 2" carriage bolts with wingnuts and washers |

**Misc.:** White glue, 4d finishing nails, 4 bullet catches, 4 recessed finger pulls, urethane finish.

# What hand tools do you need?

**Experienced craftsmen often began with a basic tool kit and added units as skills developed. Householders and budding crafters can save money following this procedure**

By W. CLYDE LAMMEY

EVERY HOUSEHOLD HAS NEED for a small kit of tools for practical applications and the simple joys of using them for repair and maintenance of the home. Over a period of time the savings of doing-it-yourself can add up to an impressive figure in which the tool kit will have long since paid for itself. But sooner or later the beginner becomes a craftsman, planning projects of his own design—a special table, fireside bench, cabinet, or perhaps a reproduction of a cherished antique, using the methods and procedures of the craftsmen of old. It is then that his tool needs expand.

Any listing of basic tools is never really complete or all-inclusive. This is true of the lists given here. The household kit is quite complete for most home-repair jobs and such simple joinery as one might do at the bench, but there are

SEE ALSO
**Caddies, tool . . . Calipers . . . Jeweler's saws . . . Micrometers . . . Scrapers . . . Screwdrivers . . . Sharpening, tool . . . Shop tools . . . Toolboxes . . . Workshops**

## HOUSEHOLD KIT

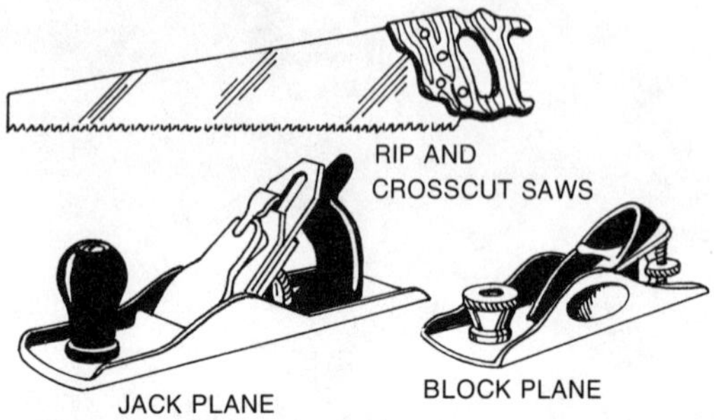


**Nail hammer, curved claw, 10 or 16-oz. head**
**Hand crosscut saw, 12 point**
**Hand ripping saw, 5 point**
**Jack plane, 14 in.**
**Block plane, 6 in.**
**Ratchet brace, 8 or 10-in. sweep**
**Auger bit set, ¼ to 1 in. by 16ths**
**Screwdrivers, 4 and 8-in. blades**
**Tape rule, or folding rule, as desired**
**Combination square, 12-in. blade**
**Combination pliers**
**Soldering gun, or propane torch, or both**
**Solder, nonacid and acid core**
**Adjustable wrenches, sizes as needed**
**Pipe wrenches, 10 and 14-in. sizes**
**Hand drill, with fluted bits**
**Carpenter's level**
**C-clamps, sizes as needed**
**Nailset**
**Files, single and double-cut**
**Putty knife**

## HOME-SHOP KIT

**All the above and the following:**

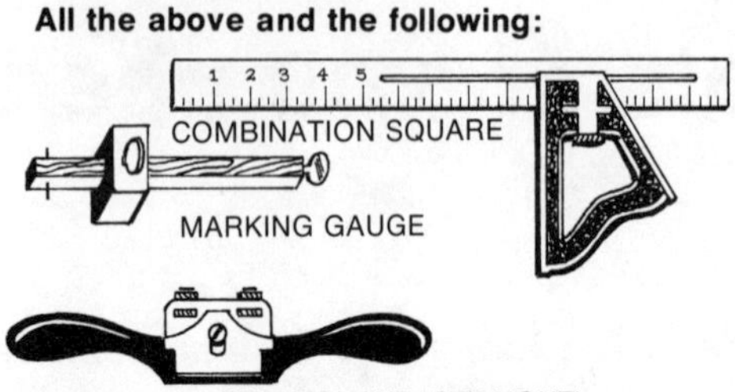


**Steel square, 24 in.**
**Twist-drill set, 1/16 to ¼ in.**
**Tinsnips, plain or duckbill type, or both**
**Cold chisels, ¼, ⅜ and ½ in.**
**Marking gauge**
**Scratch awl**
**Knife, retractable blade, or pocket knife**
**Bar clamps, pair, 24 or 36 in. or both sizes**
**Adjustable clamps, 2 to 8 in.**
**Miterbox with backsaw**
**Rose countersink**
**Combination oilstone**
**Wood chisels, butt or mortising type, or both**
**Dowel centers**
**Miter clamp**
**Spokeshave, straight blade**
**Magnetic brad driver "Pop" rivet tool, rivets**

many hand tools that might be added to the list as you will see from the homeshop kit and the cabinetmaker's kit. Both the latter are suggested for the convenience and information of the more advanced craftsman.

There are, of course, alternate choices. For example, in the homeshop kit you will see a 24-in. steel square listed, but in the household kit a combination square with 12-in. blade. The former may be more suited to your immediate needs but the latter is also useful in a wide range of applications. In time you will likely find need for both, yet in the beginning the combination square is probably the better choice.

Likewise, in the cabinetmaker's kit there is listed the choice of a "soft" hammer or a wooden mallet. Most advanced craftsmen prefer the soft hammer for working a chisel when

## CABINETMAKER'S KIT

**All the above and the following:**

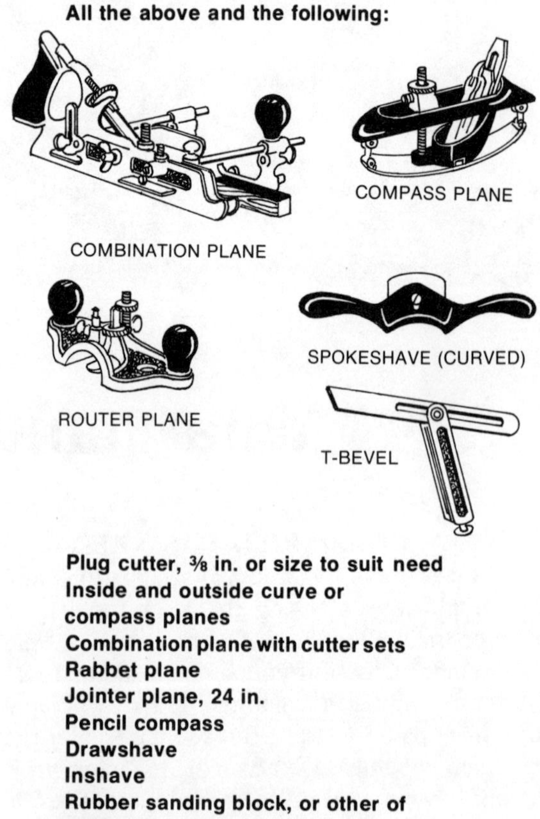


**Plug cutter, ⅜ in. or size to suit need**
**Inside and outside curve or compass planes**
**Combination plane with cutter sets**
**Rabbet plane**
**Jointer plane, 24 in.**
**Pencil compass**
**Drawshave**
**Inshave**
**Rubber sanding block, or other of choice**
**Cabinet scrapers, gooseneck, convex and straight**
**"Surform" contour tools**
**Gimlets, set of varying sizes**
**Dovetail saw**
**Coping saw, or bow saw, as desired**
**Router plane**
**Dowel jig**
**Dowel pointer**

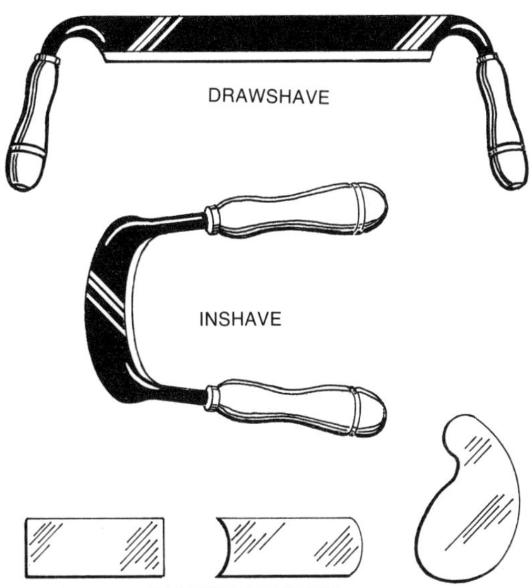


**Gouges, ¼, ½, and ¾ in.**
**Tap and die, ¾ or 1 in., for wood threads**
**Sloyd knife**
**Trammel points, for fitting on hardwood strip**
**Band clamp**
**Flexible ruler, for drawing curves**
**Stapler, with staple assortment**
**Universal woodworker's vise**
**Burnisher**
**Miter clamp**
**Pad saw**
**Spokeshave, curved**
**"Soft" hammer, plastic faces, or wood mallet**
**T-bevel**
**Wood rasps**
**Denim, canvas, or leather apron**

## HOME PLUMBING KIT

**In addition to adjustable wrenches, pipe wrenches listed above:**
**Plumber's force cup**
**Closet-bowl auger, 5½ ft. length**
**Graphited packing, for faucets, still cocks**
**Pipe-joint compound**
**Faucet washers, assorted sizes**
**Seat reamer**

## CAULKING AND GLAZING KIT

**Caulking gun, with spare cartridges**
**Wire brush with attached scraper**
**Glass cutter, with diamond point**
**Glazier's points (box)**
**Linseed oil, 1 pint**
**Glazier's putty, 1 to 5 lbs.**
**Yardstick, for measuring and cutting glass**

## GENERAL SUPPLIES

**White polyvinyl glue**
**Epoxy glue**
**Household cement**
**Assorted stove bolts and small machine screws**
**Assorted wood screws, ½ in. #4 through 2-in. #10**
**Mending plates, corner braces**
**Screweyes, screw hooks, picture hangers**
**Tacks, brads, common and finishing nails, 2d to 8d**
**Assorted wall fasteners, plastic or lead anchors**
**Extra casters, furniture glides**
**Pressure-sensitive mending tape**
**Masking tape, ½ and 1-in. widths**

chop-cutting a mortise, for example. The plastic faces of the soft hammer deliver a blow without upsetting and eventually damaging the chisel handle. Yet others, equally skilled, would choose the wood mallet for this purpose. However, in the end the soft hammer is perhaps the better choice as it has a somewhat wider application, such as tapping out dents in sheet metals.

For beginning craftsmen it's usually best to choose only a few tools, such as a hammer, saws, a plane, brace and bits, pliers, whatever is immediately needed and then add to the kit as tool requirements develop. In this way you avoid a high initial investment, gradually build a kit of the most useful units, eliminate those of only marginal use and save some money in the end. The more inclusive homeshop kit and the cabinetmaker's kit are, of course, for those who acquire skills and who wish to go all-out in building a more nearly complete set of hand tools.

For beginners certain of these may be more or less unfamiliar in type and application. The compass plane, combination plane, router plane and inshave are specialized tools used in advanced cabinet work; in chair-making and in making shallow bowls and trays where it is necessary to work concave and curved edges and surfaces. Here one uses the compass plane—which is made in "inside" and "outside" types—for working curved edges.

The router plane is, as its name suggests, for the purpose of making dadoes and grooves of limited lengths. The combination plane comes with an array of cutters designed for making beading, sash moldings and for grooving in various widths and depths. The inshave is used by chairmakers for working chair seats and by tray and bowl makers for the necessary concavities.

# Pliers basics

THOUGH THERE ARE special-purpose pliers for almost any gripping task, the old reliable slip-joint pliers is undoubtedly the most familiar-looking and versatile gripping tool you can own.

The term "slip-joint" means the jaw pivot can be adjusted to two (or more) positions—to suit different-size pieces of work—by simply sliding the jaws apart or together. The pliers' jaw consists of three different usable surfaces: 1. The straight jaw—usually with fine serrations, but which can also be smooth. These are used when a pinching action is needed on small objects such as holding a small brad while you start driving it with a hammer. 2. The curved jaw which has rugged looking teeth that will provide a sure grip on irregular pieces, and for extra power when you have to securely grasp and shift a stubborn object. 3. The crimper—that portion of the jaw nearest the pivot point. As the name suggests, this is used for any crimping chore such as for closing an electric terminal connection. The crimper can also be used to straighten out kinked wire and bent nails and for cutting light-gauge wire such as aluminum and soft copper.

Though pliers can hold a nut while you turn a screw or bolt with screwdriver, don't mistake the pliers for a wrench. For safety reasons, the latter should be used—instead of pliers—when tightening or loosening a stubborn nut. Under extreme pressure pliers can slip off the nut—easier than you might suspect—with resultant severe damage to knuckles and or fingers. When using a pair of pliers to hold a nut that might scratch or burr, it is a good idea to wrap electrician's or friction tape around the nut for the pliers' jaws to grip. The tape will prevent unwanted scratches.

When you want to hold a workpiece with pliers, grip the object with the teeth—as close to the pivot point as possible—to get the maximum handle squeeze.

Do make it your practice to use your pliers for its intended purpose. Do not try to increase leverage by adding pipe "helpers," or the like, to extend handles. If your pliers lack insulating sleeves, you can create a cushioned handle by slipping rubber tubing over the handles.

If the teeth in your pliers become worn or damaged you can restore them by filing with a three-square file. Keep your pliers clean. Every so often, wipe it with a light coat of oil to prevent rust and work in a drop or two of oil around the pivot pin.

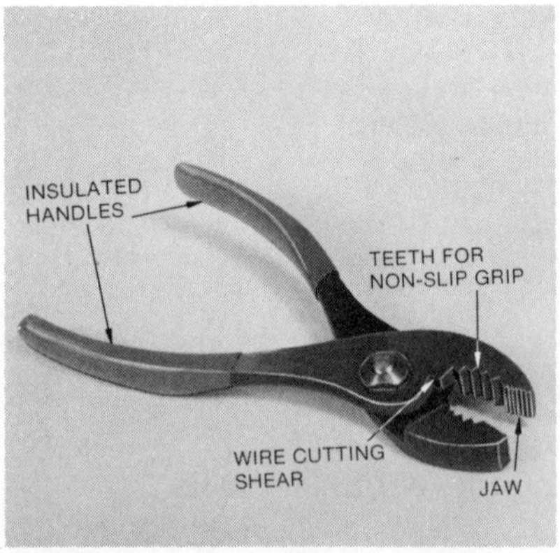


**SLIP-JOINT** pliers have two-position pivot for normal and wide jaw openings.

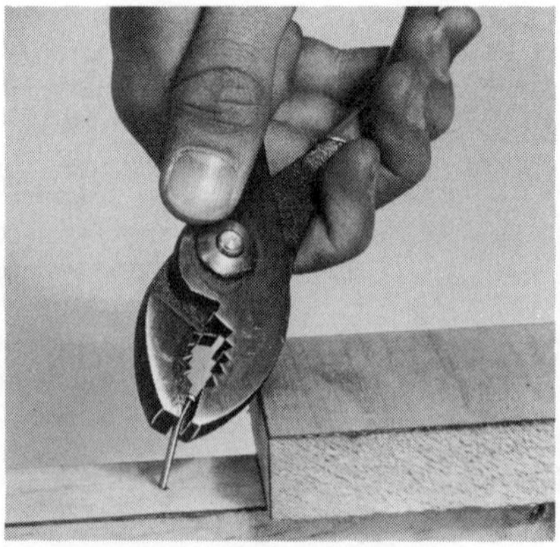

**TO REMOVE** small nail, pull at same angle it was driven, use block.

**HERE, PLIERS** hold a nut while a screwdriver is used to turn the bolt.

**IN SOME CASES,** pliers can be used to tighten a nut—but do this with caution.

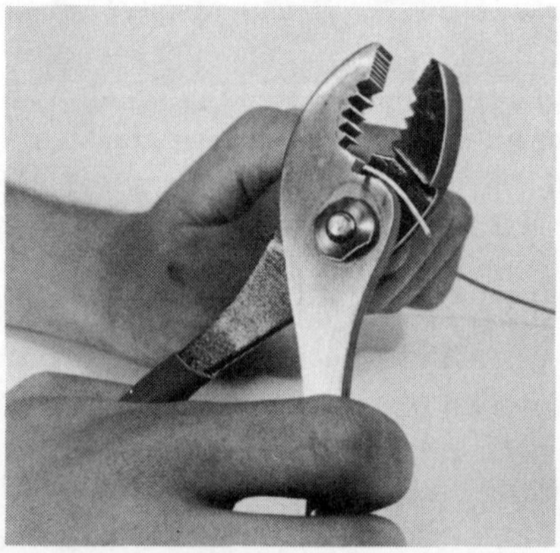

**YOU CAN** use crimping jaw to bend or cut a wire, or straighten a nail.

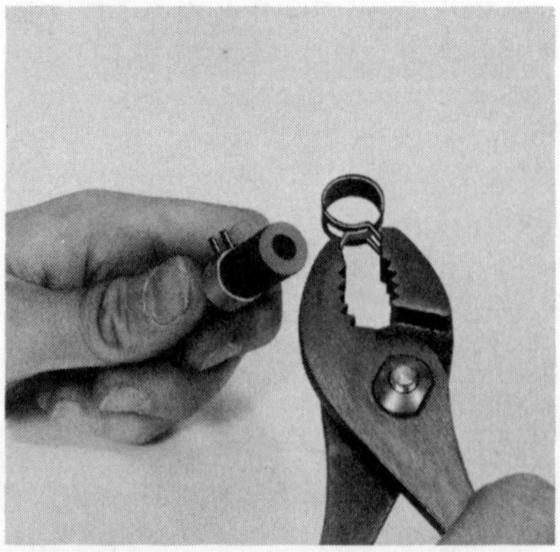

**PLIERS CAN** be used to compress small spring clamp for hose installation.

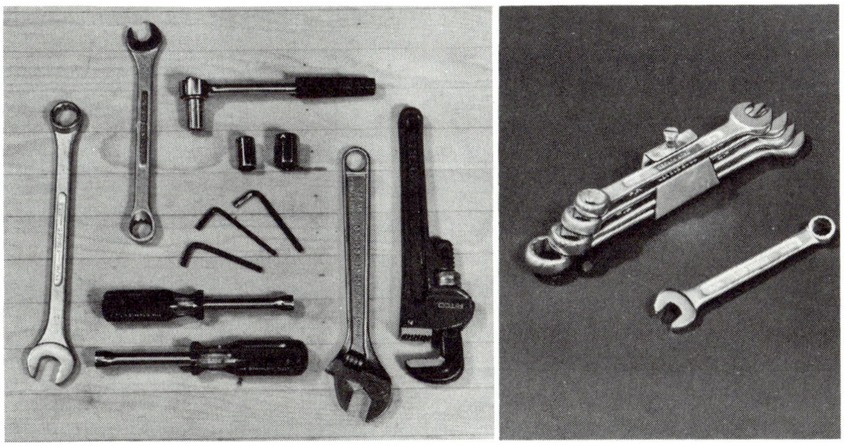

**TYPICAL WRENCHES,** starting at 12 o'clock: Hand socket, pipe, adjustable, nut drivers, open-end and box combination; in center, assorted Allen wrenches. Combo set, right, has five wrenches size 3/8, 7/16, 1/2, 9/16 and 5/8 inches.

**WRONG.** Using an oversize box wrench will quickly round off the nut corners and make it nonremovable.

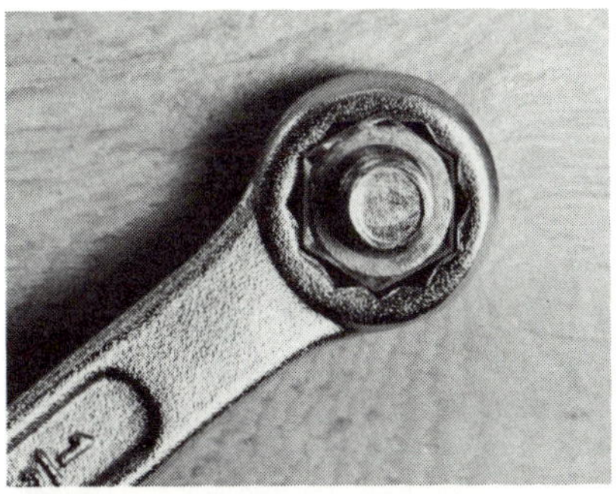

**RIGHT.** Correct size fully engages nut and will not slip off.

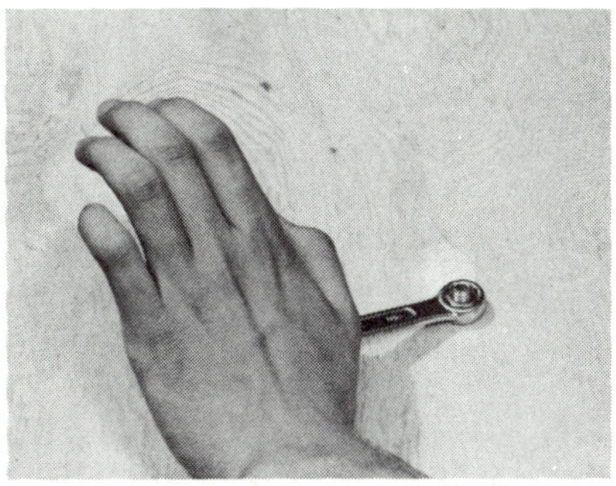

**WRONG.** Never push on a wrench because a slip could mean a fall.

**WRONG.** Oversize wrench will slip off, cause severe knuckle damage.

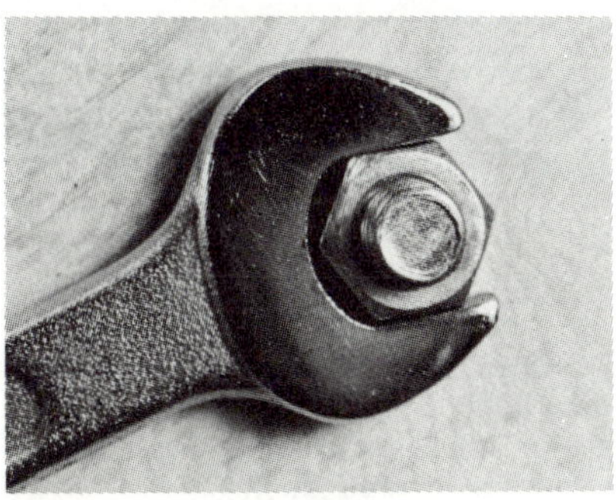

**RIGHT.** Nut is fully seated in wrench to prevent damage to either.

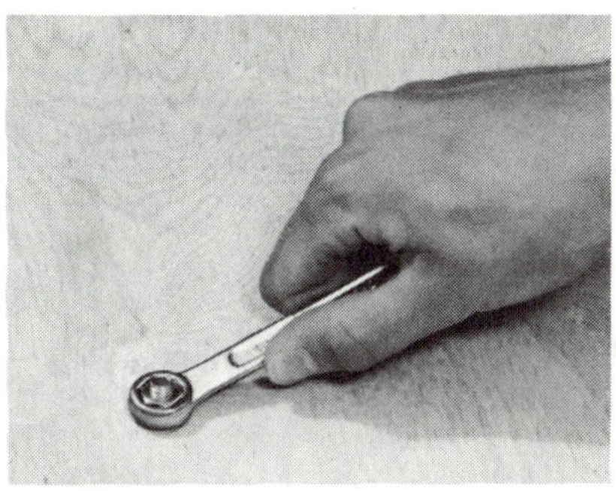

**RIGHT.** Position yourself to pull, whether loosening or tightening.

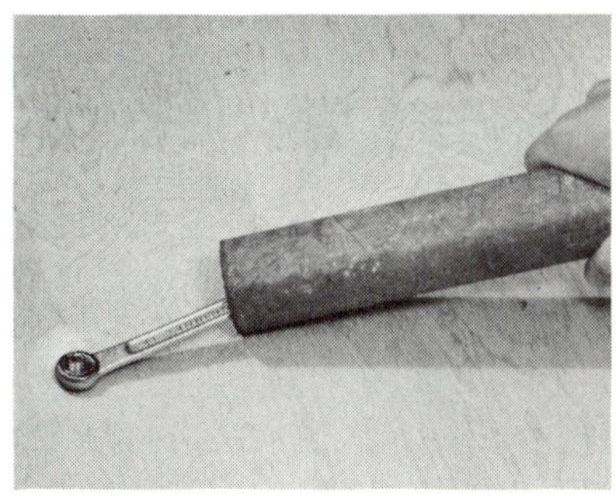

**WRONG.** *Never* use a pipe or other extension to increase leverage.

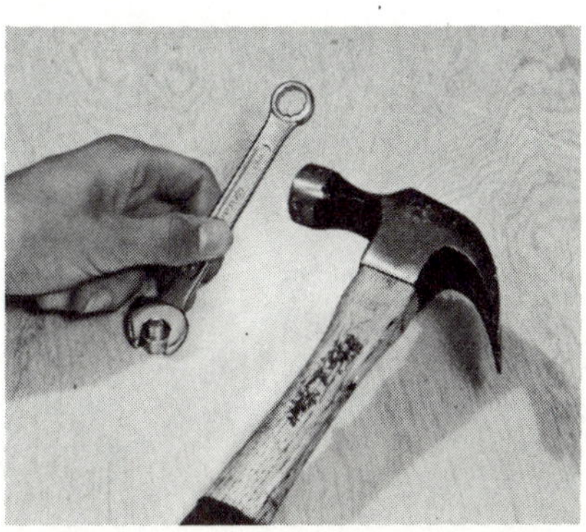

**WRONG.** *Never* hit wrench with hammer unless it is of striking-face type.

# Wrench basics

■ SINCE WRENCHES are used for tightening and loosening, you will need one on any job where nuts and screws are used. Manufacturer's now offer a wide variety of wrenches to suit just about any task imaginable. But for most homeowners, a set of combination open-end/box wrenches is the wisest first-wrench purchase.

Though wrenches are hand-powered, you are well advised to use them safely. If you use an oversize open-end wrench on a frozen nut, for example, there is a strong possibility of the wrench slipping and your bashing your knuckles. Thus, the first two safety rules are: Choose the right wrench for the job.

# Wood-chisel basics

■ THERE ARE probably more tools designed for carving wood than for performing any other workshop task. Experienced carpenters are aware that a good set of chisels plus a quality knife lets you do almost all the wood carving chores you're likely to encounter. The secret for getting maximum use from a good chisel is in knowing how to use it properly—and in keeping it sharp.

It is important to know that actually there should be two bevels on a cared-for chisel. The larger, more visible one is ground to a 30° angle (from the flat side) while the cutting edge is whetted at 30° to 35°. This is accomplished by lifting the back edge slightly as shown below. When the cutting edge is honed smooth, turn the chisel over and remove the wire formed by whetting with a couple of strokes on the flat side. Don't grind a chisel every time it feels a *bit* dull. Whetting with a couple of figure-8 strokes will usually restore the cutting edge. A chisel should be ground only when its cutting edge has been nicked or damaged by striking a nail or the like.

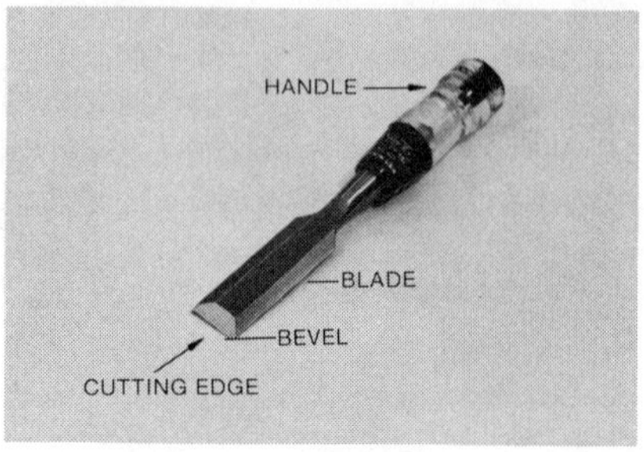


**BUTT CHISEL** is designed for use with a hammer or wooden mallet.

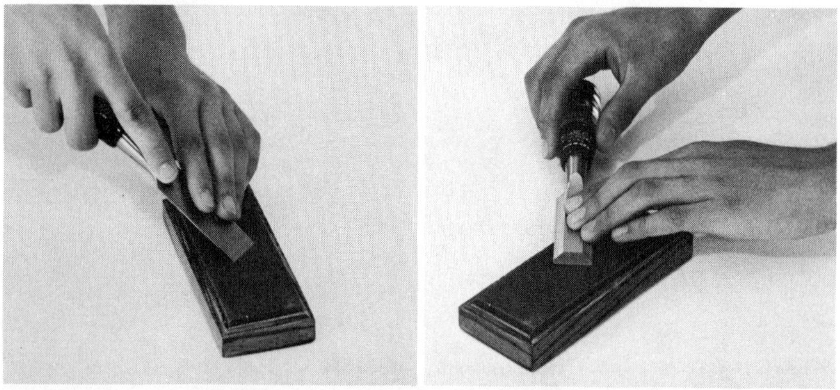

**TO WHET** a chisel, hold the bevel flat against the stone and raise the back edge *slightly*. Using both hands, rub the iron in a figure-8 motion. Next, to remove "wire" formed, hold the flat edge against the same stone and take a few strokes.

**TO CHISEL** a dado, alternately work from both edges, start with bevel side down. Rotate chisel and use paring cuts to assure accurate depth.

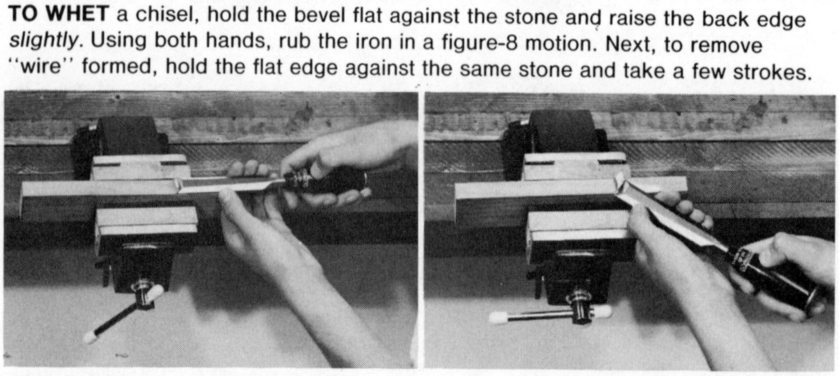

**DON'T STEER** the chisel straight into the workpiece because it increases cutting edge. The right way is to slant the cutting edge slightly in the direction of the cut.

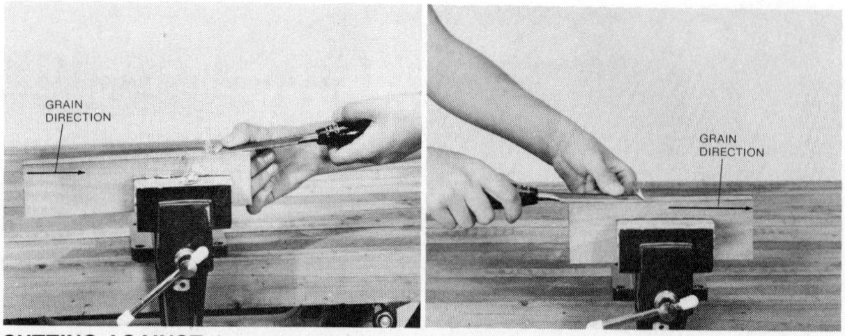


**CUTTING AGAINST** the grain leaves a rough surface and, in many cases severe tears. When chisel cuts with the grain, wood fibers are neatly severed.

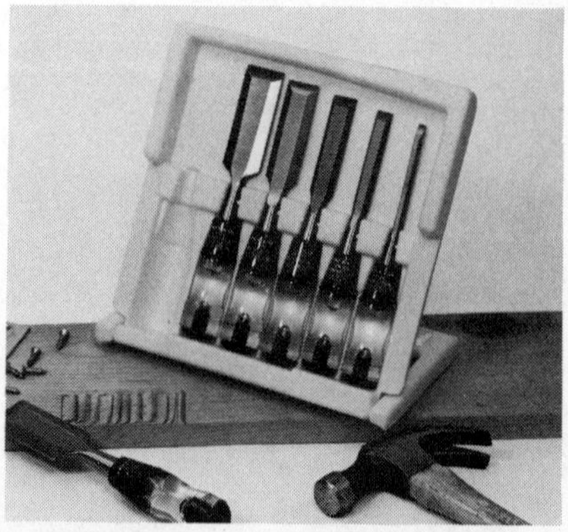

**SIX-CHISEL SET** from Stanley Tools comes with case that protects edges.

# A stand for your propane torch

**This stand holds your torch at a convenient angle for working and also storage. It is constructed from one-inch stock. The tray below holds accessories**

**By HAROLD JACKSON**

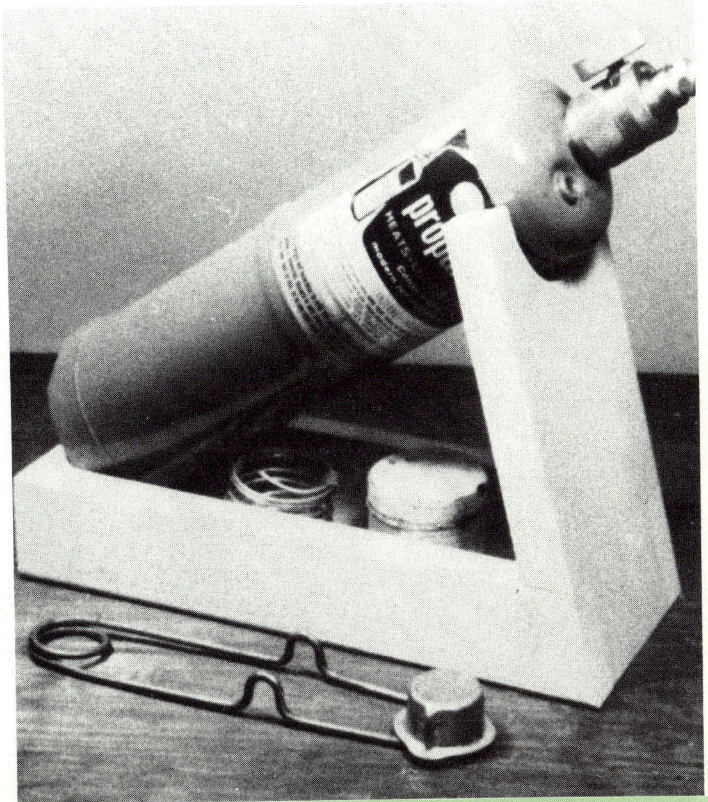

A PROPANE TORCH has an important place in every home workshop, but I've found that it is easily tipped over and presents a constant hazard once it is lit. To remedy this, I constructed the simple rack at left. It holds the torch at a convenient angle and leaves both hands free. In addition, when the torch is not in use it can remain in the stand for storage. The torch can be readily lifted out when desired and the tray in the base provides handy storage for the lighter, solder, flux and other torch-related items.

All parts of nominal one-inch stock and assembly is with glue and 4d finishing nails. You may want to build several stands, altering the angle of the rest so that the torch can be used for special jobs. If you decide to make a rest that will hold the torch nearer to the vertical, I recommend that you notch the small board at the other end in order to cradle the tank bottom securely.

If desired, you can add a torch stand as a permanent fixture to your workbench by attaching it with a large flathead screw. You can turn stand to whatever direction is most convenient for the job at hand.

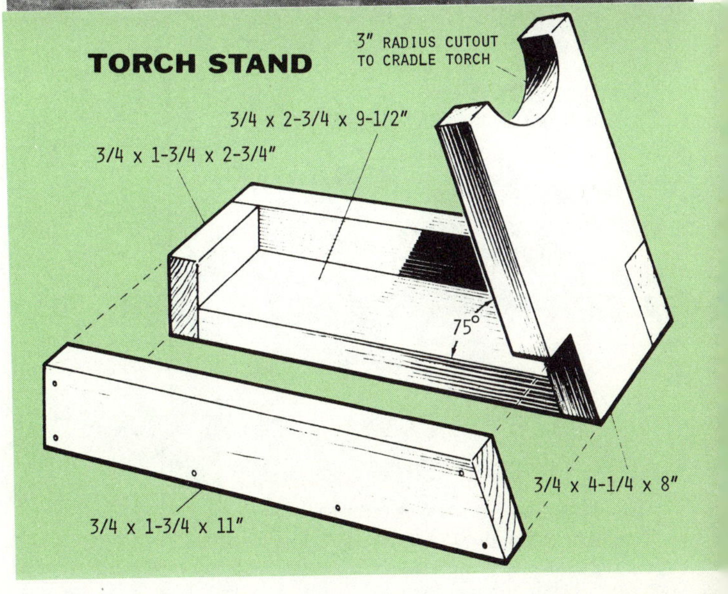


SEE ALSO

**Cutoff machines . . . Metalworking . . . Power hacksaws . . . Sheet metal . . . Shop tools . . . Workbenches**

# Three attractive towel racks

I STARTED MAKING towel racks like the ones shown here when a friend complained that he couldn't buy anything that was attractive and well constructed.

The kitchen towel rack shown at left is made of maple, with a Danish oil finish. I've made others of white pine and walnut.

Rather than purchase towel racks for the bathroom in our new home, I designed the inexpensive towel bars shown at the lower left. They are easy to make and their blind construction and attachment give a clean, modern look.

I turned my 1⅝-in.-dia. bars on the lathe from glued-up 1½-in. stock, but purchased rounds are fine. Each bracket is made from two pieces of wood glued together with their grain directions at right angles for strength. Brackets and bars were stained and finished with two coats of urethane varnish, rubbed lightly with steel wool between coats.

**EARLY AMERICAN** rack lets you swing towels against wall or into easy reach.

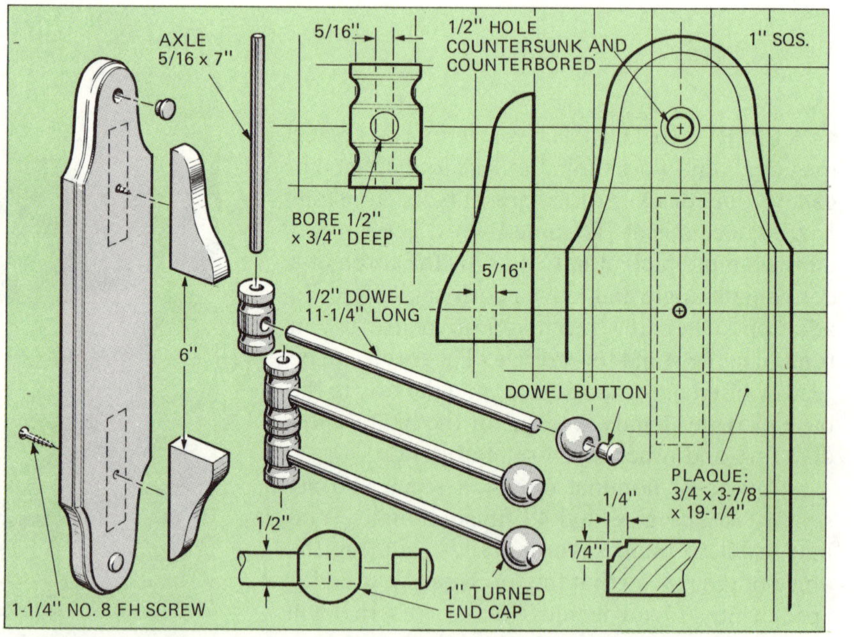


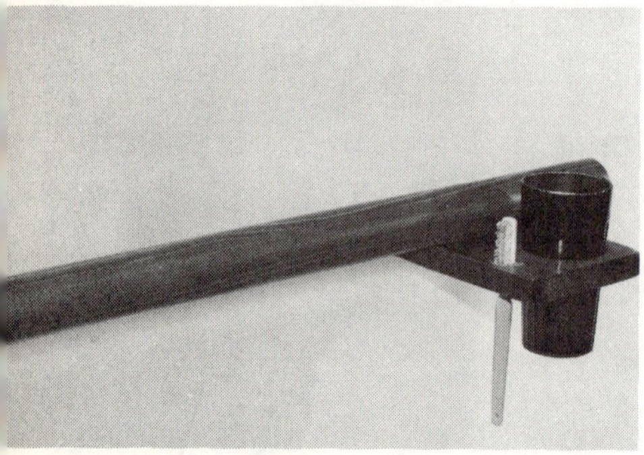

**CANTILEVERED** towel bar has places for toothbrush and drinking cup.

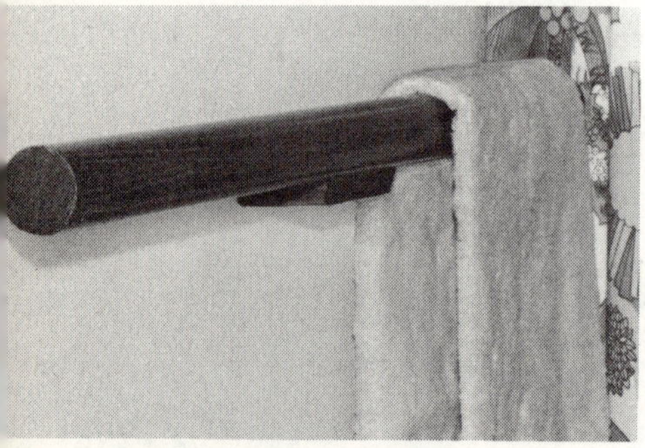

**DOUBLE-ENDED** version of towel bar omits brush and cup holder.

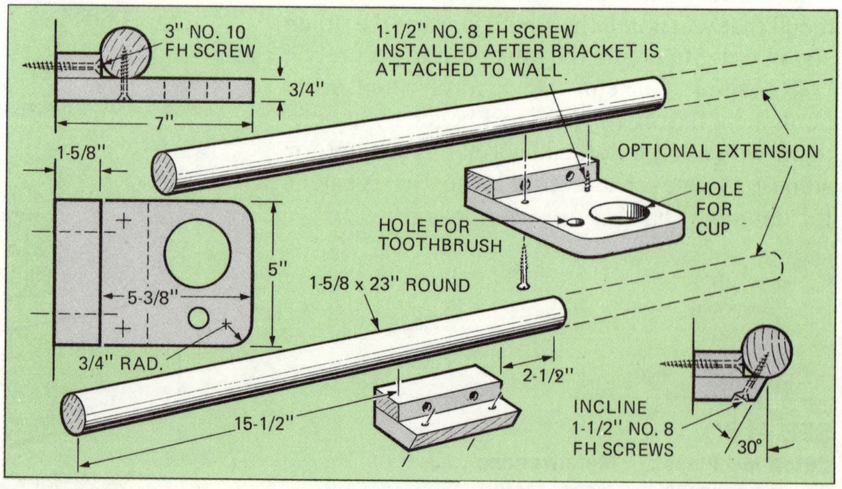

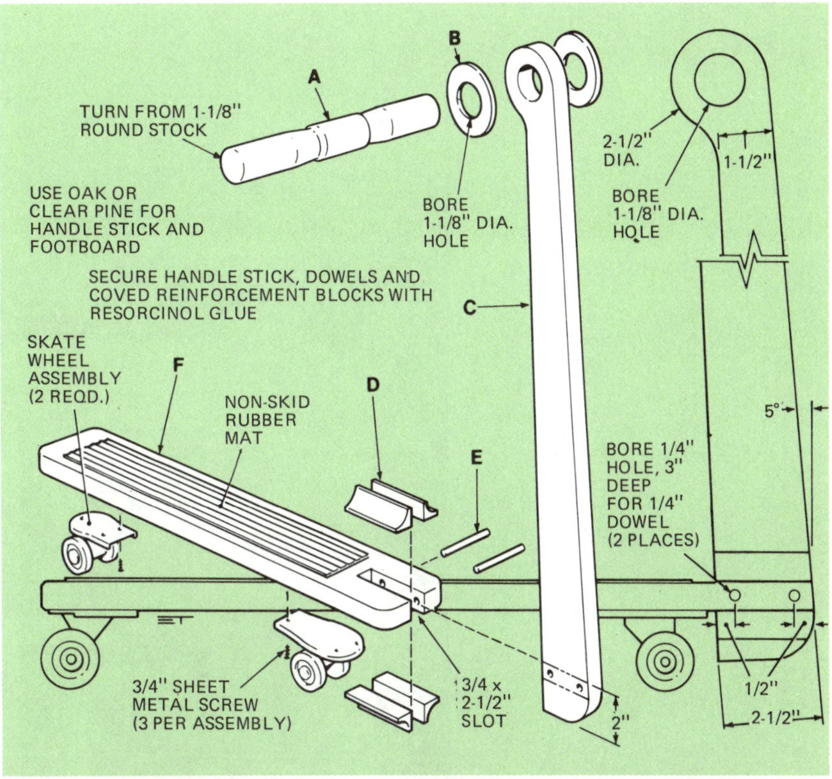


# Scooters from skates

By ELMER J. LOISELLE

THIS ROLLER-SKATE scooter is fun both for tots too small to safely use skateboards and for older ones who ride at full speed. Since fixed wheels give it a limited turning radius, there is little danger of the scooter veering sharply.

Using scrap wood and an old pair of roller skates, you can make two of these scooters in short order. Separate the wheel assemblies from the skates and remove or cut off projections from the flat mounting plates. Drill three holes in each plate for attaching to the footboard.

Cut pieces itemized in the materials list from 1-in. scrap wood. Or modify dimensions to suit stock on hand and size of user. Round the lower edge of the handle post to ride over small obstacles. Slightly round and sand all edges.

Turn the handle grip from 1⅛-in.-dia. round stock. Glue the grip into the hole in the handle post, along with a plywood washer on both sides to strengthen assembly.

Draw a centerline on underside of the footboard to position the wheel assemblies but do not attach them yet. Locate the front wheels as close as possible to the handle slot. Position the rear wheels at the very end of the footboard. Hold a straight-edge against the sides of a front and a rear wheel to keep the assemblies aligned while marking for screws. Make holes for the mounting screws with an awl, but don't install them.

Secure the handle post in the footboard slot with glue and dowels. Reinforce this joint at the four 90° corners by gluing in 2½-in.-long pieces of ¾x¾-in. cove stock.

Sand assembly, round all sharp corners and fill dents with wood putty. Finish with exterior paint.

When paint dries, attach the wheel assemblies. Glue rubber padding to top of the footboard for nonslip footing.

**MATERIALS LIST—SCOOTER**

| Key | Pcs. | Size and description (use) |
|---|---|---|
| A | 1 | 1⅛"-dia. x 8" hardwood (handle grip) |
| B | 2 | ¼ x 2½"-dia. (shop-made washers) |
| C | 1 | ¾ x 2½ x 27" (handle post) |
| D | 4 | ¾ x ¾ x 2½" (cove reinforcement blocks) |
| E | 2 | ¼"-dia. x 3"-long dowels |
| F | 1 | ¾ x 4 x 20" (footboard) |

Misc.: Resorcinol glue; ¾-in. No. 6 sheet metal screws; 1 roller skate; piece of nonskid rubber mat.

SEE ALSO

**Gifts, Christmas . . . Kites . . . Playgrounds . . . Toys . . . Weekend projects**

# Small-fry kitchen appliances

**THE MINIATURE KITCHEN** furniture consists of a two-door refrigerator, a sink with faucet, and a stove with play dials and an oven. All are constructed alike—¼-in. chipboard over ¾ x 1¼-in. framework. Appliances can be painted to match your full-size ones.

**What daughter or granddaughter wouldn't love these sturdy toy appliances made up to look just like full-size ones?**

**By TERENCE E. HOGAN**

STURDY, REALISTIC-LOOKING and sure to please your little gal is this set of pint-sized kitchen appliances you can build in a weekend or two. Unlike the flimsy metal or corrugated cardboard counterparts available commercially, these scaled-down versions of major appliances have enough movable parts to keep the youngest lady of the house occupied for months.

Because the units are constructed of pine stock and skinned with ¼-in. chip and hardboard, they are light enough to be easily moved, yet rugged enough to take the punishment small fry can dish out. All units are assembled using glue as well as nails. To fasten the outer covering, also use white glue and ¾-in. finishing nails.

Since the three units are basically alike, you can save time by using jigs, gang-cutting and other production-line methods wherever possible. For example, after roughing out the hardboard and chipboard, all frame pieces of a given dimension can be clamped together and cut simultaneously on the table saw. To avoid confusion, mark all pieces as they are cut. With all pieces of the frames cut, these parts can be sanded and prime painted

SEE ALSO
**Children's furniture . . . Desks . . .
Gifts, Christmas . . . Miniature houses . . .
Playhouses . . . Pull toys . . . Weekend projects**

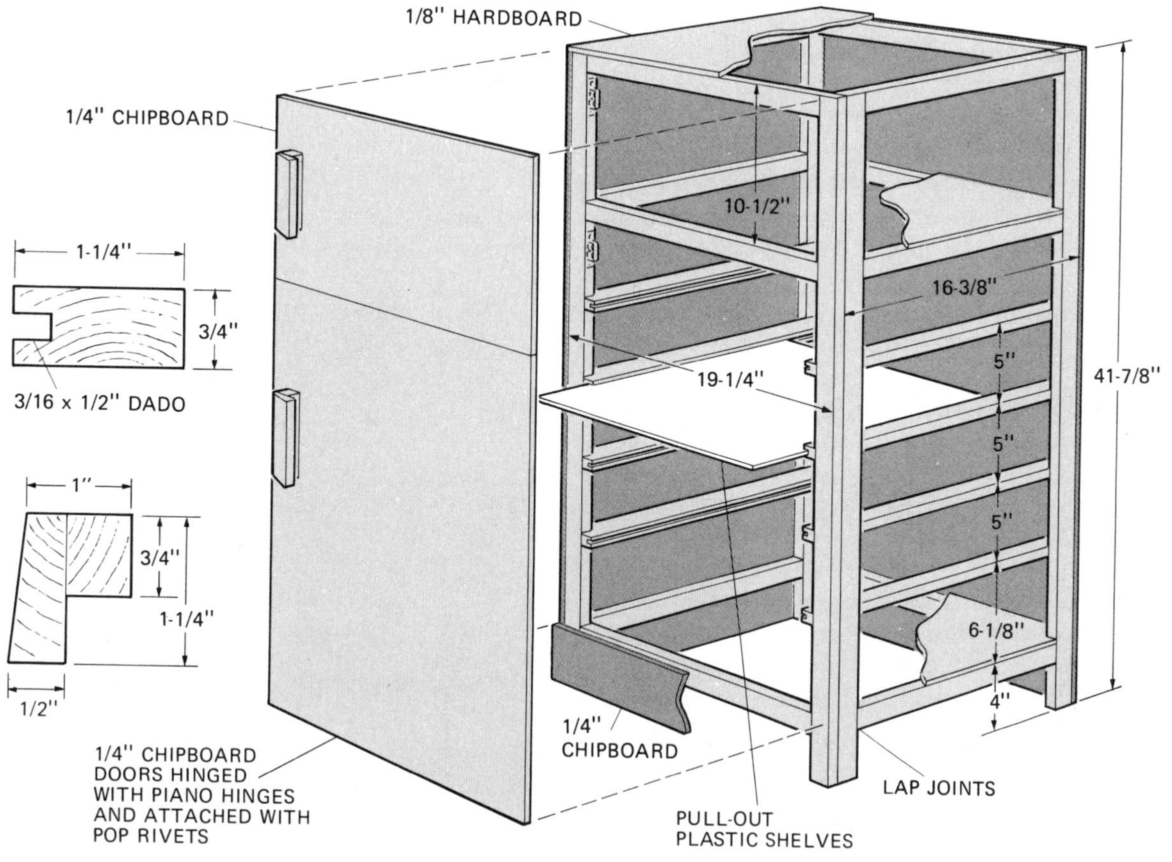
1/8" HARDBOARD
1/4" CHIPBOARD
1-1/4"
3/4"
3/16 x 1/2" DADO
1"
3/4"
1-1/4"
1/2"
10-1/2"
16-3/8"
19-1/4"
5"
5"
5"
6-1/8"
4"
41-7/8"
1/4" CHIPBOARD
1/4" CHIPBOARD DOORS HINGED WITH PIANO HINGES AND ATTACHED WITH POP RIVETS
PULL-OUT PLASTIC SHELVES
LAP JOINTS

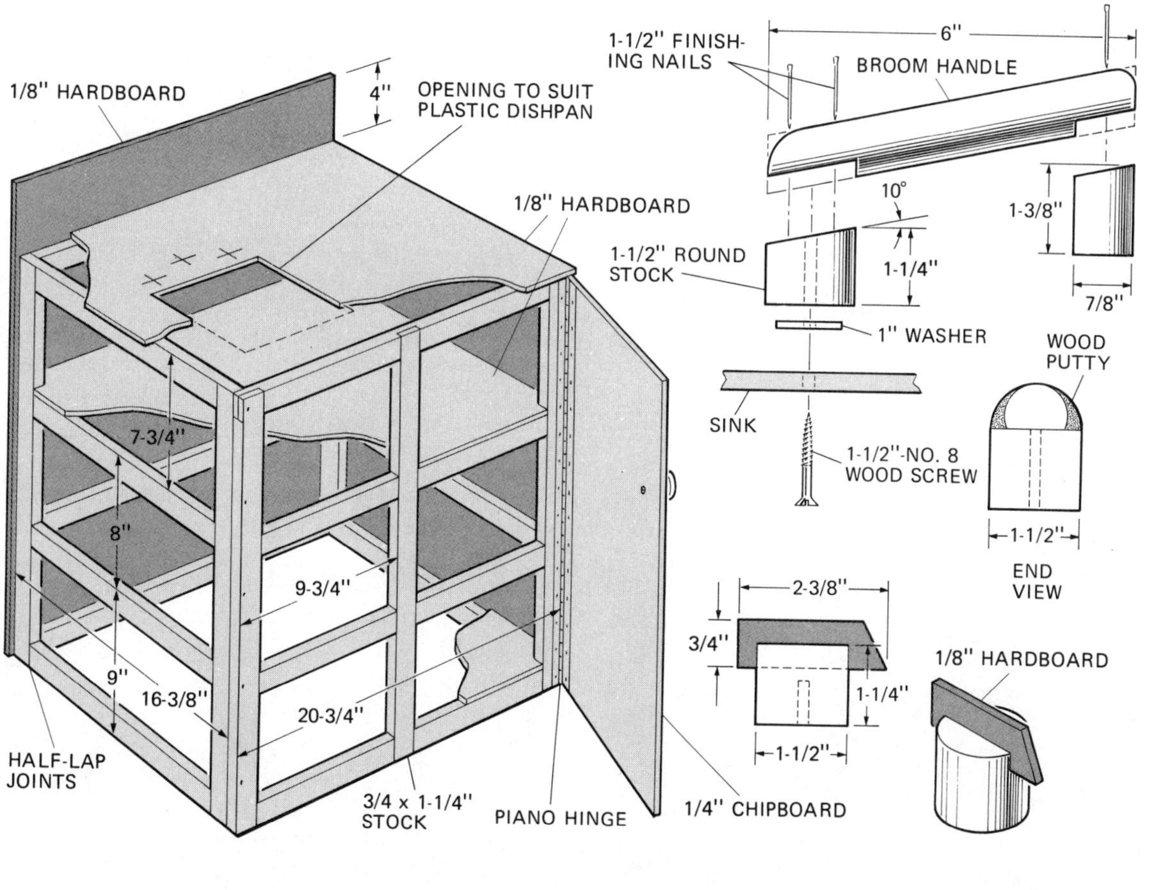
1/8" HARDBOARD
4"
OPENING TO SUIT PLASTIC DISHPAN
1/8" HARDBOARD
7-3/4"
8"
9"
9-3/4"
16-3/8"
20-3/4"
HALF-LAP JOINTS
3/4 x 1-1/4" STOCK
PIANO HINGE
1/4" CHIPBOARD
1-1/2" FINISHING NAILS
6"
BROOM HANDLE
10°
1-3/8"
1-1/2" ROUND STOCK
1-1/4"
7/8"
1" WASHER
WOOD PUTTY
SINK
1-1/2"-NO. 8 WOOD SCREW
1-1/2"
END VIEW
2-3/8"
3/4"
1-1/4"
1-1/2"
1/8" HARDBOARD

prior to assembly. But make certain you do not prime those areas that will be glue-joined.

*Range.* To mark the range for the clocks and dials as shown, use a center punch to locate exact centers. After painting the front, the circles, clock dials and other details can be applied using India ink and an artist's brush. When this "artwork" is dry, apply clear varnish. The window on the chipboard door is simply a piece of plexiglass set in the rabbet with bathtub caulk.

*Sink.* On the unit shown, the sink is a 2¼ x 7½ x 7½-in. bowl that came with a 49-cent vegetable grater. Before cutting out your sinktop, have your "sink" on hand to assure a neat fit. The sink trim requires a little effort using a chisel and coping saw to do the notching. After assembling these parts, fill any voids with a wood filler and sand smooth. Trim can be finish-painted with aluminum paint for realism.

*Refrigerator.* This is the easiest unit to construct because it is really just a box with two doors. As with all units, sand all surfaces and edges absolutely smooth before applying a *nontoxic paint.*

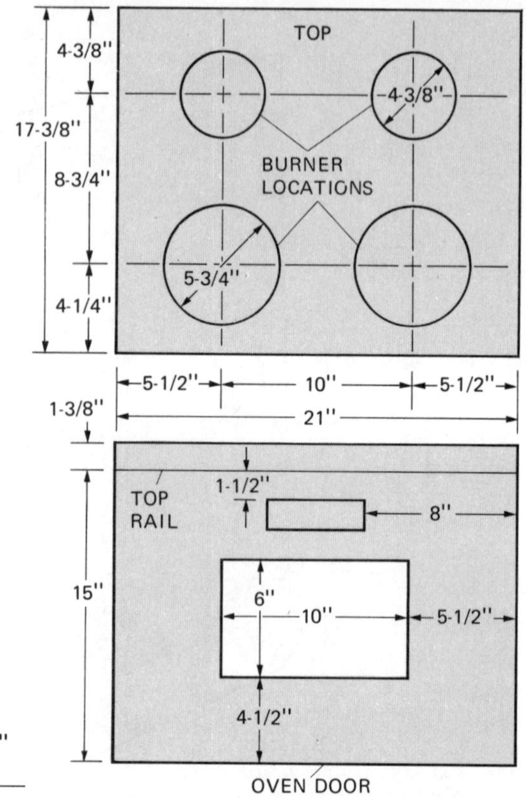


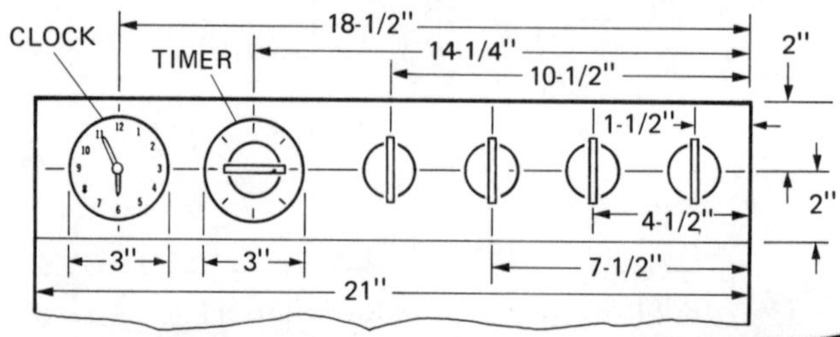


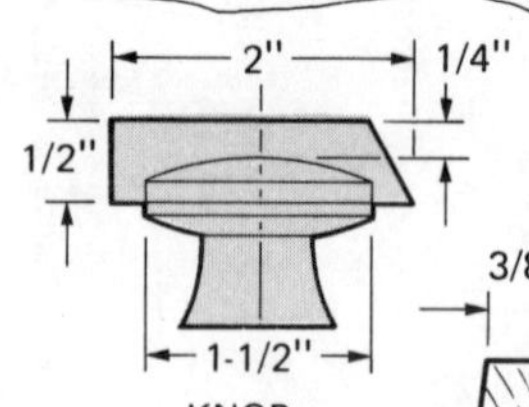


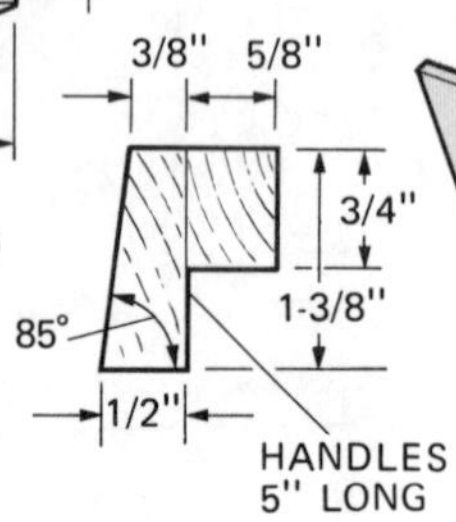


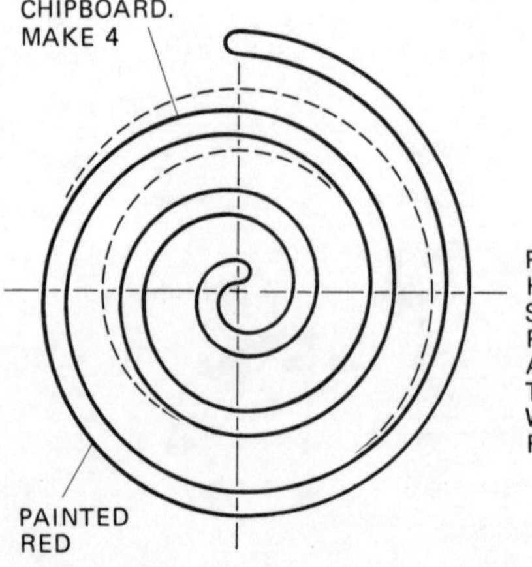


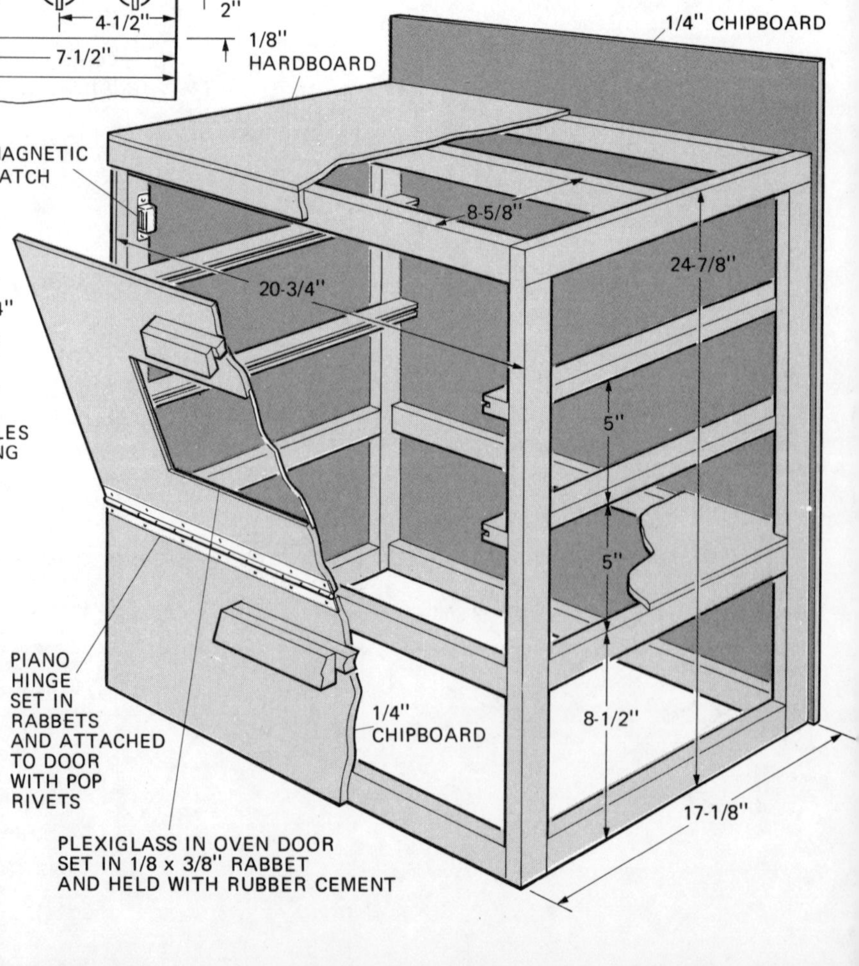

# Build a fleet of blockmobiles

By WILLARD WALTNER

A FLEET of these classy blockmobiles will provide hours of fun for a 4-year-old, and they can be made for practically nothing from scraps of 3/4 and 1 1/2-in. pine found in your woodbox. They are also practically unbreakable.

All are made by first gluing up blocks of varying thicknesses after precutting them to shape. All fender "wells" are bored 1/2 in. deep with a 1 3/8-in. spade power bit. Then 5/16-in. holes are drilled from each side for free-turning axles of 1/4-in. dowel rod.

SEE ALSO
**Dump trucks, toy . . . Gifts, Christmas . . . Playgrounds . . . Pull toys . . . Weekend projects**

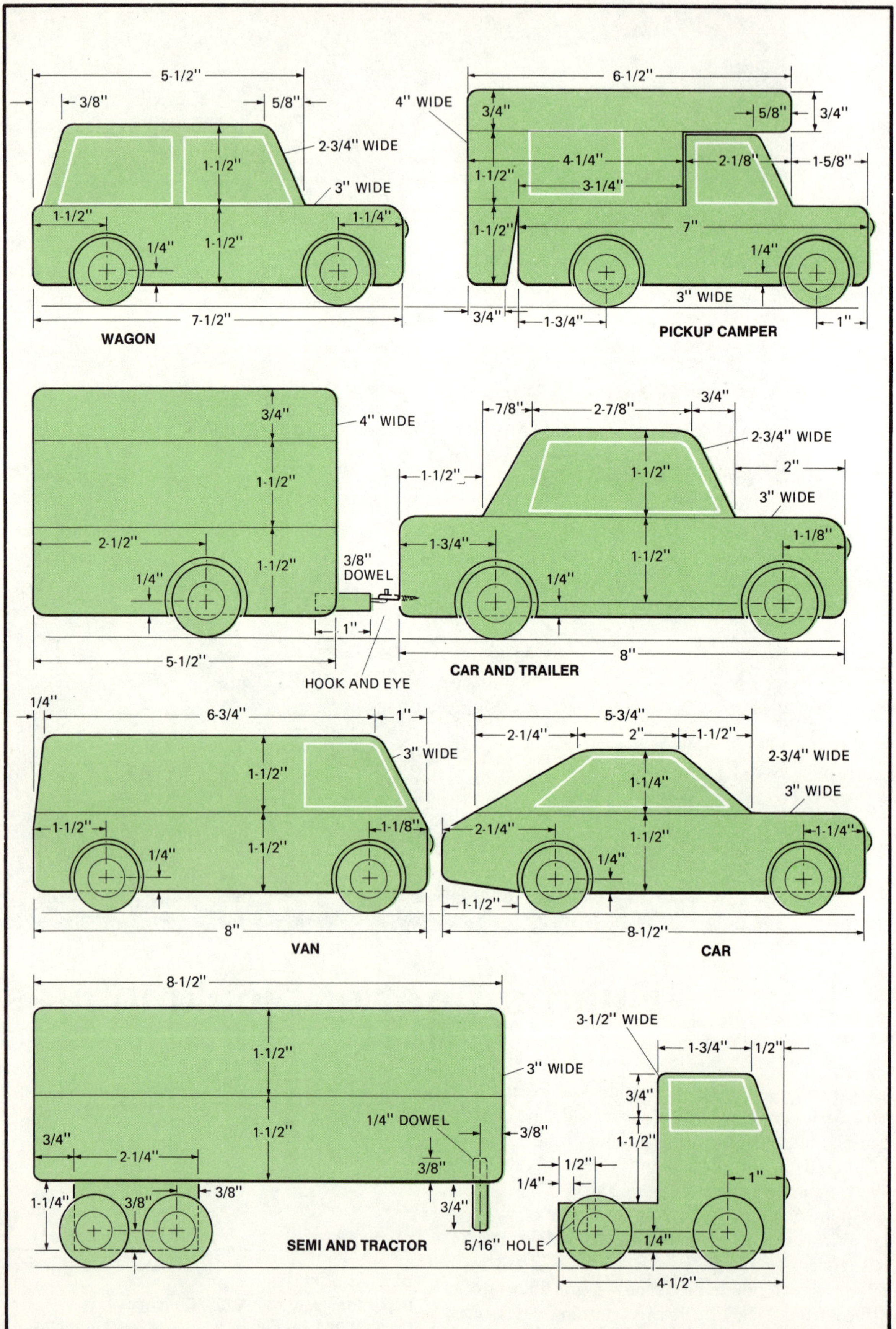

5-1/2"
3/8"
5/8"
2-3/4" WIDE
1-1/2"
3" WIDE
1-1/2"
1-1/4"
1/4"
1-1/2"
7-1/2"
WAGON
6-1/2"
4" WIDE
3/4"
5/8"
3/4"
4-1/4"
2-1/8"
1-5/8"
1-1/2"
3-1/4"
1-1/2"
7"
1/4"
3" WIDE
3/4"
1-3/4"
1"
PICKUP CAMPER
3/4"
4" WIDE
1-1/2"
2-1/2"
1-1/2"
1/4"
3/8" DOWEL
1"
5-1/2"
HOOK AND EYE
7/8"
2-7/8"
3/4"
2-3/4" WIDE
1-1/2"
1-1/2"
2"
3" WIDE
1-3/4"
1-1/8"
1-1/2"
1/4"
8"
CAR AND TRAILER
1/4"
6-3/4"
1"
3" WIDE
1-1/2"
1-1/2"
1-1/8"
1/4"
1-1/2"
8"
VAN
5-3/4"
2-1/4"
2"
1-1/2"
2-3/4" WIDE
1-1/4"
3" WIDE
2-1/4"
1-1/2"
1-1/4"
1/4"
1-1/2"
8-1/2"
CAR
8-1/2"
1-1/2"
3" WIDE
1/4" DOWEL
3/8"
3/4"
2-1/4"
1-1/2"
3/8"
1-1/4"
3/8"
3/8"
3/4"
SEMI AND TRACTOR
5/16" HOLE
3-1/2" WIDE
1-3/4"
1/2"
3/4"
1-1/2"
1/2"
1/4"
1"
1/4"
4-1/2"

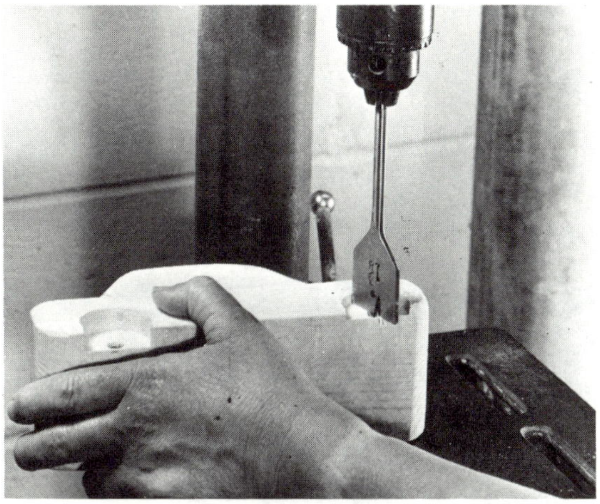

**FENDER WELLS** for wheels are made ½ in. deep with 1⅜-in. spade-type bit chucked in drill press.

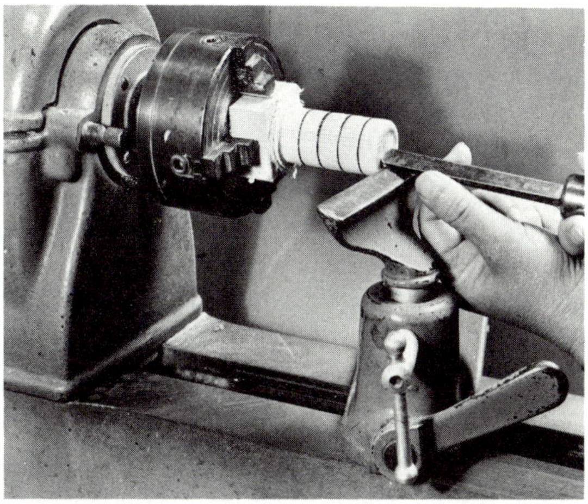

**WHEELS** are turned one at a time from chucked turning. Shape hub and tire first, then cut it off.

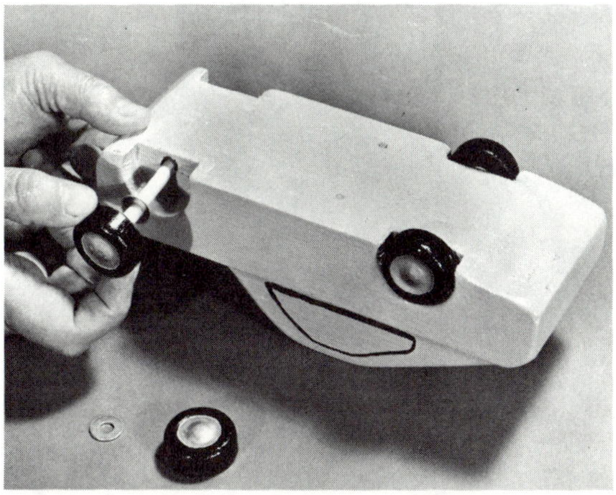

**GLUE WHEELS** to axles after inserting axles in their holes and slipping washers over the ends.

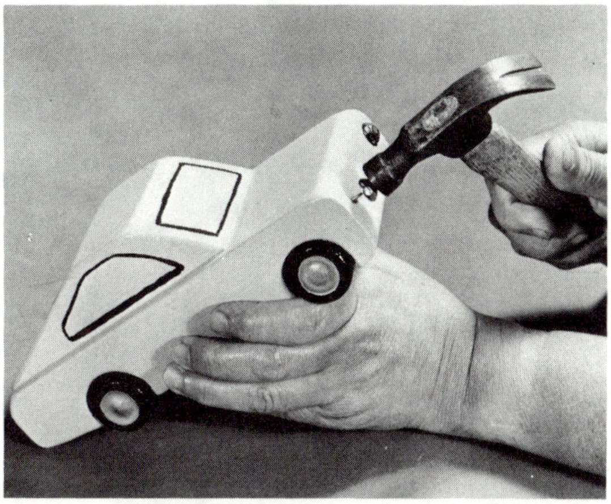

**FANCY-HEAD** upholstery nails make perfect headlights. Wooden screw-hole buttons, painted, can also be used.

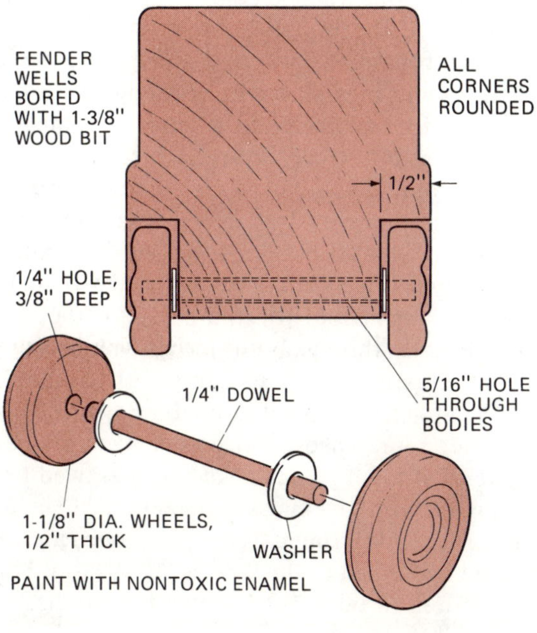


The wheels are easy to make if you own a lathe, but there are other ways to make them. One way is with a hole cutter in a drill press; another is with a pivot jig clamped to the table of a disc sander. In a pinch, checkers could be used for wheels.

The best way to turn the wheels is to gang-turn them from a single turning as shown in the photo above. Here the wheels are cut off one by one after you form a hub on the face of the wheels and round the edges to form a tire. The wheels are glued onto the ends of the dowel axles after being drilled ⅜ in. deep from the inside. Washers keep the wheels from rubbing and sticking. It's best to paint the wheels beforehand.

It's important, of course, to round all sharp edges, sand the wood smooth and paint the vehicles with a *nontoxic* paint.

Upholstery tacks are used for headlights, and a small L-hook and screw eye are used as a hitch for the car and trailer.

CIRCUS-WAGON TOY BOX

GIRAFFE CLOTHES TREE

# It's fun to make toys

SEE ALSO

**Children's furniture . . . Desks . . . Gifts, Christmas . . . Miniature houses . . . Playhouses . . . Pull toys . . . Weekend projects**

A MOST PRACTICAL GIFT is a toy box—even Mom might like to have it to corral the many toys Santa leaves. This one, a classy little circus wagon, will add color to any kid's room.

Sides of the wagon are carbon copies. The holes for the nine bars are drilled before the top and bottom members are sabre-sawed. In fact, each side can be made a simple rectangular frame to start before any of the pieces are bored and sawed. If you have a doweling jig, use it to bore mating holes dead-center and 3 in. apart. Make a full-size pattern from the half pattern given and trace the curves on your wood. For perfect alignment, drill the holes for the ¾-in. dowel axles through both side assemblies at one time. Enlarge the holes slightly with a round file or sandpaper wrapped around a dowel.

The 7-in. wheels consist of two plywood discs and a hub. The spokes are jigsawed first, then the ¼-in. thickness is glued to the ½ in. and both are sawed round as one. The hubs are centered and glued to the wheels, then ¾-in. holes are bored through both hub and ½-in. disc.

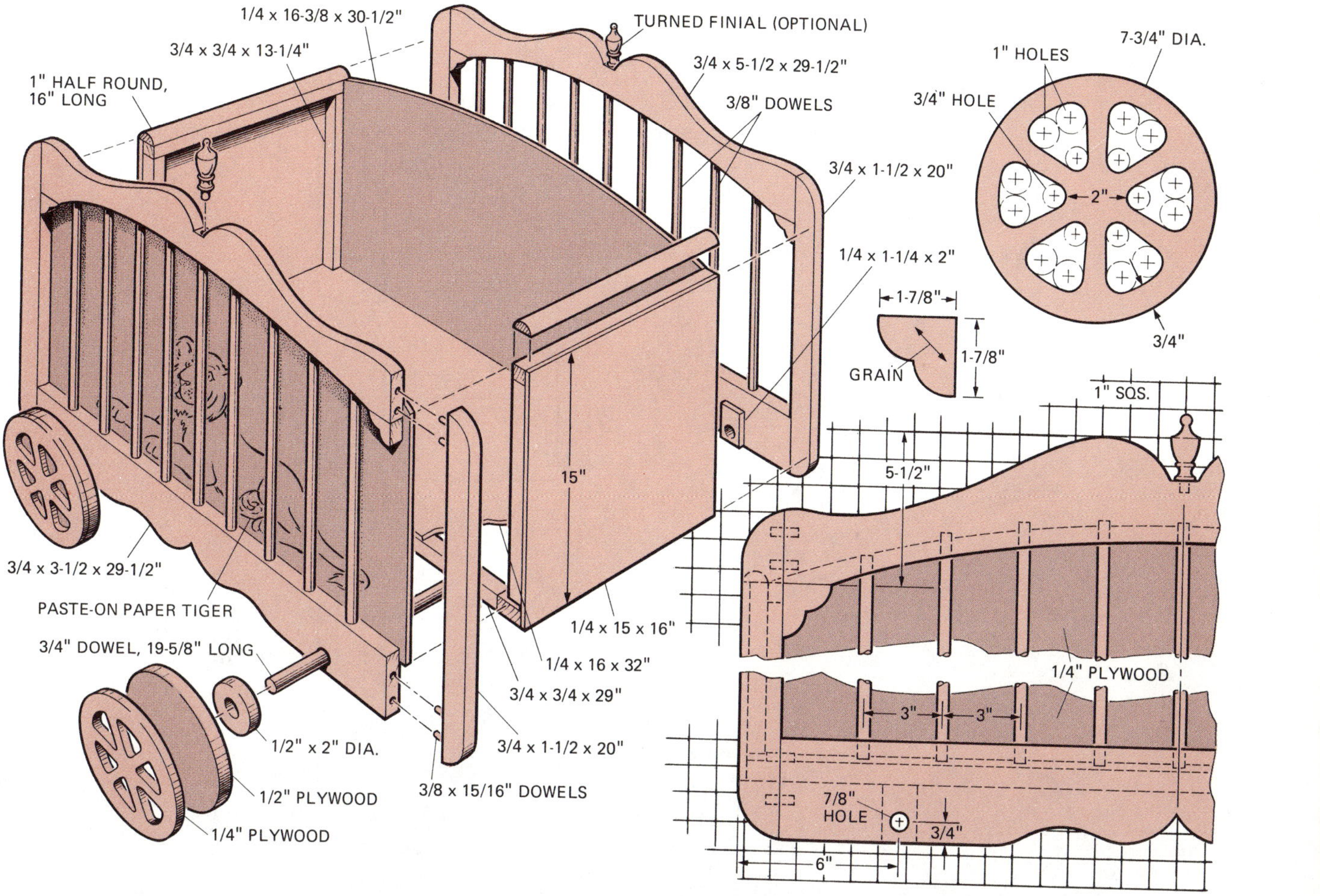

**ADJUSTABLE DOWELING JIG** simplifies drilling and aligning the mating dowel holes in the upper and the lower side members of the wagon.

**AFTER HOLES** are bored, the curves in the top and the bottom members are then cut with a sabre saw. With dowel bars in place, the ends are added.

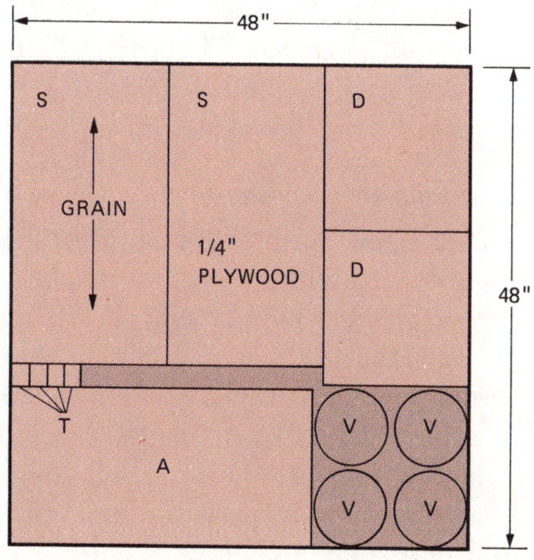


**Cutting layout**

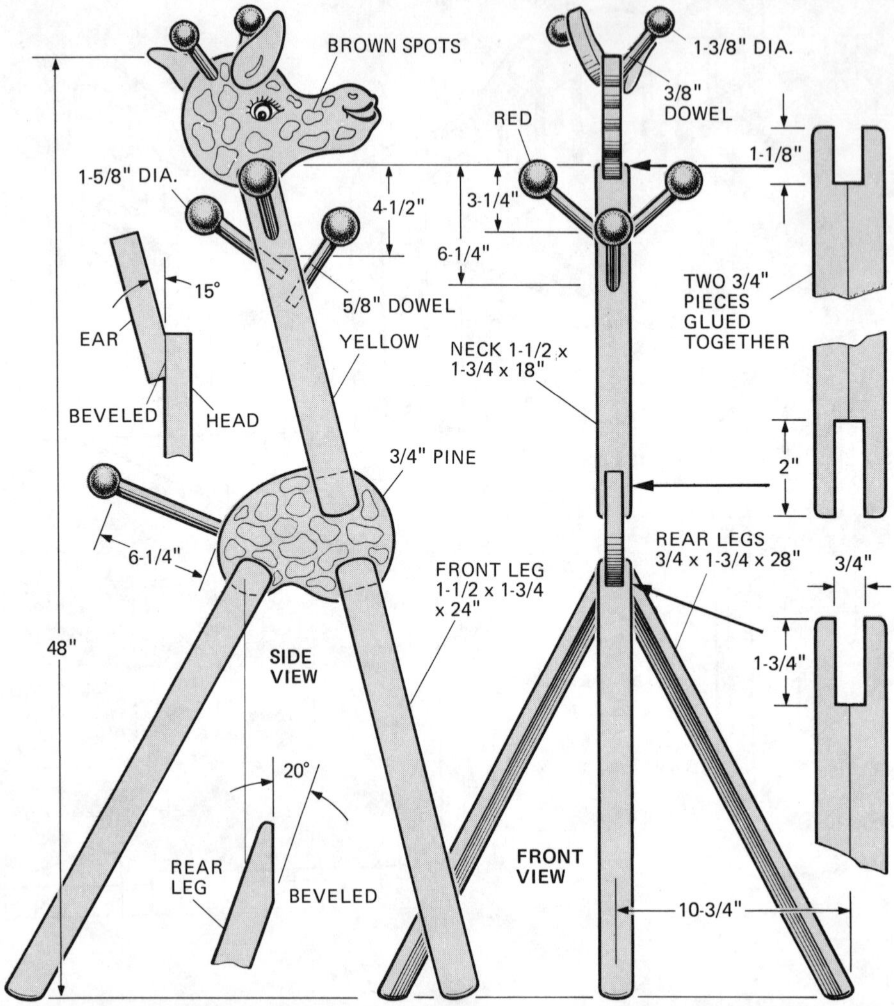


**GIRAFFE CLOTHES TREE**

The completed sides are glued to a simple ¼-in. plywood box and the cutting layout shows how the five parts can be laid out economically on a 4x4-ft. panel with wood to spare for the wheels. They are glued to ¾-in.-square members which are placed inside the ends and under the bottom. Sides of the cage are finally glued to the box; then panels S are painted white, and the paper tigers are attached with rubber cement and finally nailed in place behind the bars. Wheels are glued to the dowel axles to complete the project.

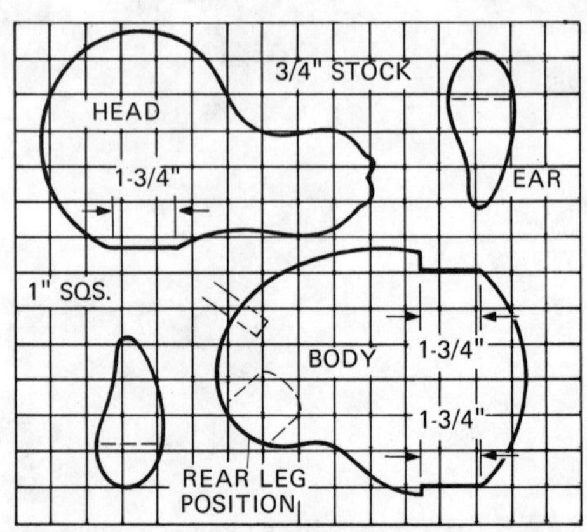


**he'll hold their clothes**

You'll be surprised how this long-necked, three-legged fellow can get little ones to hang up their clothes. Sawing the head, body and ears is hardest; the rest is easy. Ears are beveled on the inside to point outward when glued in place. Front leg and neck are two 1x2 pieces notched at ends, then glued together. Balls on ends of the pegs are wood finials you'll find at lumberyards and craft centers. Note that the top balls are smaller than others. Paint him yellow and add brown spots to make him look like a giraffe.

**any little girl's favorite**

Next to a doll, a dollhouse is perhaps the most wanted gift for any little girl. On the following page is a simple one Dad can make in a weekend. It's designed by Mary Schreck, dollhouse furniture designer, after an early 19th century English

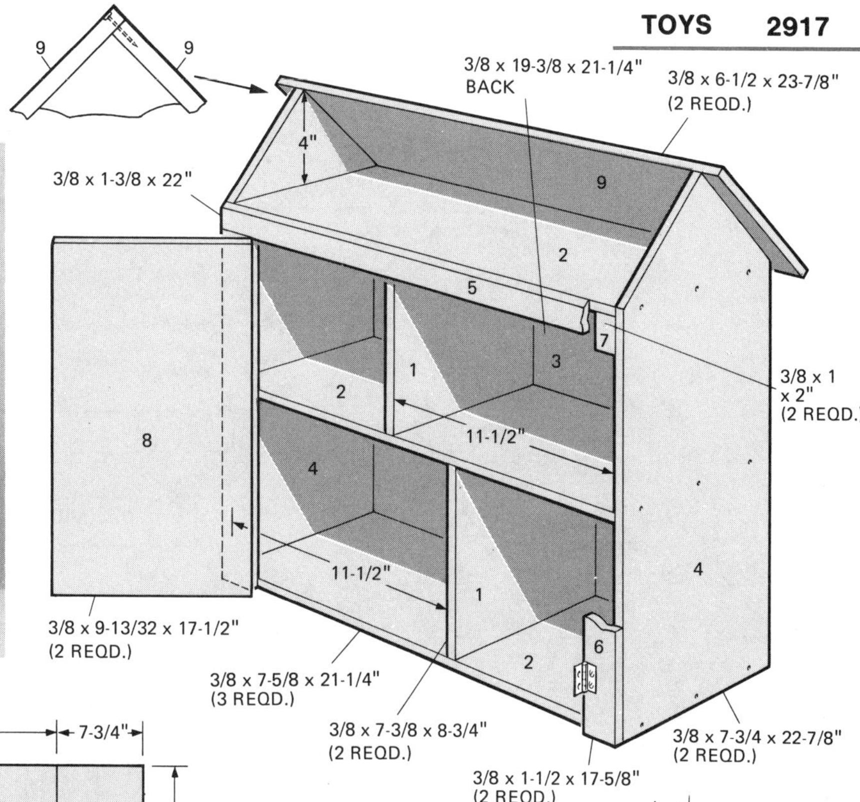


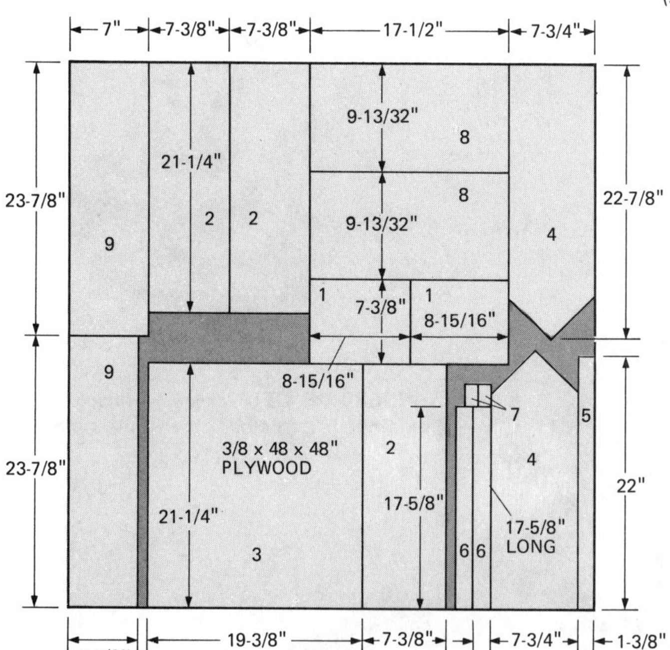

CUTTING LAYOUT

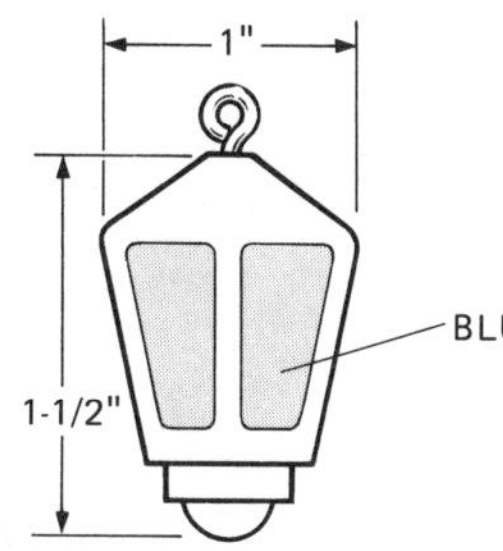


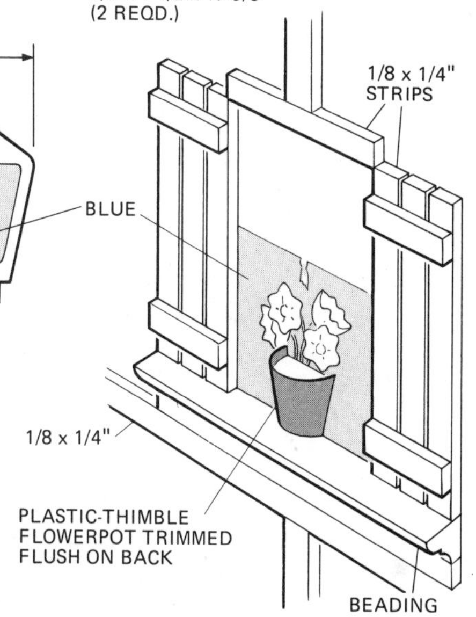


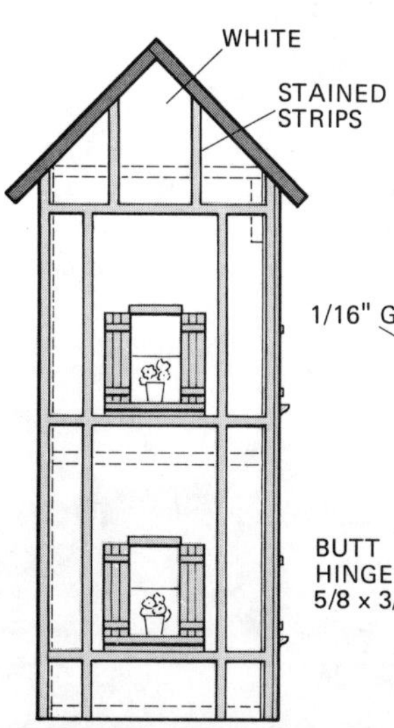

LEFT END

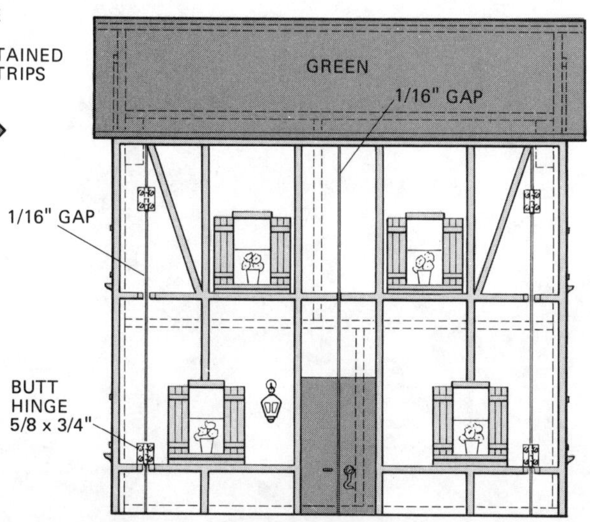

FRONT

**PUFF PUFF ENGINE**

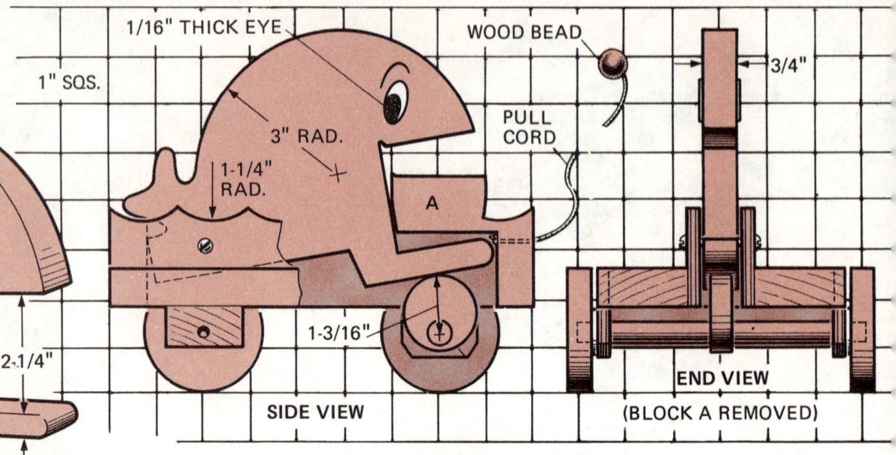


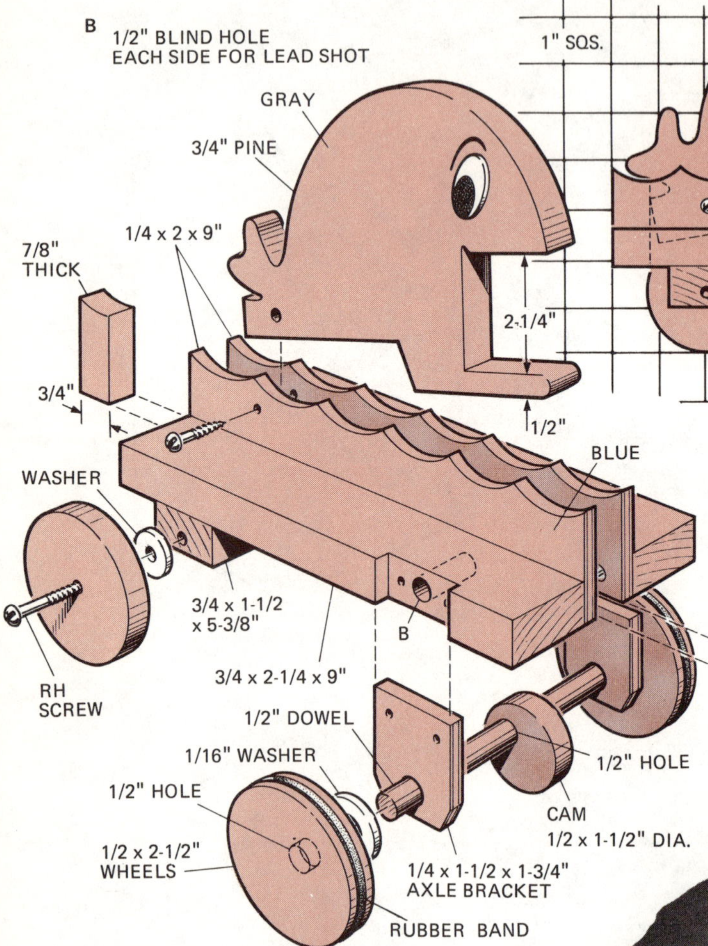


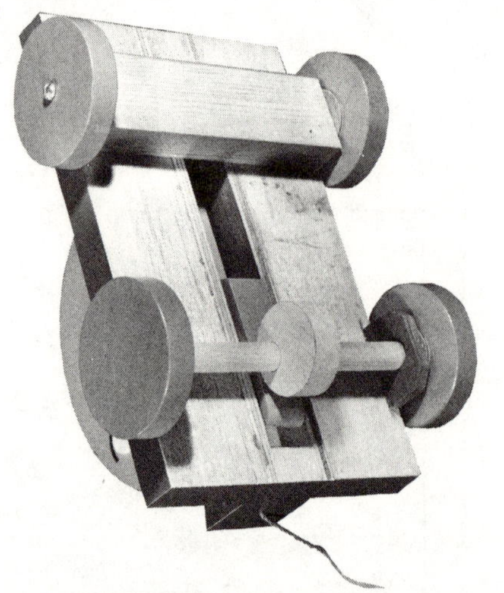

**UNDERSIDE VIEW** shows how cam on dowel axle opens and closes the whale's mouth.

**HALE THE WHALE**

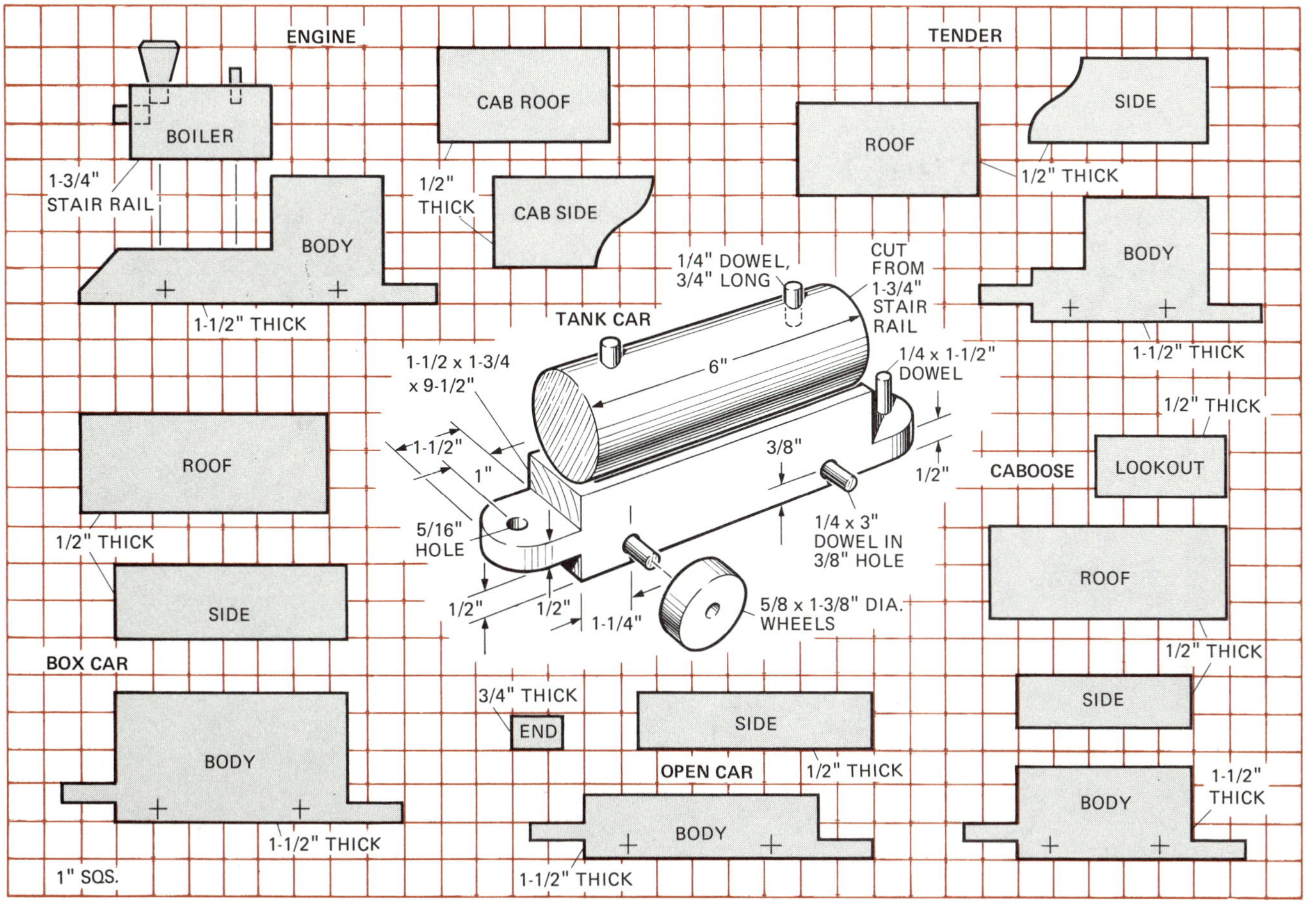


**WOOD-BLOCK TRAIN**

farmhouse. The front opens wide to provide full access to four rooms.

The 17 parts can be cut from a 4x4-ft. piece of ⅜-in. plywood. Follow the diagram when laying out the parts, but follow the dimensions when cutting.

Start assembly by nailing and gluing the three floors to one end, inserting partitions as you go. Then add the second end and the back. Glue parts 7 next, then part 5, and parts 6. Hinge panels 8 to the front and add the roof.

Paint the house white; then decorate ends and front with stained wood strips as shown in front and end views. Paint on windows and doors and fit them with shutters, window boxes and plastic thimble flowerpots.

**'smokes' as it rides along**

Puff puff engine is a toy which puffs "smoke" as it is pulled along. The illusion is created by a 7-in. clear plastic disc which rests on two inner wheels and turns clockwise when the wheels turn. Four "puffs" of blue tape are stuck to each side of the plastic disc at 12, 3, 6 and 9 o'clock, and a ⅛-in. wire shaft in an elongated center hole holds the disc in place.

The body is a sandwich of five layers, two ¾-in. thick, two ½-in. and one ¼ in. Spacers A and B form the ¼-in.-wide slot for the disc. The ½-in. pieces are made right and left hand, and the cab's roof is slotted for the disc. Blind holes are made in the four drive wheels and the wheels glued to their axles.

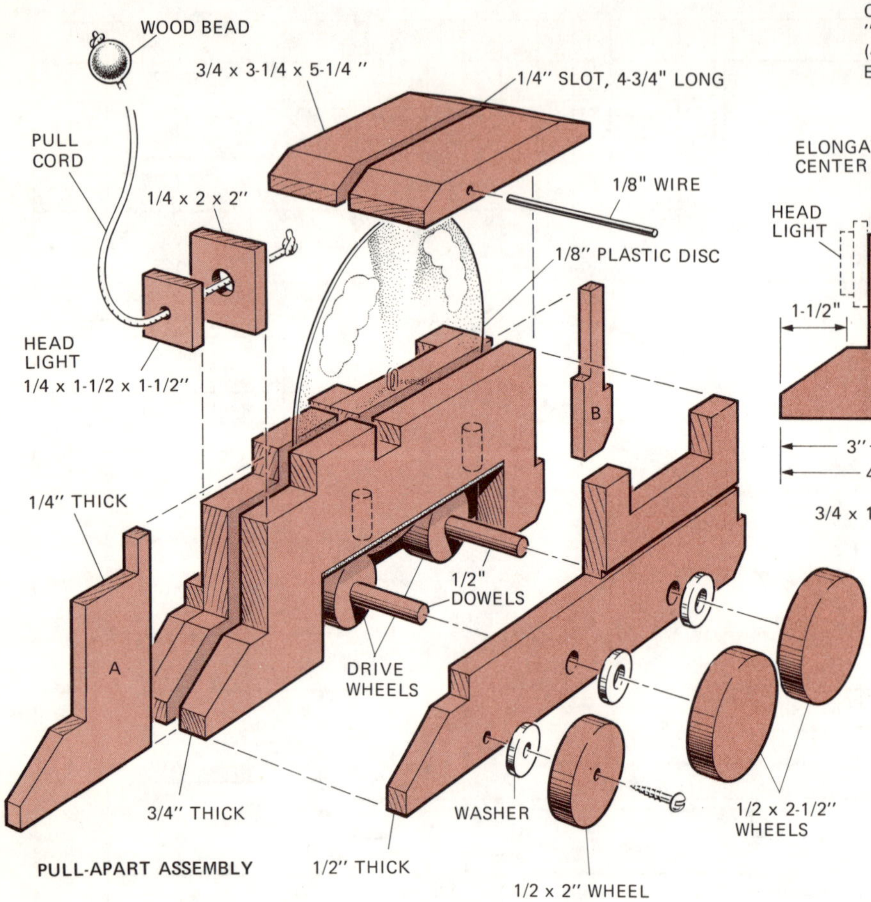


PULL-APART ASSEMBLY

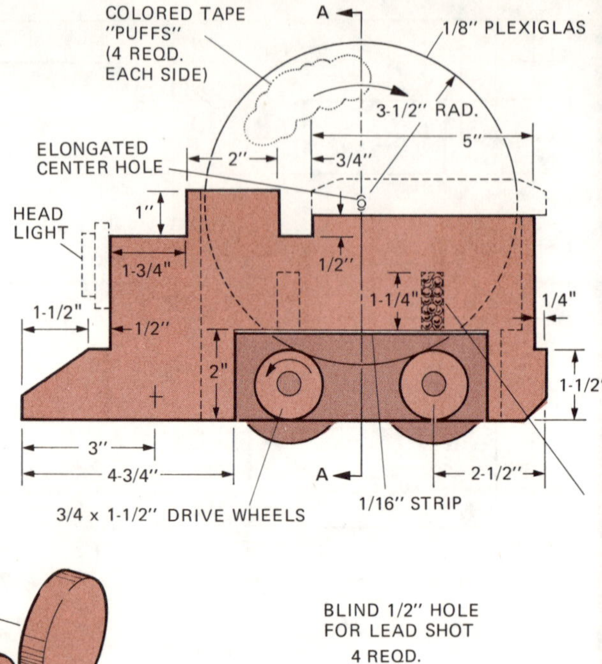


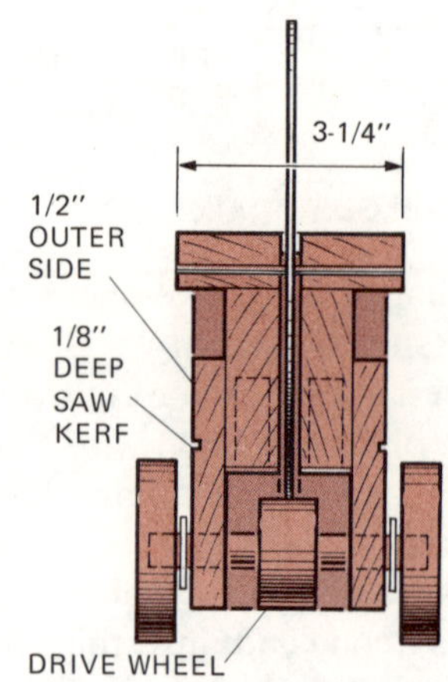


SECTION A-A

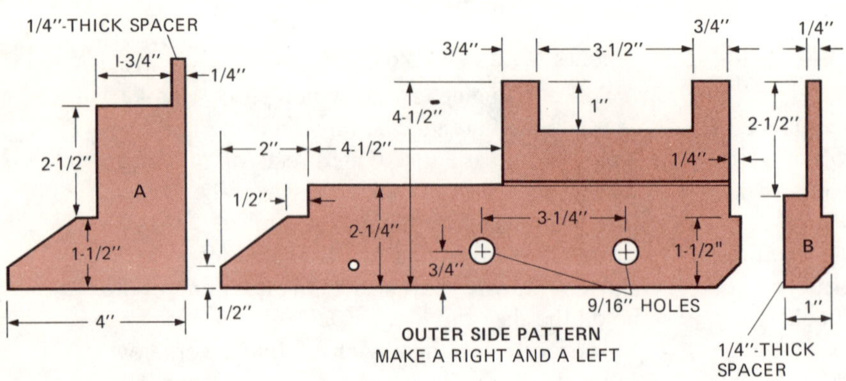


OUTER SIDE PATTERN
MAKE A RIGHT AND A LEFT

**his mouth is always moving**

Opening and closing his mouth as he swims along at the end of a string, Hale the Whale is an irresistible toy small fry will go for in a big way. A wood cam between the front wheels works the mouth up and down as the toy is pulled; ⅞-in. spacer blocks A and B allow free movement for the ¾-in. pivoted body.

A circle cutter in a drill press will cut the ½-in.-thick plywood wheels quickly. Round-head screws serve as axles for the rear wheels; blind holes in the front wheels fit the dowel axle and the wheels are glued on. Enlarge holes in the brackets slightly so the axle turns freely.

**fast freight from scrap wood**

Little guys always like trains for Christmas. The wood-block freight train can be made from scrap found in your woodbox. If you plan to make several as gifts, it will pay you to buy a length of 1⅜-in. wood closet pole and slice the ¾-in. wheels from it. Likewise a length of 1¾-in. stair rail will save time in making several engine boilers and tanks for tank cars.

# A toy plane for mini-pilots

BY H. R. HAGGERTY

THIS CHUNKY LITTLE BLOCK AIRPLANE for a chunky little aeronaut is a simple, nearly indestructible toy with just enough realism to excite his interest—including a prop that spins. It can be built in a couple of evenings. Wing and tail sections call for 2 feet of ½ x 6-in. clear pine; about 14 inches of 1 x 6 are needed for the fuselage. Propeller pin and wheel axle call for 8 inches of ¼-in. dowel. All remaining parts can be made from scraps of ¾-in. stock. Follow the plans below for dimensioning and cutting each piece. Sand all edges until round to avoid splinters. The propeller is easily made on a drill press. A plain block jig, beveled to 45°, is clamped to the table as shown. The ¾-in.-sq. blank is then held against the bevel and run past a sanding drum on the drill-press spindle. Leave enough hub for a 5/16-in. hole for prop pin and hub cowl. Assemble parts with brads and epoxy. The plane can be finished with clear finish or painted with a bright enamel.

**This all-wood airplane will be a hit with any kid you give it to. It's made from pine and features a prop and wheels that really turn**

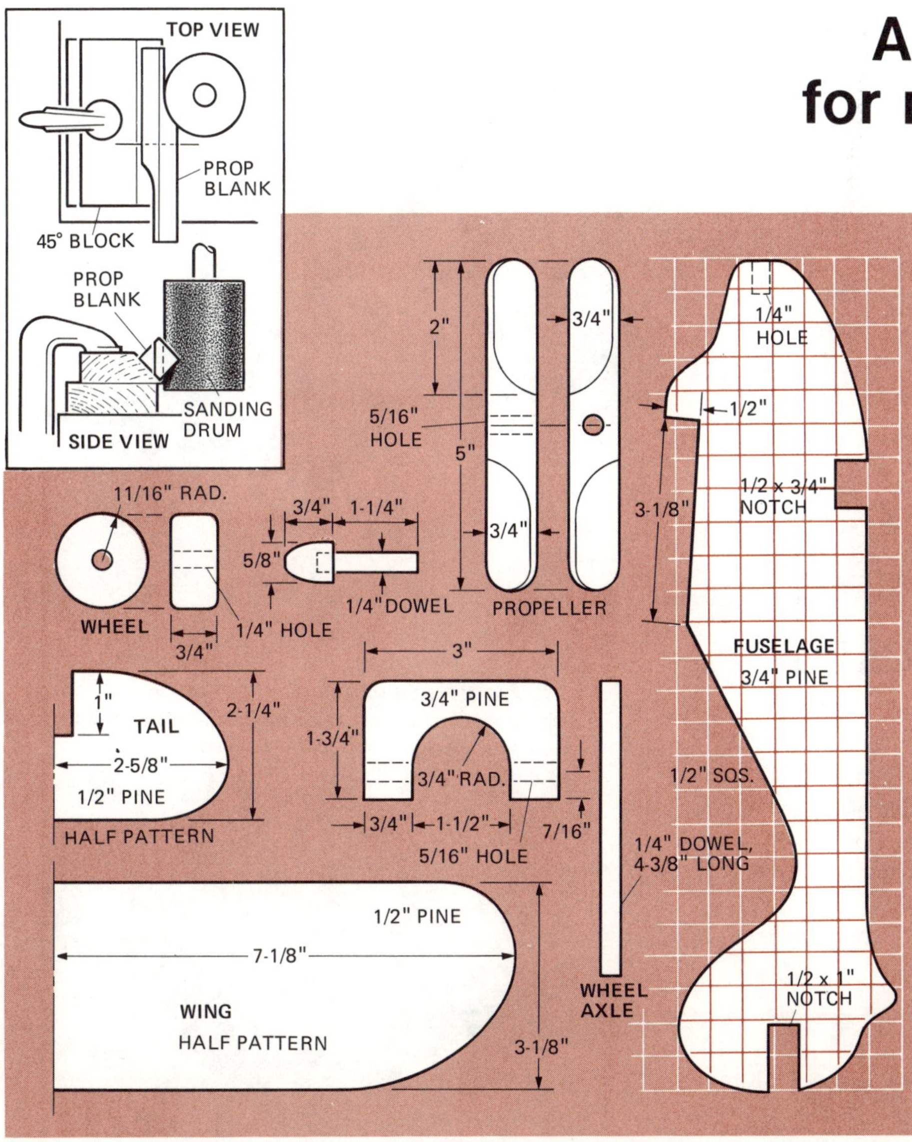

# Toy racetrack

By NELLO J. ORSINI

■ HERE'S AN EXCITING toy that will provide youngsters with all the thrills of a real speedway. I call it the Derby Hill 500. Four plastic cars are sent roaring down the track by two or four "drivers," each pulling one or two spring plungers. The car that goes the farthest or crosses the checkered finish line first wins.

SEE ALSO
**Dump trucks, toy . . . Gifts, Christmas . . . Kites . . . Playgrounds . . . Pull toys**

**STOVEBOLT SLIPPED** through coil spring and capped with drawer knob makes a plunger to propel the cars. Holes for plungers are centered in each track lane.

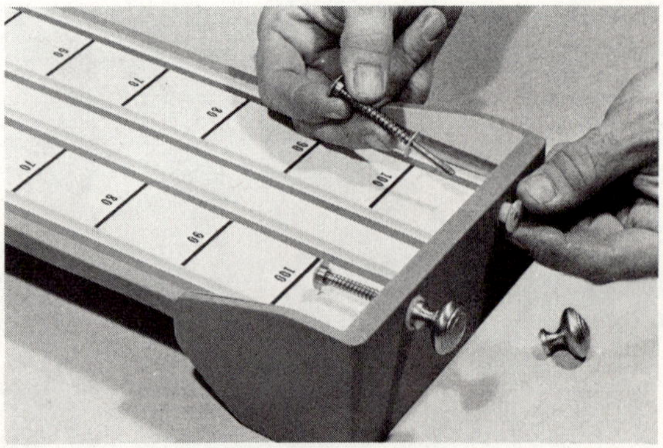

The four roadbed sections required can be placed either side by side or end to end to vary the fun. Placed in pairs side by side, the sections provide a four-track raceway 36-in. long. Hooked end to end, the sections provide a 6-ft.-long raceway. In the latter case, only two cars are driven and drivers are stationed at opposite ends, each taking turns racing his car down and up the inclined track. The driver who scores a total of 500 points first wins.

Each roadbed section measures 7-in. wide by 18-in. long and has four ½-in.-wide grooves spaced to suit the wheels of the particular plastic race cars used. The cars I used were purchased at Woolworth's and are about 6-in. long.

The drawings show how the roadbed sections are supported and how they hook together. Metal angles formed from sheet aluminum engage saw kerfs in the support blocks. The outboard end of the track hooks similarly into an open fold in the metal ramp.

Stick-on scoring numerals are used for marking the track, and ⅛-in. black matte charting tape (Prestype) is used to rule off scoring divisions.

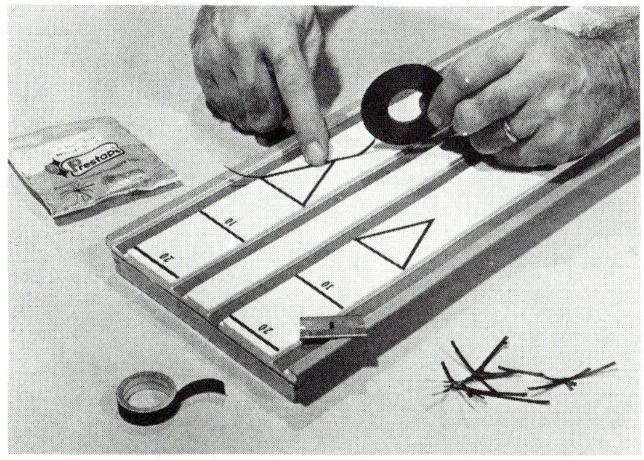

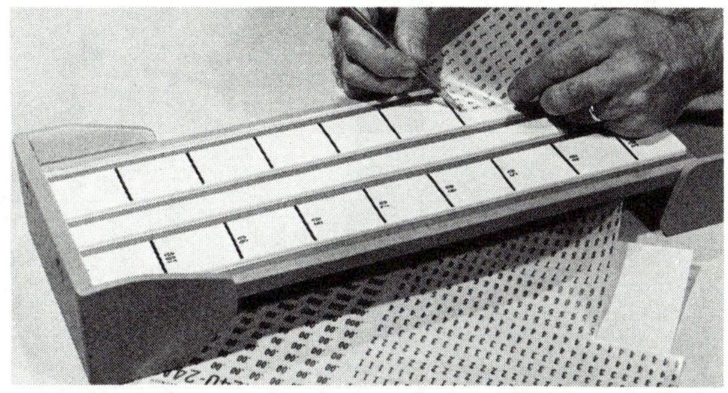

**BLACK CHARTING TAPE,** ⅛-in. wide, is used to rule lines on track surface (top). Green tape marks wheel channels; press-on numerals make neat numbering job.

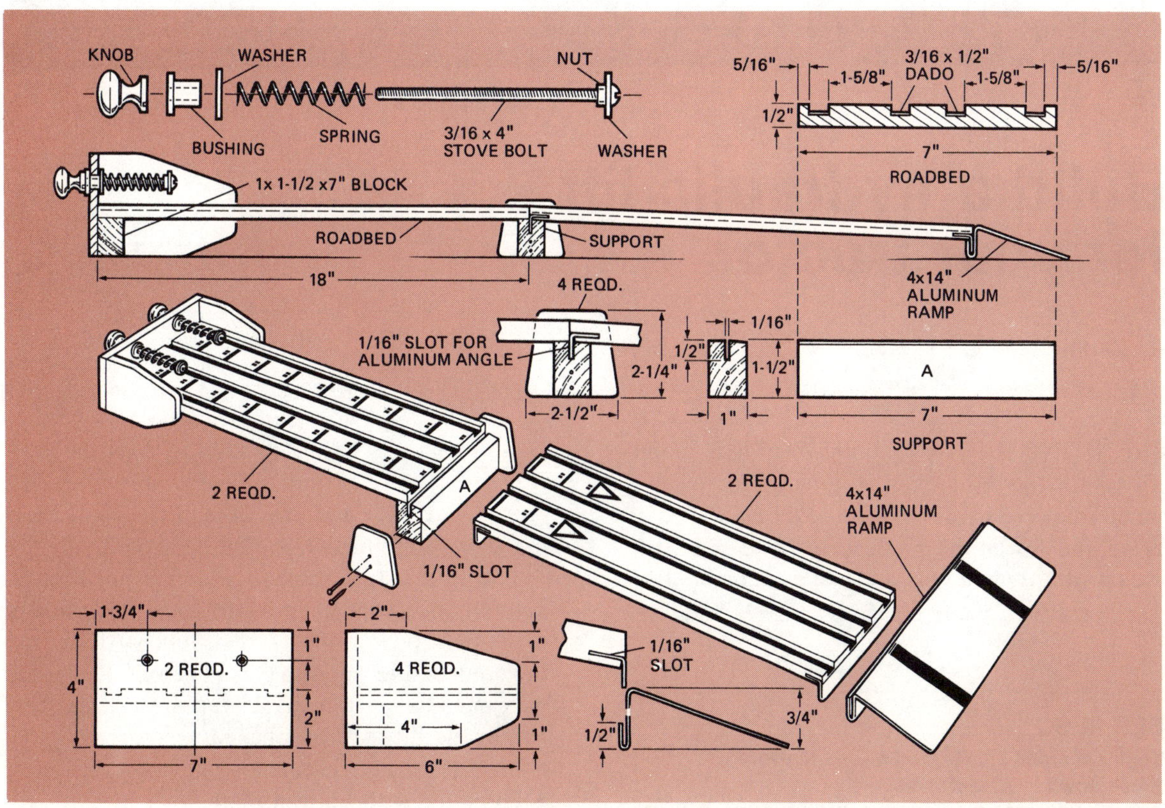

# Build a hydraulic lift for your tractor

By MAURICE ORLAREY

LIFTING A HEAVY bulldozer blade manually is for the birds even when it's only a fairly small one on a garden tractor. Pulling a lever to raise and lower the blade can make you arm-weary after only a few hours of grading or snow pushing. That's why I decided to do it the easy way and add a hydraulic lift so a mere push of a button would lift and lower the blade. Now I feel like a big-time heavy-equipment operator!

The first step I took to add this pushbutton convenience was a trip to the local junkyard to pick up the power unit—a hydraulic system from the convertible top of a car. (The one I selected happened to be from an Oldsmobile.) At the time I built the lift, $10 purchased:

- Motor, pump, reservoir unit.
- Cylinder with bottom plate.

SEE ALSO

**Engines, small . . . Gardening . . . Mowers . . . Snowplows . . . Tractor trailers**

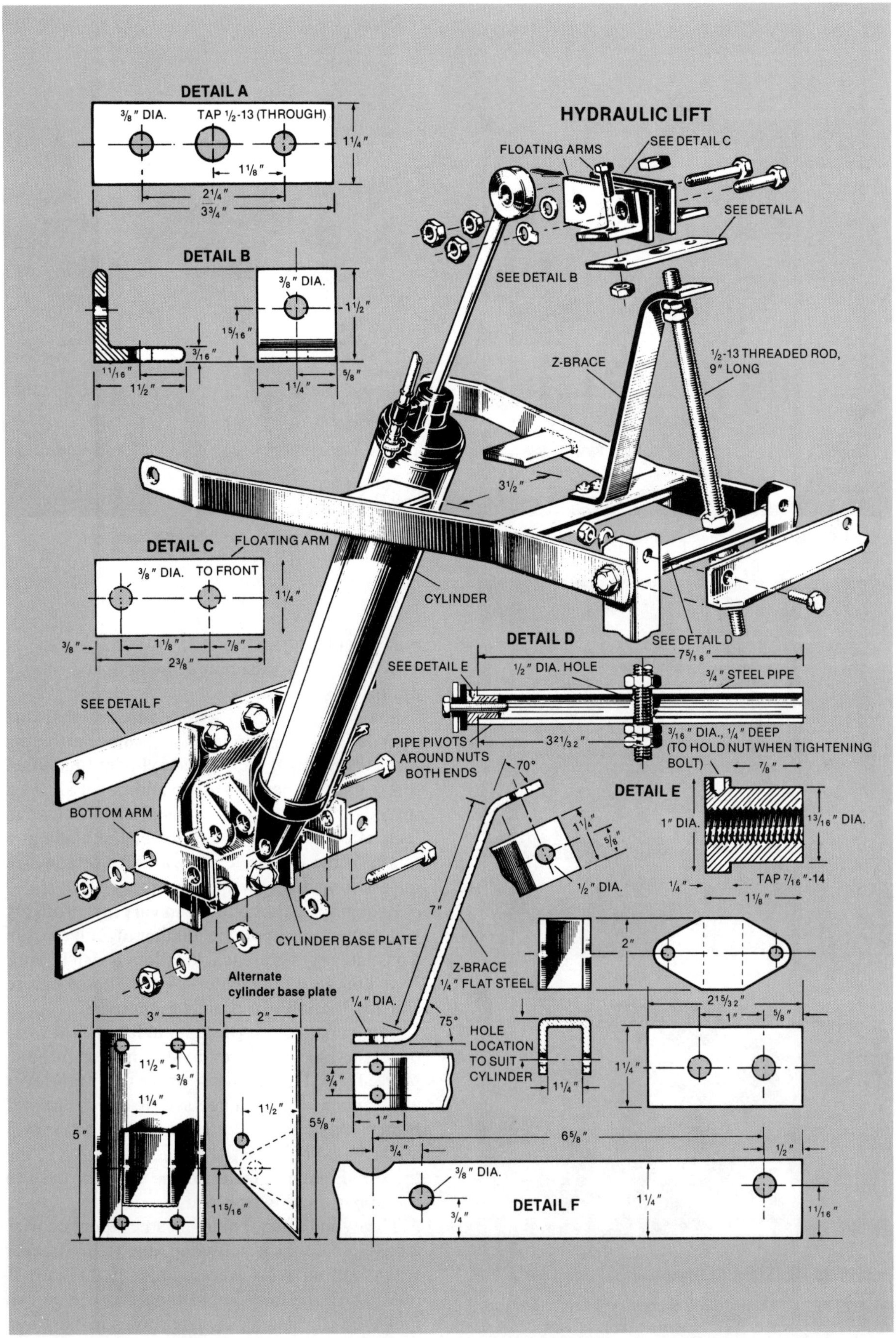
HYDRAULIC LIFT
DETAIL A
3/8" DIA.
TAP 1/2-13 (THROUGH)
1 1/4"
1 1/8"
2 1/4"
3 3/4"
DETAIL B
3/8" DIA.
1 1/2"
1 5/16"
3/16"
11/16"
1 1/2"
1 1/4"
5/8"
FLOATING ARMS
SEE DETAIL C
SEE DETAIL A
SEE DETAIL B
Z-BRACE
1/2-13 THREADED ROD, 9" LONG
3 1/2"
DETAIL C
FLOATING ARM
3/8" DIA.
TO FRONT
1 1/4"
3/8"
1 1/8"
7/8"
2 3/8"
CYLINDER
SEE DETAIL D
DETAIL D
7 5/16"
SEE DETAIL E
1/2" DIA. HOLE
3/4" STEEL PIPE
SEE DETAIL F
PIPE PIVOTS AROUND NUTS BOTH ENDS
3 21/32"
3/16" DIA., 1/4" DEEP (TO HOLD NUT WHEN TIGHTENING BOLT)
7/8"
70°
DETAIL E
1" DIA.
13/16" DIA.
1/4"
TAP 7/16"-14
1 1/8"
BOTTOM ARM
1 1/4"
5/8"
1/2" DIA.
7"
CYLINDER BASE PLATE
Z-BRACE
1/4" FLAT STEEL
2"
2 15/32"
1"
5/8"
Alternate cylinder base plate
1/4" DIA.
75°
HOLE LOCATION TO SUIT CYLINDER
1 1/4"
3"
2"
1 1/2"
3/8"
1 1/4"
1 1/2"
5 5/8"
5"
3/4"
1"
6 5/8"
3/4"
1/2"
3/8" DIA.
DETAIL F
1 1/4"
3/4"
11/16"
1 15/16"

**CYLINDER BOTTOM** arms are attached to plate with a bolt and to cylinder with shaft, washer and cotter pin.

**BLADE RESTING** on ground exposes ½-in. threaded rod. Extended down, it allows room for adjustment.

- Hydraulic hose.
- Wiring and dashboard switch for above motor.

Since at this point I wasn't sure whether one cylinder would provide enough muscle for the job, I also bought the second cylinder (manufacturers use two per car) for an additional $2. As it turned out, one cylinder was sufficient. It will, in fact, effortlessly raise and lower the blade at a touch of the button, even with an average-size male sitting atop the blade.

Recognizing that prices can vary and probably will, depending upon the number of junkyards in a particular geographical location, a visit to your local junkyard for a materials price quote before starting the job is a practical approach.

Some changes on the manual lifting unit were necessary so that the cylinder could be fitted in place. First, I had to disassemble the lifting lever and linkage that connects it to the upper-lift frame. Then, using ¼ x 1¼ x 14¼-in. flat iron, I made a flat brace (Detail F) and fastened it to the tractor. Finally, I fastened the cylinder base to the upper and lower braces.

The cylinder that I bought came equipped with a base plate which was adaptable to my tractor when bottom arms were added. If this part is missing on the unit that you purchase, you can make the alternate base plate shown in the draw-

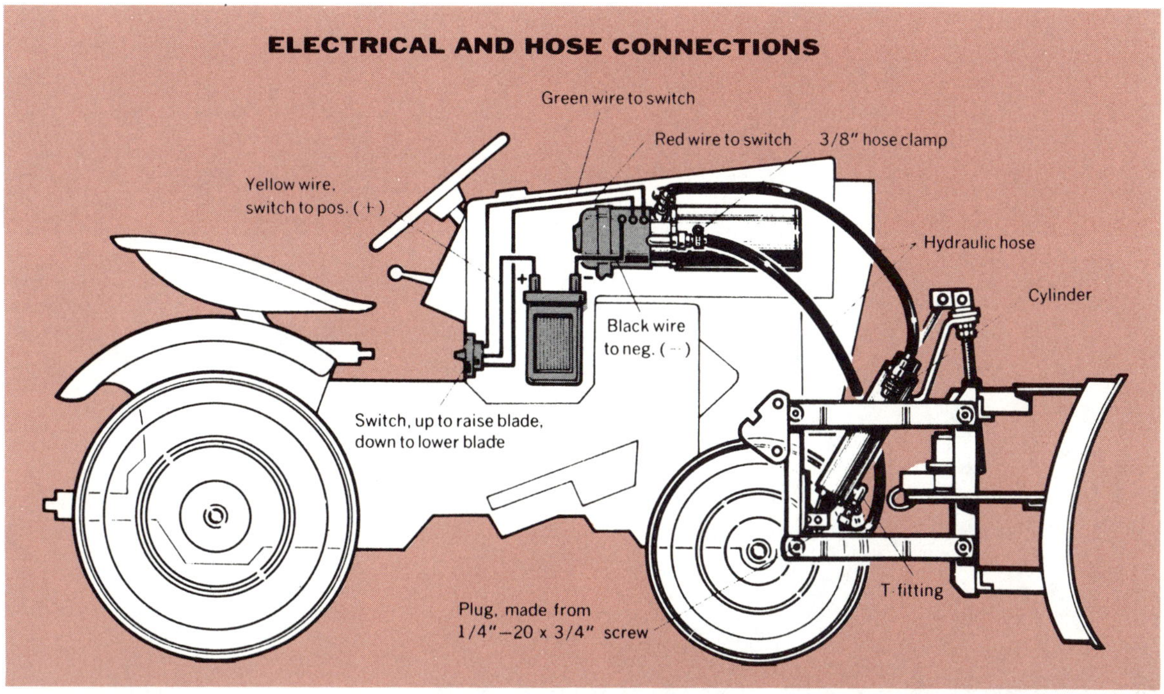


**AFTER CUTTING HOSE** to unused second cylinder, plug T-fitting with a ¼-in.-diameter bolt and a ⅜-in. clamp.

ings. With this version, the bottom arms can be eliminated since the cylinder-holding U-channel provides ample swing-clearance.

The motor-pump reservoir unit fits snugly under the tractor hood. On my rig it had to be positioned on the top left side of the engine between the air cleaner, gas tank and left headlight. To make room, it was necessary to move the air-cleaner cover slightly to the right.

Current draw is given at about 35 amps. which is no problem for my 12-v. heavy-duty battery. The "on" time is very short since the blade is lifted at a speed of roughly 2 in. per second. If your blade doesn't stay up, due to slow leakage through the pump, it can be corrected by stiffening the pivot points of the upper and lower frames by inserting spring lock washers under the bolt heads.

All of the dimensions shown were determined by trial-and-error fitting as I built the lift to suit the tractor (Sears 10-hp XL). For other makes I would recommend experimenting with cardboard and/or plywood templates to check for fit and clearance before cutting, shaping and welding the iron.

Working at a leisurely pace, I completed the setup in my spare time. I'm so pleased with the results that I feel it borders on understatement to say that my effort was worth every minute.

**WITH THREADED ROD** almost vertical, floating arm position indicates that the blade is free to float.

**POWER UNIT** fits neatly under hood on the engine's left side when the air cleaner was moved slightly.

# Make a trailer for your garden tractor

By G. R. JOBE

YOU'LL HAVE A SURE CURE for those backaches caused by heavy back-yard chores with this functional utility trailer that can be constructed of common materials to fit most any make of garden tractor.

The versatility of the trailer is mainly a result of the flexible arrangement of interlocking slatted sides and a removable rear panel. The trailer can be used with its four slatted sides, or it can be converted quickly to a three or four-sided flatbed type.

Made of four horizontal and two vertical strips of ¾ x 2¾-in. fir, the slatted sides slip into retainers of 16-ga. cold-rolled steel (CRS) permanently mounted to the four side panels of ¾-in. exterior plywood. Attached to the top slats of each side are supports of 12-ga. CRS that hook onto each other and greatly strengthen the corner joints while allowing quick and easy removal of the sides without the need for any tools.

The main section of the trailer consists of a three-sided plywood enclosure mounted on a steel frame. The fourth side (rear panel) slips into the channel formed by the lengths of 1x1 and 2x2 angle that are screwed to the inner and outer surfaces of the side panels.

The frame or chassis of the trailer is made of 1⅛-in.-square steel bar, although steel pipe, square or round tubing, angle or channel also could be used. Regardless of which material you use, however, make certain that all joints are securely welded together with fillet welds.

Almost any type of pneumatic tire and wheel assembly can be used, as long as it is at least 12 in. in diameter. Suitable wheels often can be

SEE ALSO

**Engines, small . . . Gardening . . . Lawns . . . Mowers . . . Snowplows . . . Tractor lifts**

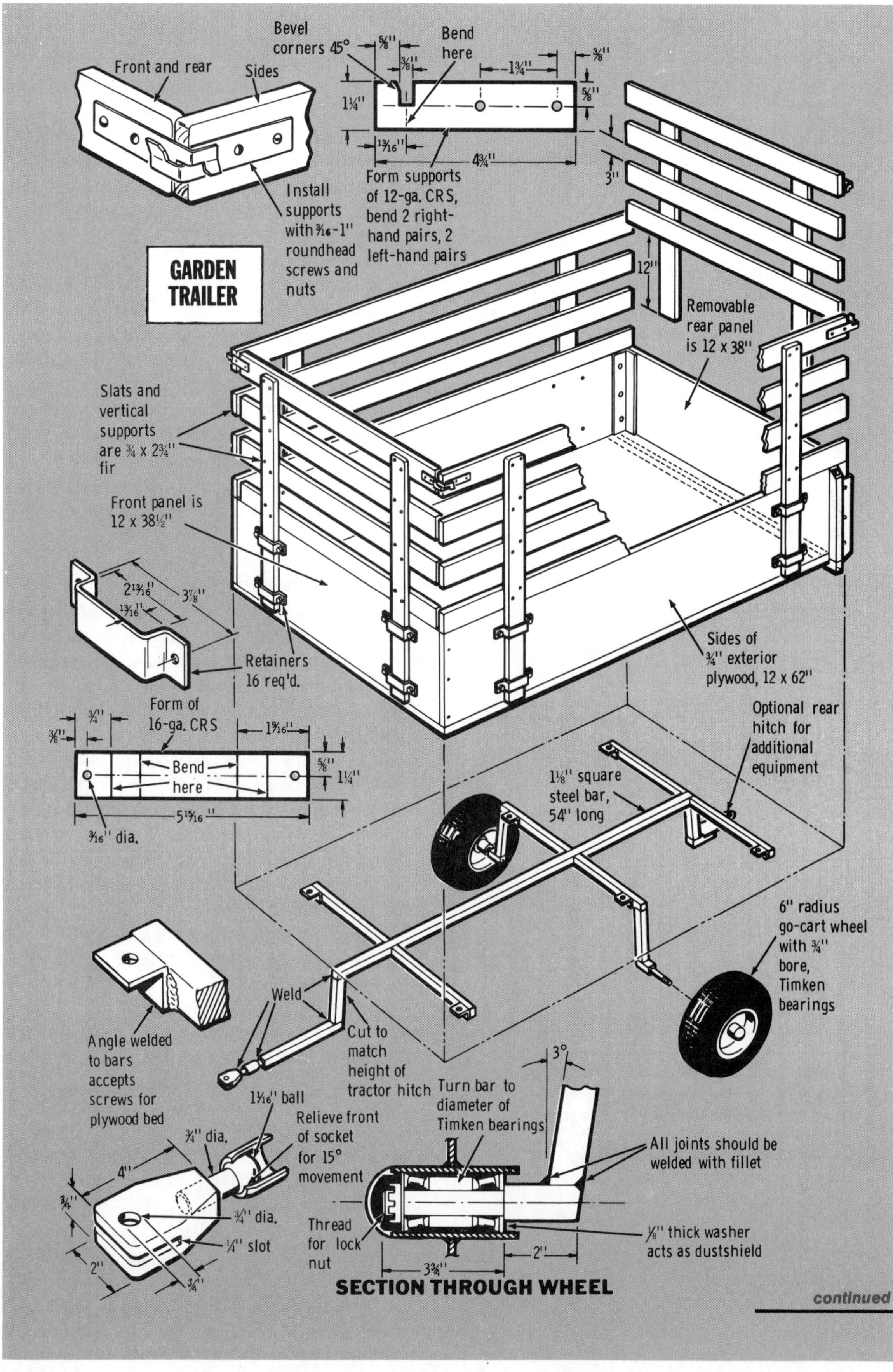
GARDEN TRAILER
Front and rear
Sides
Bevel corners 45°
Bend here
Install supports with 3/16-1" roundhead screws and nuts
Form supports of 12-ga. CRS, bend 2 right-hand pairs, 2 left-hand pairs
Removable rear panel is 12 x 38"
Slats and vertical supports are ¾ x 2¾" fir
Front panel is 12 x 38½"
Retainers 16 req'd.
Form of 16-ga. CRS
Bend here
3/16" dia.
Sides of ¾" exterior plywood, 12 x 62"
Optional rear hitch for additional equipment
1⅛" square steel bar, 54" long
6" radius go-cart wheel with ¾" bore, Timken bearings
Angle welded to bars accepts screws for plywood bed
Weld
Cut to match height of tractor hitch
1 1/16" ball
Relieve front of socket for 15° movement
Turn bar to diameter of Timken bearings
All joints should be welded with fillet
Thread for lock nut
⅛" thick washer acts as dustshield
¾" dia.
¼" slot
SECTION THROUGH WHEEL

continued

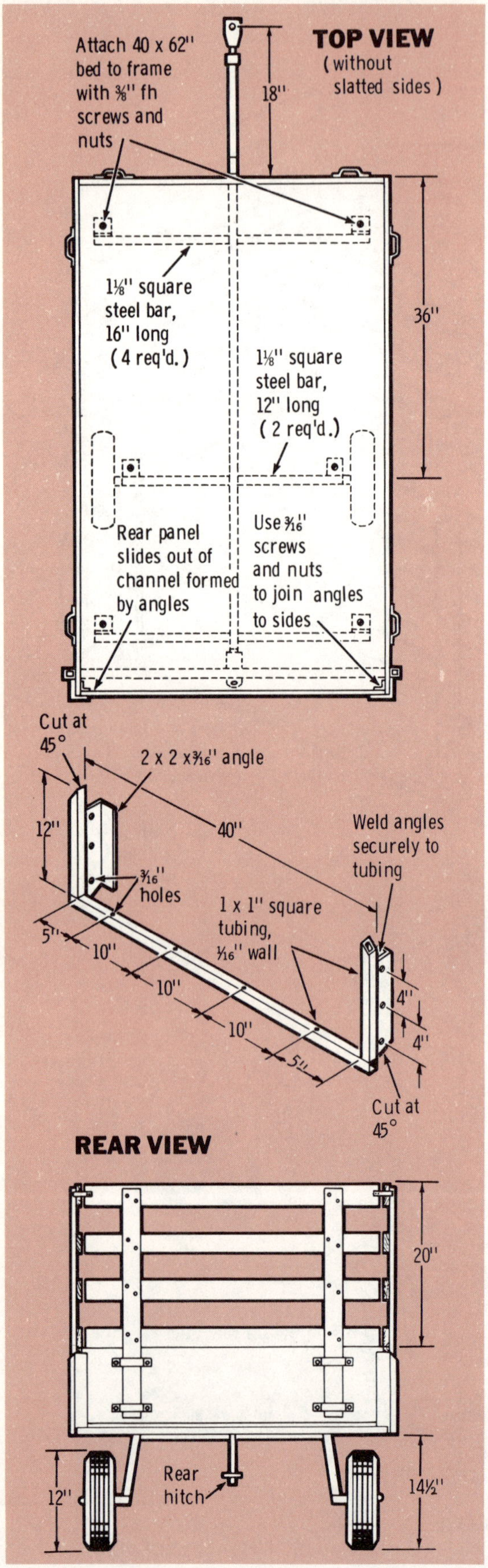


salvaged from wheelbarrows, boat trailers, golf carts or lawnmowers. Go-kart wheels are probably the best choice, especially if they are equipped with tapered roller bearings. The inner diameter of the bearings should be at least ¾ in.

Ball bearings (sealed or nonsealed) or sleeve bearings will work equally well. However, provisions must be made for lubricating and sealing any hubs not fitted with sealed, prelubricated bearings.

The spindles are turned from the square steel bar to accommodate the wheels and bearings selected. The turned length should equal the spacing between bearings, plus the space required for a grease seal, flat washer and nut. The end of the turned spindle also can be threaded and drilled for a castellated nut and cotter pin.

An alternative method to form the spindles is to weld a headless bolt in a hole drilled in the supporting arm of the chassis. Be sure, however, that the wheel will clear the arm of the steel chassis.

**construction sequence**

The steel frame and wheels should be assembled first, then fitted to your tractor so the proper vertical position of the hitch can be determined. The length of the horizontal bar connecting the hitch to the frame may also have to be modified slightly since the turning radius of your tractor might be smaller than that shown.

When completed and tested, the frame should be fitted with six short sections of angle drilled to facilitate the mounting of the bed to the frame. Then clean all welded areas, removing the slag completely, and give the frame a protective coat of zinc chromate primer.

The bed of the trailer is built upside down on a level surface. All joints should be made with waterproof glue and secured in alignment with 1¼-in. finishing nails. Then drill and drive in No. 8 1½-in. wood screws every 10 in. and allow the bed to dry before adding the U-support at the rear.

Six 3-in. blocks of scrap wood are used as spacers to insure the proper positioning of the slats on the vertical supports. Make certain the vertical supports are spaced the same distance away from the ends of the slats before gluing and screwing the sides together.

When all glued joints have dried, screw the bed to the frame. Then secure the retainers to the side panels and the locking supports to the corners of the slatted sides. Finish by painting and trimming the trailer to match the tractor's colors.

**COLORS THAT** have been mixed often dry somewhat lighter or darker than they appear in the paint can. A wet dab placed on a white blotter "dries" quickly to give you an idea of the exact hue.

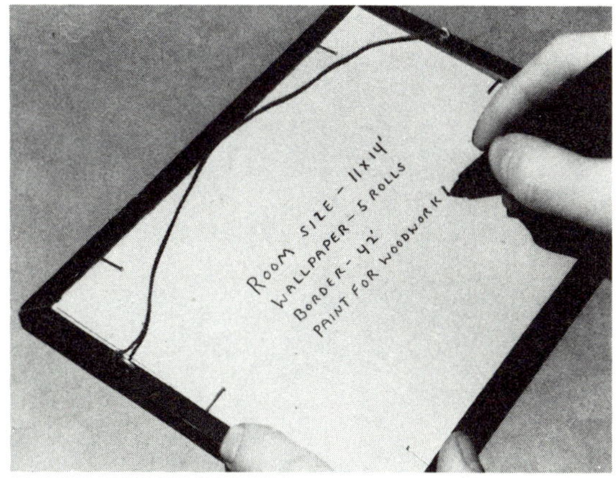


**AVOID REMEASURING** a room each time you get ready for new wallpaper with this trick. Put all of the data on the back of a wall-hung picture in the room—and the information will always be at hand.

**PLACE A JAR LID** under each leg of a chair or table to keep them from sticking to newspapers spread on the floor. When the newly painted furniture dries, simply roll up the papers and lids and throw away.

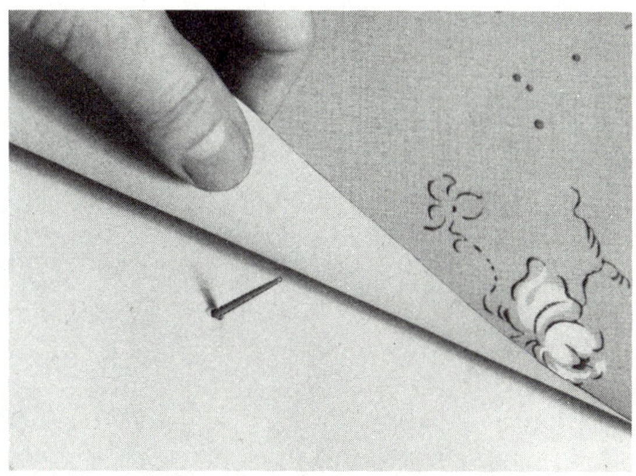

**NEXT TIME** you wallpaper, insert a toothpick in the hole as you remove each picture hook from the wall. Toothpicks, left in place, will protrude through the new paper, making hook replacement easy.

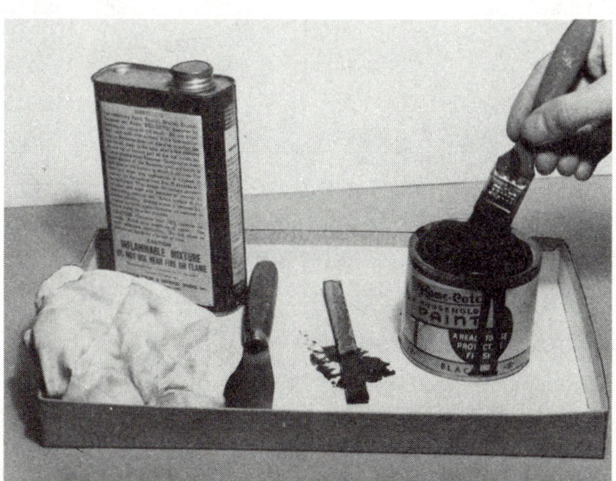

**WHEN YOU DO** a small paint job, a good way to keep paint and other equipment together is to place them in a cardboard box cover. All is handy, and you'll save steps going for forgotten items.

**USE A DISC** of wire screen cut slightly smaller than the diameter of your paint can to save yourself the trouble of straining lumpy paint. The round pieces of screen takes the lumps with it as it sinks.

# We built our own tent trailer

**Camping can make for an inexpensive and interesting vacation. This four-sleeper tent trailer is just the thing for your next trip. You can build it yourself in your garage. It unfolds easily when you get to the campsite**

By JAMES L. BENNETT

SEE ALSO
**Campers . . . Camping . . . Recreational vehicles . . . Vacation homes**

BECAUSE WE THINK camping is the best and least expensive way to take vacations, my wife and I decided to put together this tent trailer.

With an 8½-foot trailer, we thought we could take our two children and dog on fun trips for less money.

So with my wife's help, I built our first tent trailer. It took me four weekends and it cost \$335—at the time we did it.

I purchased the open A-frame chassis for \$145. You can build the whole tent trailer for about \$250 if you make the chassis yourself. I decided to purchase the chassis because I am not that experienced in metalwork. But I do know woodworking.

I found that building the trailer box was simple once the plywood and lumber are cut to size. The plywood sections are so designed that you can use every bit of eight 4x8-ft. pieces of plywood. This means that you don't have extra bits and pieces left over after construction. It also means that you will not have the expense of extra sheets of plywood.

To start, you need the trailer chassis. You can get this from a number of commercial metal works. Better still, you can scavenge it from an old beat-up trailer. Or you can build it from scratch—but you will need metalworking equipment.

Should you want to build the chassis, the materials you'll need include two 10½-foot sections of 2½-inch pipe. The trailer bed is 8 feet long, but you'll need an additional 2½ feet of length for the trailer tongue. Next, you need six 6½-foot

**BUILD THE CHASSIS,** then attach floor pieces. The trailer stands are attached to the forward portion.

**FLOORING** is laid on the joists. Attach floor and joists to angle iron with bolts or wood screws.

**PREFABBING SIDES** is a good idea. Note the position of the structural supports for cabinets.

pieces of angle-iron stringers. These must be welded to the piping. Suspension springs, brackets, axle and wheels come next. (See diagram.) Positioning of the axle is critical. You want the completed trailer to tow straight behind the car, and be so balanced that only 50 to 60 pounds of weight rests on the hitch. The trailer tires should be 4.80/4.00 x 8-in., which are rated to carry 1200-pound loads at 60 mph. You want to try to

## PLYWOOD PATTERNS

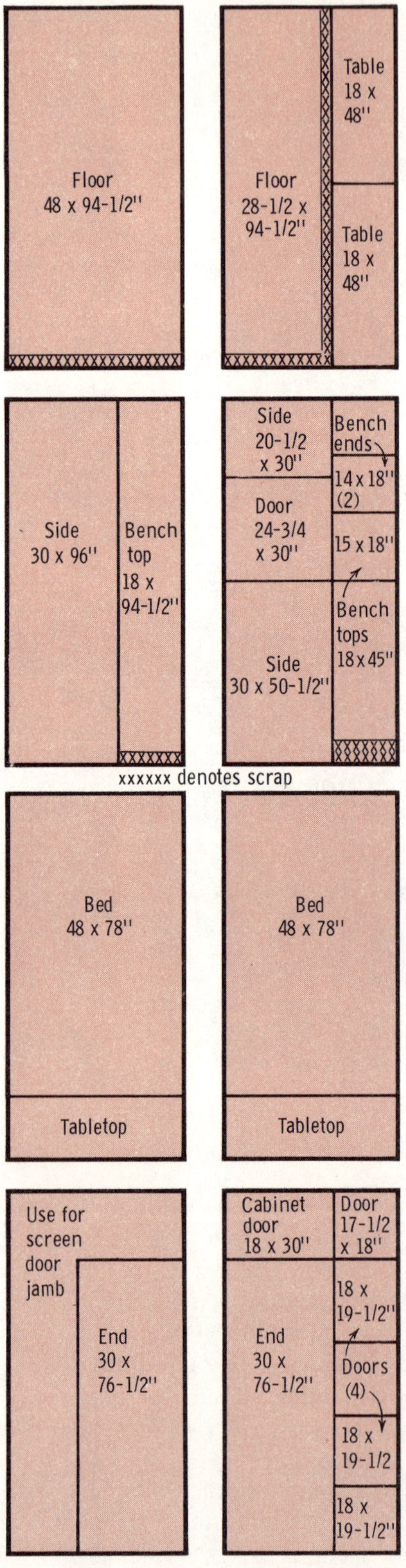

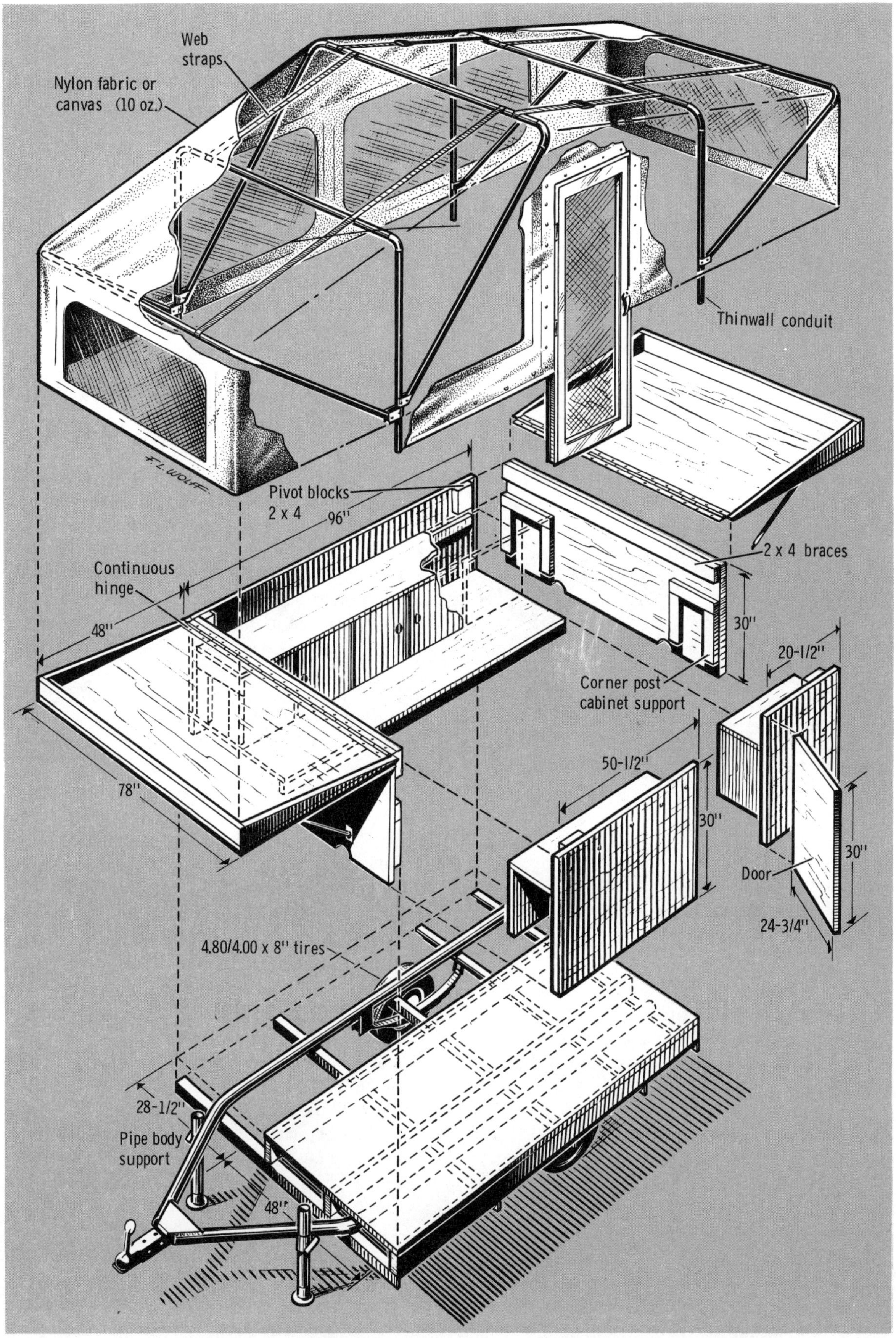
Web straps
Nylon fabric or canvas (10 oz.)
Thinwall conduit
Pivot blocks 2 x 4
96''
2 x 4 braces
Continuous hinge
48''
30''
20-1/2''
Corner post cabinet support
78''
50-1/2''
30''
30''
Door
24-3/4''
4.80/4.00 x 8'' tires
28-1/2''
Pipe body support
48''

**A SCREEN DOOR** can be mounted. This door is removed and laid on the floor when you collapse the trailer.

**PIVOT BLOCKS AND BOLTS** are necessary for tent pole. Note steel straps that attach oblique pole.

keep away from large tires as they call for wheel wells in the camper box for wheel clearance.

The trailer body is basically a box made of plywood with 2x4-in. lumber used as joists under the floor.

The floor should be of ⅝-in. plywood, while the trailer sides, top and cabinets can be of ⅝-in. or ½-in. Once you've cut all your wood, start by laying floors on joists and drilling through floor, joist and angle iron. Bolt together securely. Remember, this trailer will take a lot of bouncing.

To finish off the floor, it's a good idea to lay tile. Remember to arrange the tile so the joint between the two plywood floor sheets is covered. Also lay the tile before adding cabinets. This avoids intricate tile cutting and assures proper fit.

For the cabinets, use strips of 1x3-in. lumber as supports and lengths of 2x2-in. as structural supports in the corners and at the ends. Cabinet doors can be covered with vinyl to spruce up the trailer interior.

For extra sleeping space, make the table so the support leg can be folded under and the table can be detached from trailer bracket. Then lay the tabletop across the cabinet tops or benches. This can make up into another bed.

Here are some other trailer building tips:

Remember to keep the door handle low enough so there is enough space for collapsed tent poles and canvas.

Use heavy 2½-in. continuous piano-type hinges to secure bedwings to the trailer box.

Use awning brackets as sockets for bedwing support rods.

Use pivot blocks in corners so tent poles fall within the trailer box. Use pivot bolts to secure poles.

Cement sponge-rubber weatherstripping around the top edge of the trailer box. When the trailer is closed in the travel position, this stripping will absorb shock and help keep road dust out.

Paint the chassis so it will not rust and so it can be hosed off after long, muddy trips.

Now you're ready for the tough part—the tent canvas.

It is possible that you may want some professional help on this important section. Few people have sewing machines capable of double stitching 10-oz. canvas. Rug-binding and hand awls may also present a problem to the average builder. A good awning and tentmaker can turn out a first-rate job for you when given the dimensions of your trailer. Remember, the tent poles, from pivot to peak, cannot be longer than the interior dimensions of the trailer box.

Electrician's thinwall conduit—about 9 cents a foot—can be used for tent poles and ribs. This material can be bent with a plumber's bending tool. Or you can have formed corners of $^{13}/_{16}$-in. bar inserted in saw-cut tubing ends. Wrap all joints with tape to prevent wear on canvas. Web luggage straps can serve to hold poles in the correct standing position.

There is a helpful source for those of you who might have trouble building the chassis and sewing the canvas. It's the Stratford Fabricating Co. in Bridgeport, CT. This firm manufactures the open A-frame chassis and the tent.

**Stucco 'blisters'**

*My sand-stuccoed home is quite old and lately a couple of bulges or blisters, each about a foot in diameter, have appeared on one wall. How can I do the repair myself?*–W.W., Ind.

Stucco patching is rather tricky; I hesitate to get you involved. I assume that by "sand-stuccoed" you mean sand-finished and by "old" you mean the stucco is applied over wood lath.

Using a hammer and cold chisel, chip away all loose material back to solid edges and then undercut these edges to "key" new patching. Drive scaffold nails in a pattern over the opening; the projecting heads will serve as anchors.

Mix one part portland cement and three parts coarse, clean sand with just enough water to make an easy troweling mixture. Dampen opening and edges, then trowel the mixture into the opening, using enough pressure to force the material into contact well under the undercut edges. Fill to within ¼ in. of the original surface. Score the fresh mix lightly in crisscross pattern with trowel point or a piece of heavy wire. Cure at least two days, keeping patch damp with a fine water spray.

Dampen again and apply a second coat of the mix, building it up to within ⅛ in. of the old surface. Leave this application smooth and cure it as before. For a final coat add about ¾-part lime to the mix and, after building it slightly above level of the surface, strike off the excess with a straightedged board. Let coat stiffen slightly, make a float by attaching a handle to a short length of 1x4, sprinkle water on the patch and work the float until you get a matching surface.

**Air-curing walnut planks**

*I'm having two walnut trees in our yard cut down and the logs sawed into planks 2 inches thick. What is the best and surest way to cure this lumber for a home-shop project I have in mind? How long should the planks cure?—R. D. Jordan, Lexington, Ky.*

Have the planks kiln-dried where temperature and moisture can be controlled. Lacking the facilities to do this, you could air-dry the wood overhead in your garage or attic. In the latter procedure, ends of the planks must be coated with asphalt—preferably hot—to prevent checking. Then the planks should be stacked with ¾ x ¾-inch strips in between to permit air circulation. Keep strips no more than 2 feet apart. Normal curing time will vary from one to two years, depending on the drying conditions that prevail. It's well to turn the planks occasionally during this period.

**Wet attic**

*Last winter, my attic was dripping water. I've checked for roof leaks and have been told the water comes from sleet blown in the vents—that it may work in under shingles during a driving rain. But the shingles have sealed tabs. I've even watched during the rain and no leaks are visible. Where can the water come from?—W.H., Miss.*

The water comes from inside the house, not through the roof or in the vents. Every time you or other family members exhale, shower, prepare food, boil the teakettle or do the laundry you contribute to moisture in the room air. This can build up to several gallons in a 24-hour period. Warm, moist air seeks the colder, drier air outside the house and forces its way through common building materials and insulation by what is known as vapor pressure.Unless your attic vents are of ample size, this moisture-laden air is trapped in the attic. It condenses on any material—rafters, roof boards and nail tips, mainly because these areas are at a lower temperature.

Attic vents or louvers should provide at least one square foot of free area for each 100 square feet of attic floor space. This is minimum, especially where there are low pitched roofs. Enlarge the louvers, if necessary, and do everything else possible to lower the moisture content of air in rooms. Don't let the teakettle boil; install a fan in your bath or shower stall; air the house after laundering, and if you have a clothes dryer or your house is heated by a gas floor furnace, be sure they are properly vented to the outside.

**Leaky water pipe**

*How can I stop a slow leak in a water pipe?—J.J., Utah.*

It's best to replace the leaking pipe or have your plumber do it. Should replacement be delayed for some reason, there is a device that can be clamped around a pipe for stopping a leak temporarily.

**Use a carbide-tip blade**

*I've ruined a circular-saw blade cutting hardboard panels. What should I use for this job?—E.P. Hardy, Waco, Tex.*

"Ruined" may not be the right word, unless teeth have been broken. Hardboard, especially the tempered variety, will dull ordinary blades quickly, but usually they can be resharpened. However, if you have much hardboard cutting to do it will pay you to buy a carbide-tip blade, which can take it almost indefinitely.

**1. FLYWHEEL COVER** is removed for access to drain plug for torque converter. Some cars lack a converter drain on the transmission. Consult owner's manual.

**2. ROTATE CONVERTER** to get plug in 6:00 position. Kick it around using starter or, as shown here, inch it around with ring-gear teeth using a screwdriver.

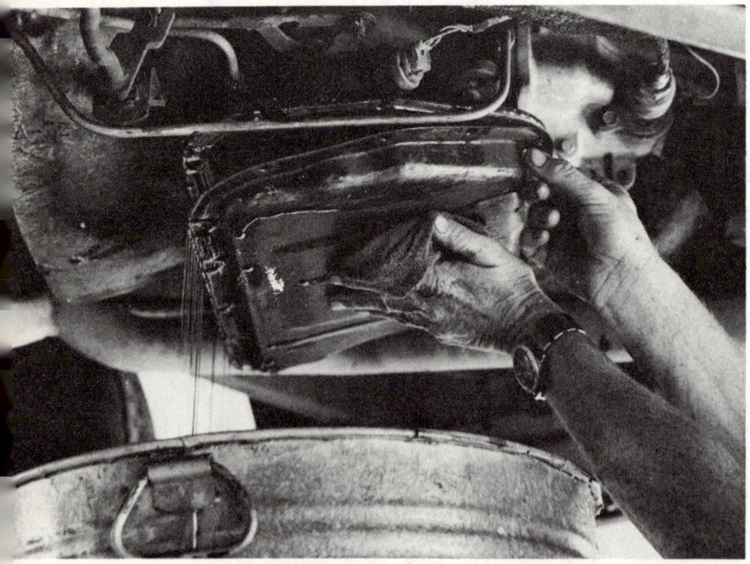

**5. REMOVE ALL BOLTS** except two at the back of the pan. They should be loose but not removed so the pan will tip down at the front to drain fluid into a catch basin without making a mess. That's the theory, but it takes extraordinary care to make it work.

**6. REMOVE THE FILTER** or screen after the pan has been taken off. A screen may be cleaned in solvent, but filters must be replaced. The Mopar filter shown here must be replaced.

# How to avoid automatic transmission problems

By MICHAEL LAMM

SEE ALSO

**Differentials, auto . . . Lubrication, auto . . . Noises, auto . . . Power-train noise, auto . . . Ramps, auto repair . . . Tune-up, auto**

**3. REMOVE** the drain plug and drain fluid into a catch basin. After draining the fluid, replace the plug and tighten to manufacturer's specification.

**4. LOOSEN ALL** the bolts that hold the transmission pan. If the pan has a drain plug, use it to drain fluid first, and then replace and tighten the plug.

**7. OLD GASKET** must be scraped away from the transmission body. Use a conventional putty knife or a sharp scraper for this task.

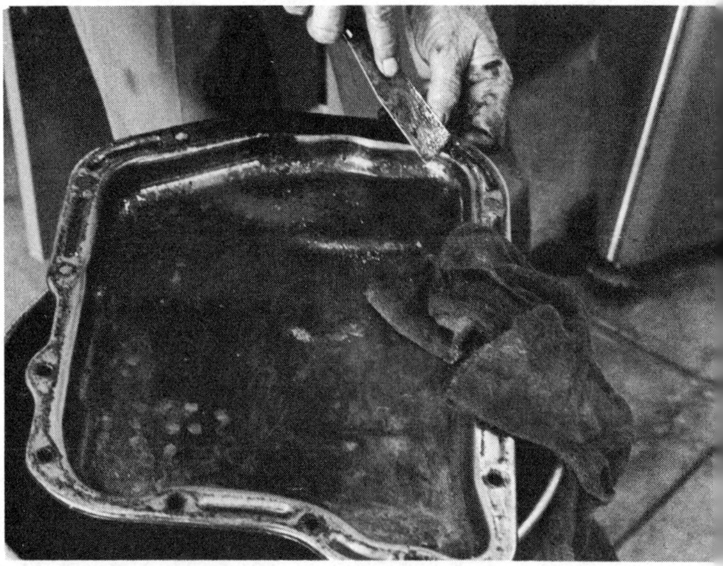

**8. THE OLD GASKET** should also be scraped away from the transmission pan.

■ A TRANSMISSION-SHOP owner told me recently that three quarters of the overhauls he performs could be prevented if car owners would change their automatic transmission fluid (ATF) more often. How often? Every 12,000 miles, he recommends, with new filters or screens cleaned every 24,000 miles, no matter what the books say.

Most car owners not only neglect changing fluid—most don't even know how. The photos and captions should clear up the major mysteries. Also helpful are the following tips on the care of automatic transmissions.

■ Changing fluid yourself can save you between $10 and $20 per change. Filling stations usually charge about $10 for labor plus 25 to 50-percent markups on fluid, filters and gaskets.

■ Expect *some* metal filings in the bottom of your transmission pan. A few filings are normal. It takes a good transmission man to "read" the filings for signs of wear, but don't let anyone sell

**9. INSTALL A NEW** transmission filter or put back the cleaned screen. This procedure depends on the design of your car's automatic transmission.

**10. CLEAN THE** transmission pan thoroughly in solvent before you put it back on the transmission body.

you an overhaul simply because you see a pinch of filings.

■ If your transmission hasn't been shifting properly—if it slips, clunks, makes noises, lags—don't change fluid. Let a transmission shop check things out first. If you do need a band adjustment or other work, you'll have to change ATF again, so you'll be paying for fluid twice.

■ Be sure you buy a name-brand fluid because the cheaper brands break down quickly. Be aware, too, that ATF comes in two main types: Type F and Type A/Dexron. Dexron is a type, not a brand, and different brands of Dexron *will* mix. It's the same with different brands of Type F.

■ When refilling, use only the type of fluid called for in your owner's manual. Basically, Type A/Dexron fluid is used in cars made by General Motors, AMC, Chrysler, BMW, Datsun, Fiat, Mercedes, Opel, Saab, Volkswagen, Audi, Simca, Hillman and Sunbeam. Type F is recommended for all Ford products plus Austin, Jaguar, Toyota and Volvo.

■ Some transmission pans have drain plugs. Use these plugs, but to get out all the ATF and also to get at filters and screens, you'll have to remove the pan. Pans without plugs have to come off, of course.

■ The trick to removing a no-drain-plug pan without slopping fluid all over the floor is: Place a big catch basin under the pan; remove all pan bolts except two at the rear corners; loosen but do not remove these two bolts; tap or pry the front of the pan so it drops down. The two loose rear bolts will hold the pan and fluid will run out the front into the basin. Or that's the theory at any rate (see photos).

■ On the GM Turbo Hydra-Matic 400 and other automatics with can-type filters, replace filters *every other* fluid change. And note that no GM automatic has provision for draining torque converter. Ford and Chrysler converters all drain and demand more fluid when refilling.

■ In Ford products using the C-4 or C-6 automatics, don't touch the filter unless you can see that it's plugged. People have a habit of tightening these filters too tight, thus doing more harm than good. Also, if you remove the screen on a 1970 or later C-4, be sure not to lose the valve and spring under the screen. The valve is held by a spring up against the screen.

■ Screen-type filters inside automatic transmissions can be cleaned in kerosene or solvent and don't need to be replaced. Paper or can-type fil-

**11. REPLACE THE PAN** using a cork or a neoprene gasket, and don't use any adhesive on the gasket. Run up a couple of bolts to hold the pan while you align the gasket, and then tighten all bolts in a crisscross pattern to prevent any warping of the pan.

**12. HALF FILL** the transmission with recommended fluid. Start engine and run it in neutral; then continue filling until you read a pint below the full mark. Shift through all gears and recheck. When engine is hot, fluid should expand to the full mark.

ters do need to be replaced. To tell whether your transmission uses a screen, refer again to the chart.

■ Install only cork or neoprene pan gaskets—never paper ones. And never use an adhesive or grease to help seal. Pan gaskets usually come complete with filters and gasket, but check the pack when you buy it. And always be sure you buy everything you need before you start the job: fluid, filters, gasket and so on.

■ Check your transmission's vacuum modulator for leaks. If there's oil in the vacuum line or modulator, replace the modulator. And be careful not to lose the modulator pin.

■ In transmissions with converter drains (only), refill with four quarts initially, then keep filling until your trans dipstick shows one pint below full. At this point, run your engine and shift slowly through all ranges, including reverse. Check the fluid level again and refill to one pint below the full mark. This allows for fluid expansion when the transmission gets hot. Never overfill, because when the fluid gets hot, it'll expand and be thrown out.

■ Check your pan for leaks, and keep an eye on your garage floor to check for leaks.

After changing the fluid, it's important that the level be maintained at the proper point. Consult your owner's manual for the correct procedure to follow in making the fluid-level check. Usually, the transmission must first be warmed up to normal operating temperature. The transmission lever is then placed in Park or Neutral. The car should be parked on a perfectly flat surface.

The automatic transmission dipstick, which is usually found at the rear of the engine compartment, is pulled from the dipstick tube *after* wiping dirt from the area. Be certain that dirt does not get on the dipstick or fall into the tube.

Most transmission dipsticks have two index marks. The top one is the "Full" mark. The one lower down is the "Add" mark.

If it is necessary to add fluid, be sure to choose one that is compatible with the type already in the transmission. Don't overfill. Excessive fluid in the transmission causes aeration, which leads to slipping and other shifting problems.

Although some motorists manage to rack up 100,000 miles on their original ATF, eventually neglect will catch up with any transmission. So it makes good sense to change your fluid every 12,000 miles and maintain the proper level between changes.

# All about transplanting

■ THERE ARE SEVERAL KINDS of transplanting, but certain guidelines apply to them all. For instance, *correct planting time is extremely important, even critical*. If you do not know the correct planting time in your area for a certain plant, by all means check your catalogs or call a reputable local nursery. *Transplant only at the optimum time*. If possible, choose a cool and cloudy or rainy day without wind.

Select the sturdiest and best-shaped specimens for transplanting. Dig holes for them that are straight-sided and are deep and wide enough to accommodate the roots without crowding. Expose the roots to the air no longer than is absolutely necessary because in some cases just a few minutes of exposure is too much. Protect the roots, if the soil falls off, by putting them into water or a moistened plastic bag. Trim off broken or bruised roots with a sharp knife or shears.

For best results, prepare a good soil mixture to surround the transplant. Dig in humus like peat moss, rotted manure or compost to lighten the soil and make it hold more water. The humus will encourage the young plant—whether a tomato vine or a tree—to root quickly and well. One caution—if you use fertilizer, place it in the dirt well beneath roots or stem, so it does not touch them.

SEE ALSO
**Garden shelters . . . Gardening . . . Grass . . . House plants . . . Landscaping . . . Lawns . . . Mowers . . . Paths, garden . . . Retaining walls . . . Trees . . . Vegetable gardening**

Most plants should be set the same depth as they were growing originally. Firm the soil gently around the roots but don't pack it in. Make a surface basin, and water it thoroughly to settle the soil. Around a tree this basin should be extended each year as the roots spread.

If you have an especially large, delicate transplant, you may be able to ease the shock of transfer by a two-stage process. A few days before the actual transplanting, prune the roots by driving a spade down in a circle around the plant. This will give the plant some time to recover from the initial shock.

### balled, burlapped and potted plants

Many trees and shrubs, including evergreens, are sold balled and burlapped. The nursery encases the entire root system in burlap and ties it with twine. In handling such plants: 1. Do not bump or jar the root ball, which can cause the soil to separate from the roots. For the same reason: 2. Do not use the trunk as a handle, even though it invites you to do so. If the weight is not

**IF YOU'RE PLANNING** to transplant seedlings from a flat, water the flat the day before you start. When you are ready to transplant, jar the flat by striking one end sharply against the ground.

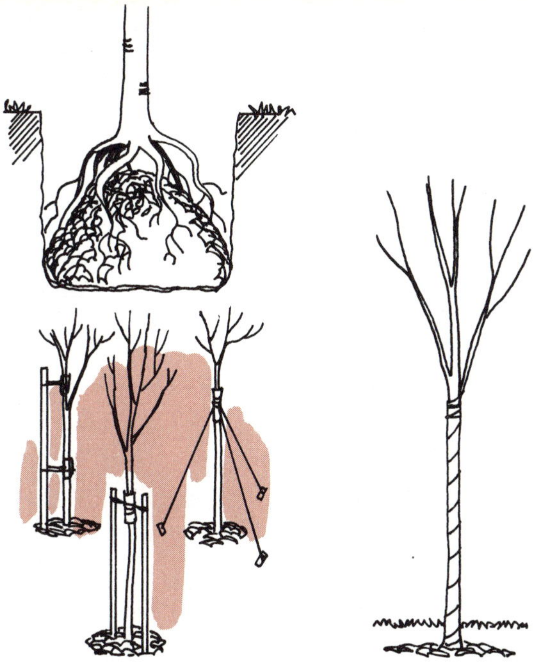

too great, cradle the root ball in your arms. Using a sling of stout cloth, two people can carry a heavier plant. If necessary, a third can support the trunk.

Dig the planting hole *about twice the diameter of the root ball,* and deep enough so there will be 8 or 10 in. of loosened soil under the ball. That loose soil is very important. Set the plant so the top of the ball is just a bit higher—say, half an inch—than the surrounding surface. This will allow for settling. Now split the burlap and fold it back from the top but leave it on the rest of the ball. It will not hurt the plant, and will gradually rot away. Fill the hole with enriched topsoil, firming it with a tamper made from a 2x4, and water thoroughly. Make sure that the plant stands straight and its best side faces in the direction you want.

If your tree or shrub comes in a large pot, allow the soil to dry out somewhat before planting. Then turn the pot on its side and grasp the trunk. Pull gently as you tap around the rim of the pot. The whole soil mass will slip out and the plant then can be handled in much the same way as a balled and burlapped one.

### bare roots and "canned" plants

During winter and early spring you can buy bareroot dormant trees and shrubs that are less expensive than plants in containers sold months later. If the ground is still frozen when you buy bare-root plants, heel them in until you can plant them.

In setting a bare-root plant, form a mound in the hole, using the native soil from the hole mixed with an equal amount of organic material such as peat moss. Spread the bare roots over this mound. Fill the hole, and water as with other plants.

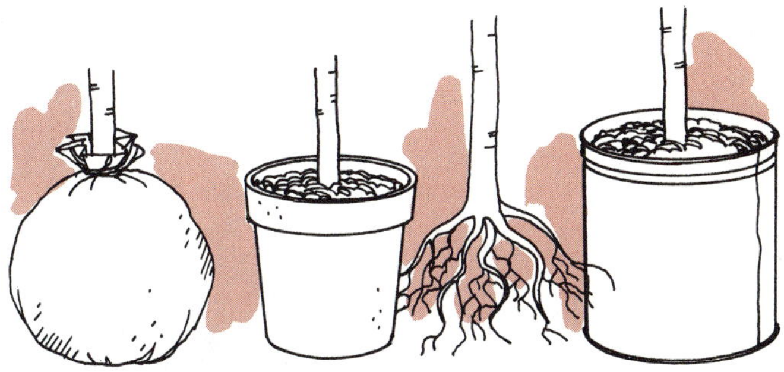

Plants are sold in cans in some areas. After preparing the planting hole, use tin shears to cut off the can (many nurseries will slit the can for you). Make two cuts directly opposite each other. While supporting the trunk, slip the can off the soil mass. Loosen the roots a bit, and set the plant. Be sure you use gloves in handling the can, as the cut edges are very sharp.

### after trees and shrubs arrive

Sometimes an emergency arises. You may not be able to set out your plants as soon as you get them. In that case, heel them in. In particular, this applies to bare-root plants.

Newly transplanted trees may need helpful support. *Before transplanting the tree,* drive a single stake 6 to 8 ft. long and 1½ to 2 in. in diameter into the transplanting hole. Position the stake on the same side of the tree as the prevailing winds. For even more support two stakes, or a combination of stakes and guy wires, may be used. Use turnbuckles to keep any wires taut. And never loop wire directly around the trunk; use cloth ties or rubber against the bark. Sometimes the trunk of a tree is wrapped with tarred paper. This conserves moisture and prevents sunscald.

### bulbs and perennials

When you transplant perennials or bulbs, resist the temptation to do it just after the plants have bloomed, while foliage is still green. That is the time the bulbs are being nourished by the leaves and developed for next year. Instead, you can fold the foliage and tie it neatly with a rubber band, then plant a shallow annual to cover the leaves when they turn brown, after which bulbs can be dug and stored.

In general, it is best to plant summer and fall-blooming perennials in the spring and to plant kinds that bloom in very early spring and summer in the autumn. But transplant irises in June or July, right after they bloom.

EARLY TIMES
Kentucky
Straight Bourbon
Whisky
BEEFEATE
LONDON DISTILL
DRY GIN

# Build a folding snack server

By WAYNE C. LECKEY

**This folding cocktail snack server can be right at the center of the action at your parties. You can make it of fine hardwood to match the rest of your furniture. After the party is over, it can be folded flat and placed out of the way in a closet**

WHEN HOME PARTIES reach the point of help yourself, this handsome hors d'oeuvre server will soon become the center of the party. Loaded with tempting cheese dips, chips and the makings of a drink or two, this self-service server will receive a standing ovation in more ways than one.

You'll find it equally as useful at bridge, or wherever snacks are served. Best of all, the server folds flat for storing. Start with the legs. These are twin assemblies which are cut in pairs, following the pattern. All four legs are bored for ¾-in.-dowel rungs, but keep in mind that the blind holes must be bored in facing surfaces. One pair of legs is drilled for four roundhead brass screws which serve as pivot-pins for the trays, and here you'll wisely drill the holes through both legs at the same time to insure identical spacing. If you own a router, run a bead cut along the curved edges of the legs; it will relieve their plainness and give that store-bought look.

One pair of legs is joined at the top with a crossrail which is shaped like the legs and then glued and screwed to the pair of legs previously drilled for the pivot screws. Two flathead screws are used at each end of the crossrail to fasten it.

Each tray consists of a hardwood-faced plywood center which is faced around the edge with a ¼ x ¾-in. molding, neatly mitered at the corners, then glued and nailed. Stop pins, made of nails with the heads cut off, are driven into the

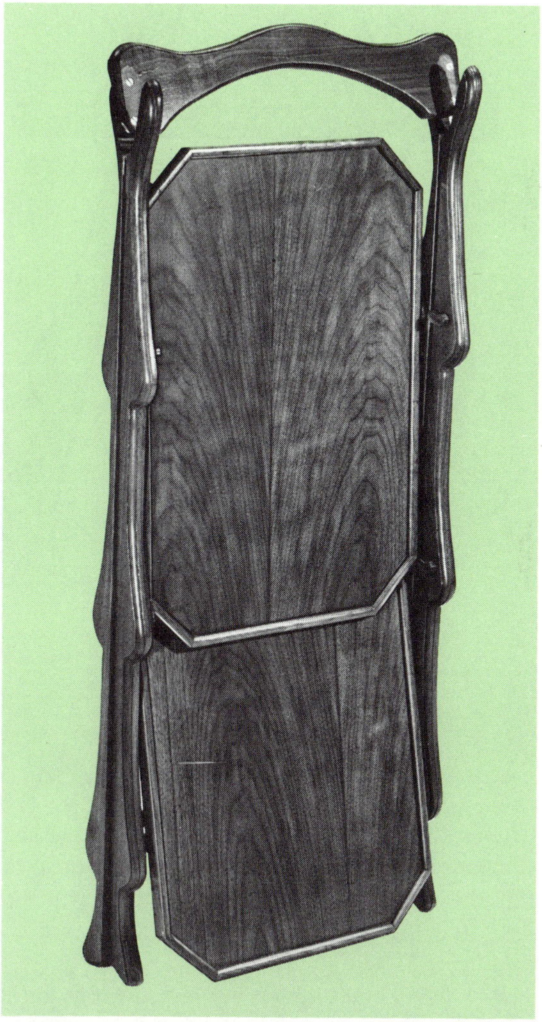

**BETWEEN PARTIES,** if you don't want it standing around, you can fold the server flat and stow it away. Trays lap and nest between the hinged legs.

**WHEN OPEN** the sturdy server gives two generous-size surfaces for holding snacks and libations. Closed (photo at the right), the space-saving table folds flat for convenient out-of-sight storage in the closet until your next party.

SEE ALSO

**Lazy Susans . . . Mobile furniture . . . Party tables . . . Servers . . . Serving carts**

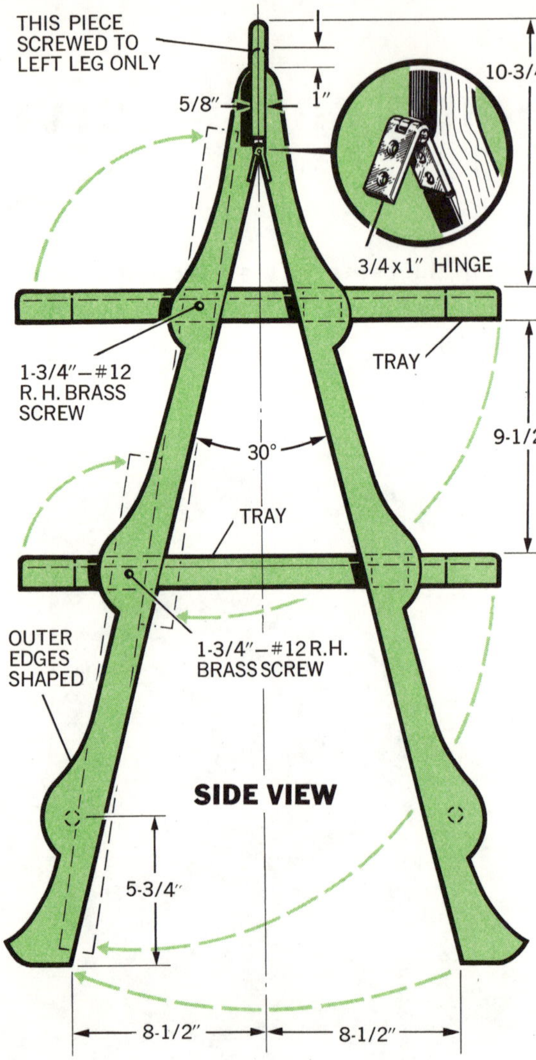


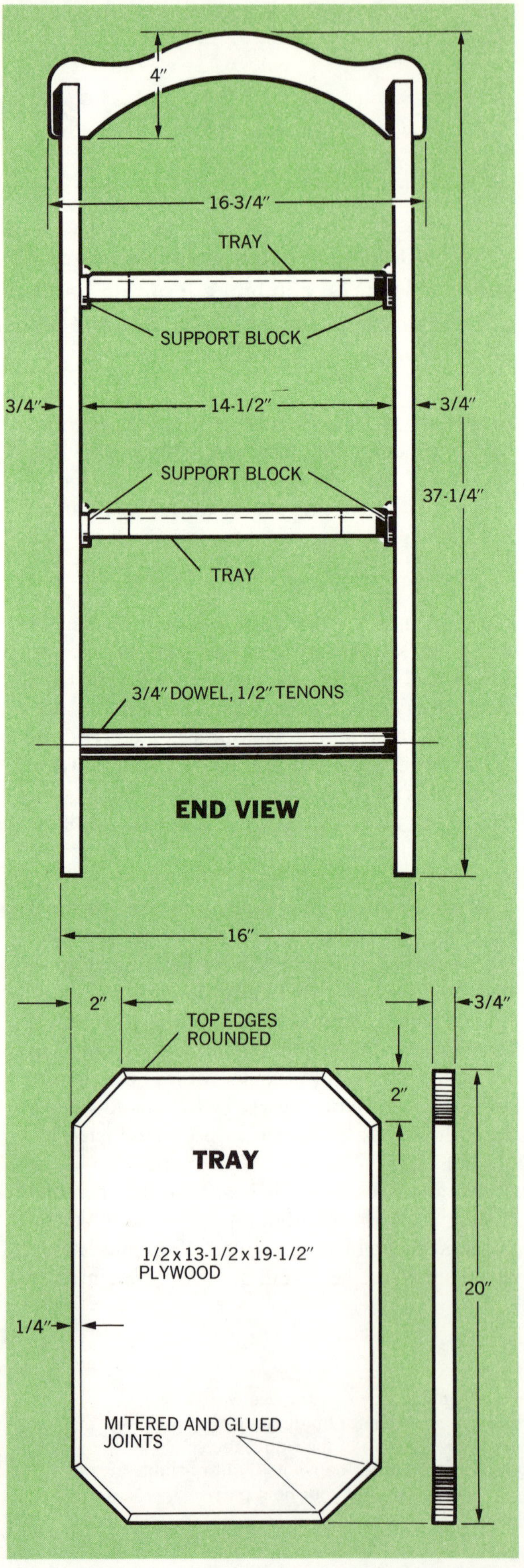


trays to rest in support blocks glued to the second pair of legs. The pins must not project so far that they rub and mar the legs. Wooden washers keep the trays from rubbing as they pivot for folding.

Pick small brass hinges to hinge the legs at the top. The hinge pins must be first driven out (if you can't get loose-pin hinges) so that the hinge leaves can be screwed in place. The pins are then replaced and your stand is completed.

Finishing the stand depends on the kind of wood you used. If it's walnut, you'll need to fill the open grain of the wood with a paste filler, then stain as desired. Two coats of rubbed-effect varnish will make a mighty handsome piece.

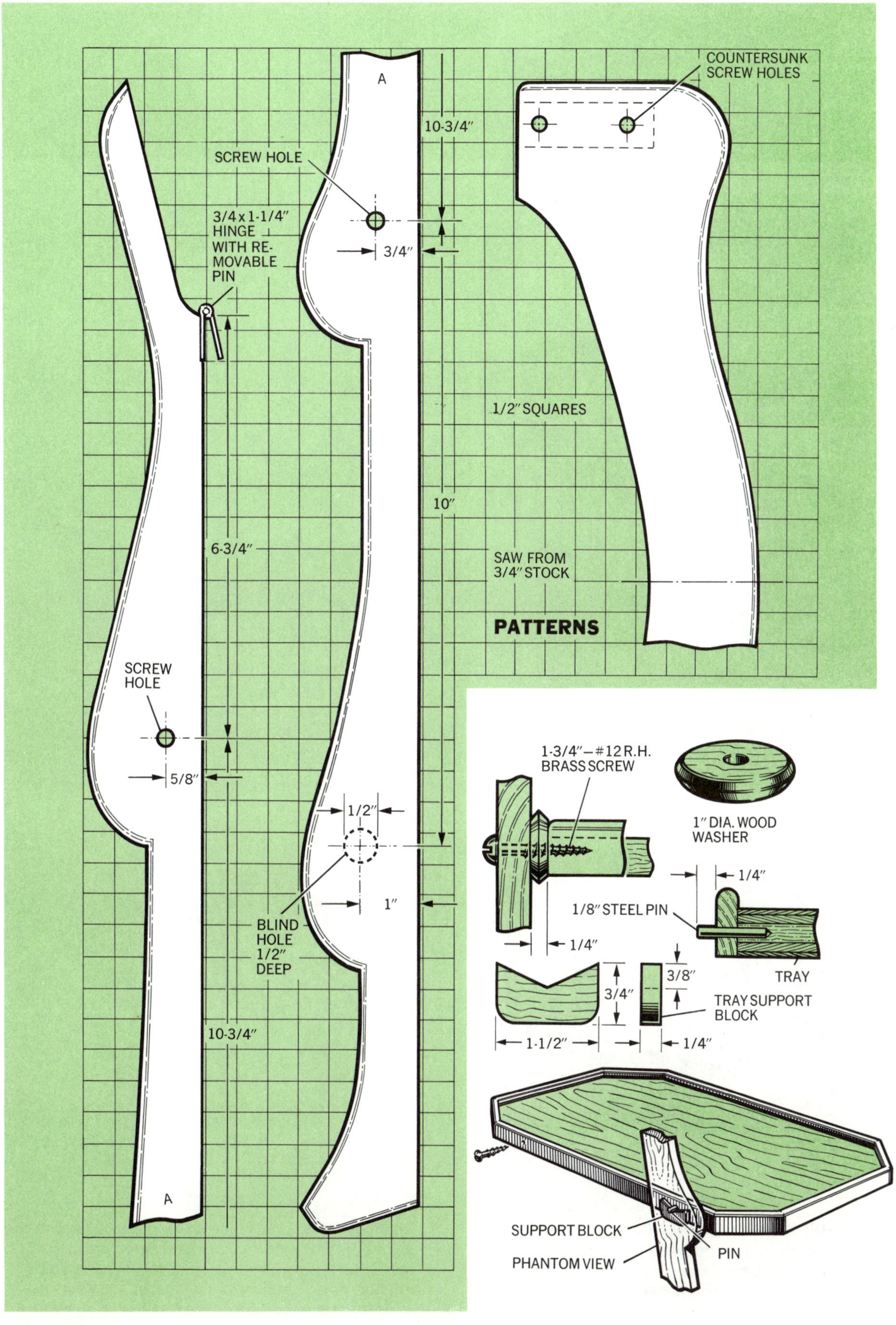
COUNTERSUNK SCREW HOLES
A
10-3/4"
SCREW HOLE
3/4 x 1-1/4" HINGE WITH RE- MOVABLE PIN
3/4"
1/2" SQUARES
10"
6-3/4"
SAW FROM 3/4" STOCK
PATTERNS
SCREW HOLE
5/8"
1/2"
1"
BLIND HOLE 1/2" DEEP
10-3/4"
A
1-3/4"—#12 R.H. BRASS SCREW
1" DIA. WOOD WASHER
1/4"
1/8" STEEL PIN
1/4"
3/8"
3/4"
TRAY
TRAY SUPPORT BLOCK
1-1/2"
1/4"
SUPPORT BLOCK
PHANTOM VIEW
PIN

**AN INSTANT BOOKCASE** for your kids can be improvised from the drawers of an old shallow chest. Just remove the pulls and stack the drawers. Deep drawers can be made shallow by installing a stop.

**HANDY BINS** for storing nails, screws, washers and other small objects in your shop are just angle-hung coffee cans. Punch a hole through the side and bottom, as shown; mount on a board between studs.

**SHARPENING THE CORNER** and a portion of one edge of the putty knife you use when you are applying wallpaper will give you a handy tool for trimming paper at the baseboard.

**BEFORE YOU START** to paint, bend a loop in the wire bail of the can to form a spring fit around the narrowest portion of the paintbrush handle. It makes a neat and dripless holder for your paintbrush.

# Build a stack of swingers

BY ROSARIO CAPOTOSTO

■ THIS ROLL-ABOUT stack of swinging trays offers handy storage for the hobbyist and the man with a home office. I made it for about $20.

The nine trays are made of ¼-in. fir plywood, butted, glued and nailed together. They swing open on a length of thinwall conduit. Use a smooth-cutting blade to mass-produce the tray parts. Use a fairly hard wood such as poplar, birch or soft maple for the tray corner blocks. Dress a square length, bevel one corner, then slice it into 3-in. pieces to project ¼ in. above the tray edges. Sand the blocks and glue in place.

Holes in the blocks must be bored squarely and identically so the trays will align and swing out evenly. Clamp a flat board to your drill-press table and two stop blocks at one corner. Hold each tray firmly against the blocks as you bore and stop when the bit's point pokes through. Turn the tray over to complete the hole. Half-inch conduit is 11/16 in. o.d. (outside diameter).

**ASSEMBLE** trays with glue and ⅝-in. (20-ga.) brads, being careful to drive them straight. Cut parts from flat plywood.

**EASE** all sharp corners of assembled trays with a block plane, then sand outside surfaces.

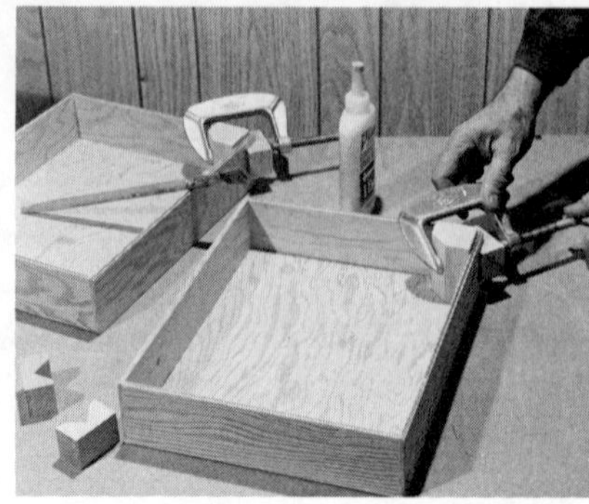

**PROTECT** outside corner with a notched 90° block when gluing and clamping pivot blocks in right front corners of trays.

**CLAMP** two stop blocks to wood drill-press table to assure identically bored holes in the corner blocks of all nine trays.

**COAT HOLES** with sanding sealer, then sand when dry. Cotton on stick makes swab. Follow with candle wax.

**SLIDE TRAYS** over conduit post. Wax coating inside holes and on tops of corner blocks assures smooth-swinging trays.

**BORE HOLES** for conduit in top and bottom sections of cabinet before final assembly. Glue the bottom section first.

**ATTACH** free-swinging, swivel plate casters to the four corner blocks. Wheels should extend about 1 in. below sides.

When the holes are bored, paint trays and insides of holes with sanding sealer, then sand lightly when dry with 220-grit paper, holes and all. Rub a wax candle in the holes and across the tops of the blocks.

Make the outer cabinet shell from ¾-in. fir plywood. Drill a ¼-in.-deep hole in the top of the base section and in underside of the upper section, and nail and glue the base section in position. Insert the conduit in the hole in the base and place the upper section over the top of the conduit. Then glue and nail the top section in place.

Now turn the unit upside down and install blocks in the corners for plate-type swivel casters.

A facing of ¼-in. plywood is attached to all surfaces except the top edges of the upper compartment. These edges are faced with ¼ x 1-in. solid pine. Ease (round slightly) all corners with a block plane and sand. You'll find the wild grain pattern of fir plywood can add an interesting effect when finished natural.

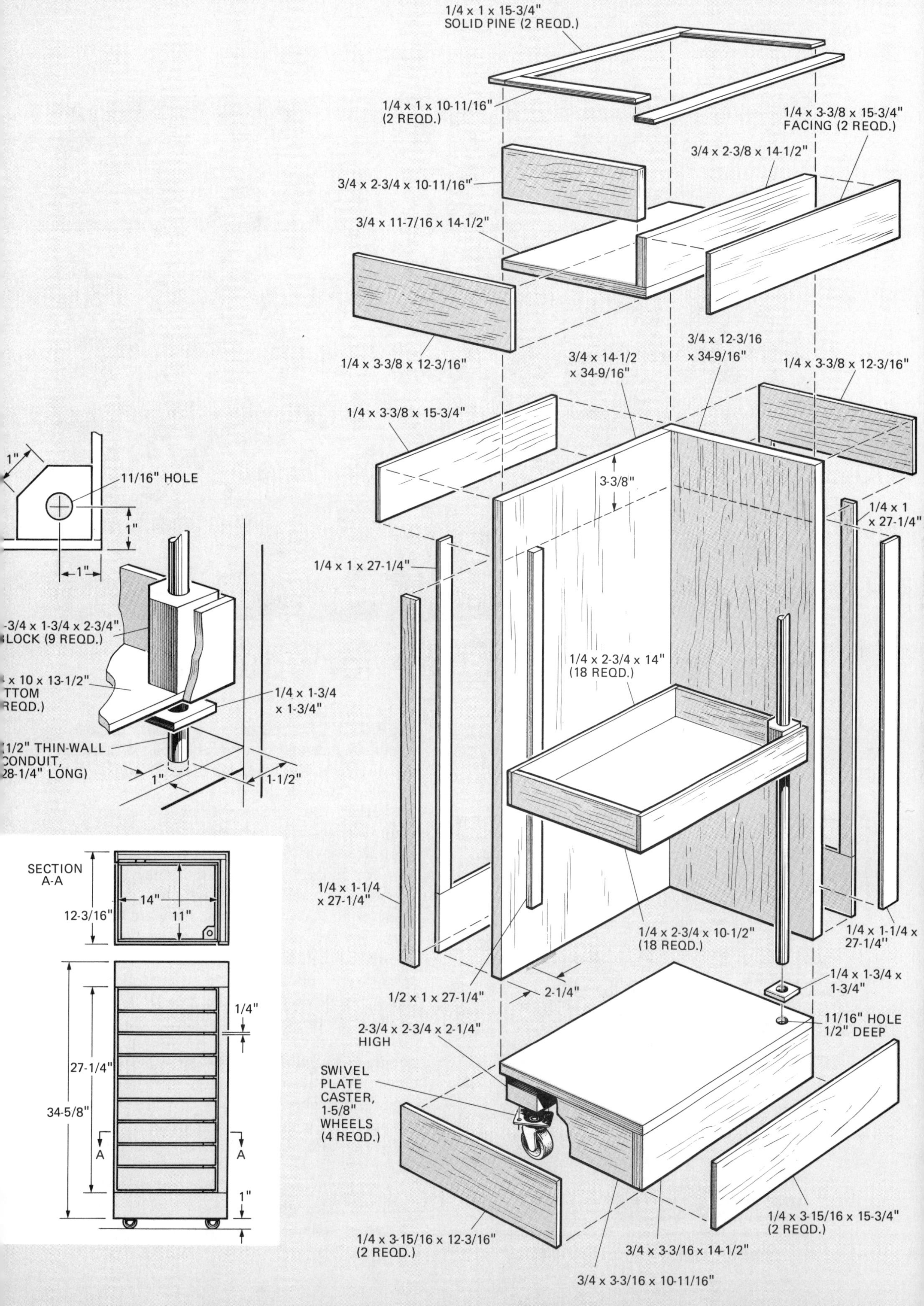
1/4 x 1 x 15-3/4"
SOLID PINE (2 REQD.)
1/4 x 1 x 10-11/16"
(2 REQD.)
1/4 x 3-3/8 x 15-3/4"
FACING (2 REQD.)
3/4 x 2-3/8 x 14-1/2"
3/4 x 2-3/4 x 10-11/16"
3/4 x 11-7/16 x 14-1/2"
1/4 x 3-3/8 x 12-3/16"
3/4 x 14-1/2
x 34-9/16"
3/4 x 12-3/16
x 34-9/16"
1/4 x 3-3/8 x 12-3/16"
1/4 x 3-3/8 x 15-3/4"
1"
11/16" HOLE
1"
1"
3-3/8"
1/4 x 1
x 27-1/4"
1/4 x 1 x 27-1/4"
-3/4 x 1-3/4 x 2-3/4"
LOCK (9 REQD.)
x 10 x 13-1/2"
TTOM
REQD.)
1/4 x 1-3/4
x 1-3/4"
1/4 x 2-3/4 x 14"
(18 REQD.)
1/2" THIN-WALL
CONDUIT,
28-1/4" LONG)
1"
1-1/2"
SECTION
A-A
14"
11"
12-3/16"
1/4 x 1-1/4
x 27-1/4"
1/4 x 2-3/4 x 10-1/2"
(18 REQD.)
1/4 x 1-1/4 x
27-1/4"
2-1/4"
1/2 x 1 x 27-1/4"
1/4 x 1-3/4 x
1-3/4"
11/16" HOLE
1/2" DEEP
1/4"
2-3/4 x 2-3/4 x 2-1/4"
HIGH
27-1/4"
SWIVEL
PLATE
CASTER,
1-5/8"
WHEELS
(4 REQD.)
34-5/8"
A
A
1"
1/4 x 3-15/16 x 15-3/4"
(2 REQD.)
1/4 x 3-15/16 x 12-3/16"
(2 REQD.)
3/4 x 3-3/16 x 14-1/2"
3/4 x 3-3/16 x 10-11/16"

# How to choose a tree for your yard

**Trees serve many different purposes. What do you want yours to do for you?**

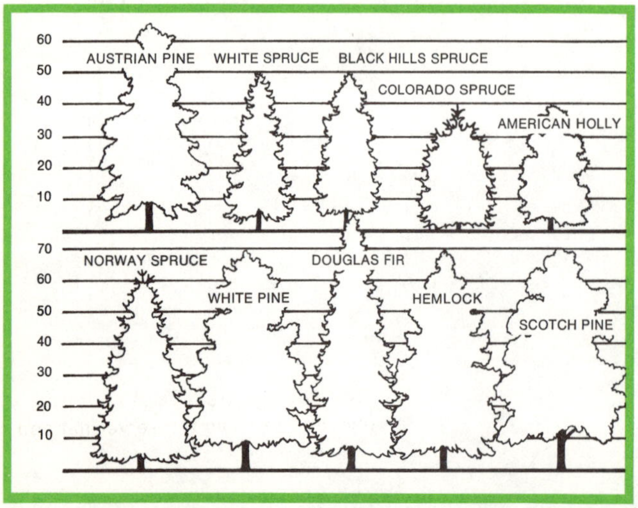


SEE ALSO

**Landscaping . . . Lawns . . . Paths, garden . . . Retaining walls . . . Transplanting**

A TREE can be the most important part of your landscaping plan. And, because there are so many kinds of trees, it can be the hardest part of the plan to decide upon.

Perhaps the best way to choose a tree is to start with the qualities you're seeking, the ''job'' you want it to do for you and your family. Trees are for cooling shade in the summer, warming windbreak in the winter, fruit, blossoms, showy berries and colorful leaves. They are for climbing, building treehouses in, swinging from.

Basic practicalities must be kept in mind. In a shade tree, for example, you want a species that grows well where you live, that leafs out early and holds leaves until late in the fall; that is deep-rooted so you can garden or grow grass beneath it; and that is resistant to pests and disease. Shade trees are undergoing major changes today, brought about by improved propagation techniques, widespread research to find varieties that are disease-resistant and pollution-tolerant.

**Local climate** is the first consideration in selecting a tree that will perform well over a long period of time. Trees native to the area are usually the very safest bet, if you don't mind limiting your selection.

Certain types of trees do better in an acid soil, others in alkaline ground (although minerals can be added to the soil to change its "sweetness"). Some trees thrive in dry soil, others in wet. For specific recommendations about the most appropriate types for your area, check with your local nursery, arboretum, or the county office of your state Agricultural Extension Service.

**Favorite shade tree** recommendations by region include: *High Plains* (as in Colorado): thornless honey locust, green ash, Norway maple, hackberry, littleleaf linden. *Midwest* (as in Minnesota): sugar maple, Norway maple, green ash, Crimean linden, white oak. *Southeast* (as in Georgia): evergreen live oak or willow oak, American holly, magnolia grandiflora, dogwood, loquat. *North Central/East* (as in Ohio): Norway maple, sugar maple, red maple, littleleaf linden, pin oak. *Desert* (as in New Mexico): Arizona ash, pecan, thornless honey locust, fruitless mulberry, Aleppo pine. *Southern California* (as in Los Angeles): fruitless mulberry, fern pine, magnolia grandiflora, Koelreuteria integrifoliola, Brazilian pepper.

**Flowering trees** stay small, give a burst of bloom in season and all are useful for light shade. They fit well into a small lot, especially at corners, make an excellent privacy screen if planted closely along the edge of the yard, and look well placed three or more in a clump to achieve a full, natural effect. Favorites include redbud, crab apple, English hawthorn, European mountain ash, flowering cherry, peach and plum, dogwood, franklinia, fringe tree, golden chain.

**Evergreens** provide shade all year and are outstanding as a winter windbreak. Kinds that mature at 30 feet or larger include American arborvitae and holly, Austrian pine, Black Hills spruce, Cedar of Lebanon, Colorado spruce, Douglas fir, Eastern hemlock, Norway pine.

Almost any variety of tree has some disadvantage that must be weighed against its good points. Thus, it's not a good idea to choose elms, willows, poplars or maples for planting near drainage pipes, because the roots of these trees can clog sewers. Species with shallow roots rob lawns of moisture and if planted near a sidewalk can break the pavement.

Some trees are extremely susceptible to insects or disease. A notable example is the graceful American elm, favorite street tree of U.S. cities until it was decimated by Dutch Elm disease.

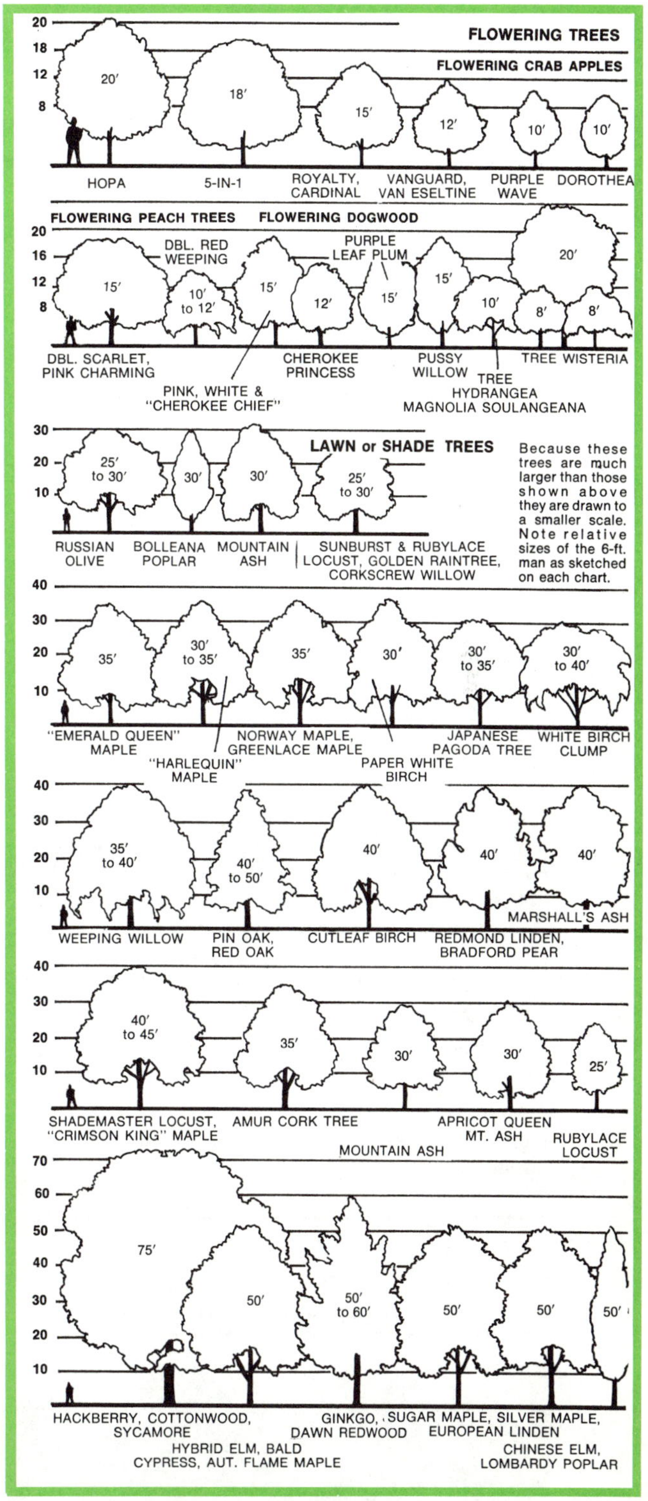


**TREES ARE THE MOST** important plantings you will make in your landscape. You plan for your own pleasure and that of future generations. Because of the long-range effects of planting a tree, consider its overall shape and expected size at maturity before you plant. For guidance, consult the chart above prepared in cooperation with the Henry Field Seed and Nursery Co., Inc., Shenandoah, IA.

# How to fell and limb a tree

**There are right and wrong methods for felling and limbing a large tree. Stick to these suggestions and you will find that the job will go easier with a lot less chance of injury**

### Basic sawing techniques—notching and felling

Done properly, it takes three cuts to fell a tree: two passes to make the undercut (notch) and a back cut on the opposite side of the trunk. If you are a beginner, mark all three cuts waist high on the tree trunk with chalk. The notch should be cut in the sequence shown above to a depth of approximately one-third tree diameter, and perpendicular to the line of fall. After making the first two cuts, remove the wedge from the trunk.

Make the back cut at least 2 in. higher than the notch so as to leave a "hinge" of uncut wood to guide the tree over. *Do not cut through the notch.* Besides guiding the tree, the hinge will also prevent the tree from twisting as it falls. As the tree starts to fall, pull your saw free. Immediately turn off power and retreat quickly along your pre-planned escape route. From here on, gravity takes over.

### When to use a felling wedge

If you suspect the tree may not fall in the desired direction, or may tilt back causing the saw to bind, do not complete the back cut. Withdraw the saw and use wood, plastic or magnesium wedges to open the cut and tilt the tree in the desired direction of fall. *Caution: When using wedges, make certain the chain saw does not come into contact with wedge or the saw will kick back.* Felling wedges are available at most chain-saw dealers or you can cut your own of hardwood.

With the tree felled, you can now trim off the waist-high stump close to the ground, repeating the three-cut method mentioned above.

SEE ALSO

**Chain saws . . . Fireplaces . . . Firewood . . . Landscaping . . . Log cutting . . . Sawbucks**

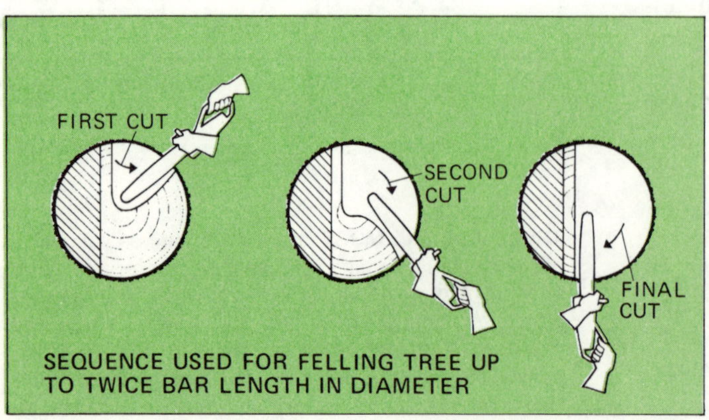


### Sawing sequence for large-diameter trunks

As a rule of thumb, large-diameter trees (up to twice the chain-saw-bar length in diameter) should be handled by a professional; cutting one down is not a job for a fledgling woodcutter. However, if you are confident of your tree-felling ability, and the tree is standing out in open terrain, you should always use felling wedges in the manner described above.

To fell a large tree, use a series of cuts as shown at left. Notice that the cuts are made so that the third and final cut leaves the hinge wood parallel to the notch cut. This is a must, so make the cuts with maximum care.

## Limbing a tree

There are two things to guard against when limbing a tree: First, the possibility that the cut branch will whip back in the direction of the woodcutter, and second, the impulse to work from an improperly positioned, thus unsafe, ladder.

To prevent the first, use the cutting sequence shown. To saw off a large limb supported only by the trunk, first cut one-third of the way through the limb on its underside. Make second cut through the limb from the top. Make certain you lash the ladder securely to the tree. Run a rope around the trunk a couple of times, then tie it securely to the top rung. Plant the ladder so that its feet are level and are placed a distance from the base of the tree that is equal to one-quarter of the vertical height.

## Stacking fireplace logs

For use as firewood, the logs should be stacked and allowed to dry. There is a difference of opinion on whether to split logs before or after they are dry. Splitting goes quickest if you use a steel splitting wedge and a wooden maul rather than an ax. And it's a lot safer.

Twelve or fourteen logs may be stored without danger of toppling over. One cord of wood equals 128 cu. ft. Assuming you've cut your logs into 24-in. lengths, it would take a pile 16 ft. long and 4 ft. high to equal this volume.

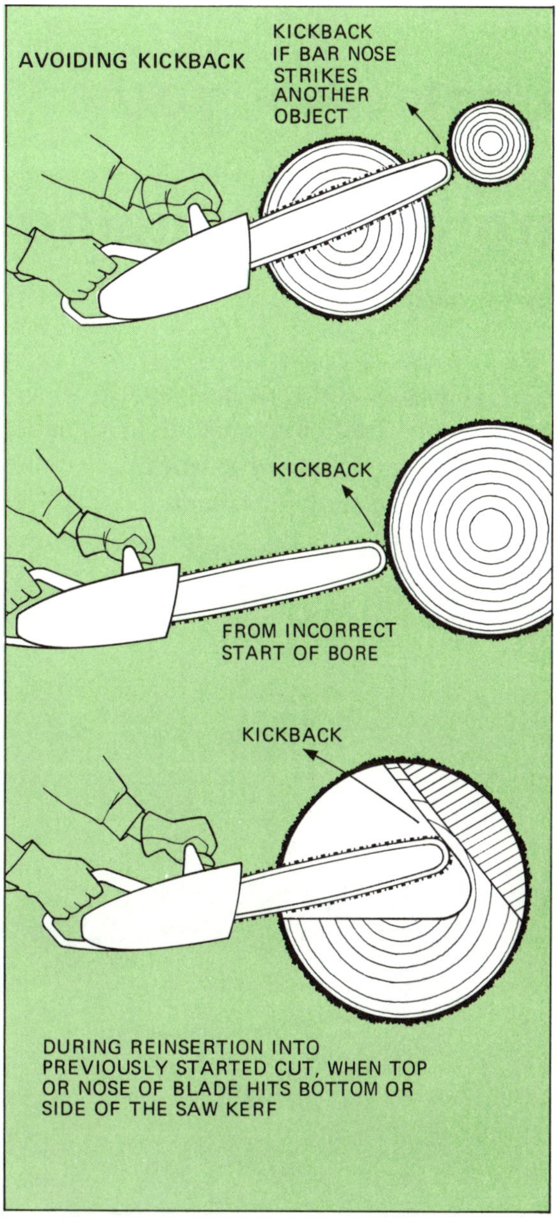


## Avoiding kickback

When cutting with the nose of the bar, take extra care to protect against chance of saw kickback. It will occur when any of the three conditions illustrated above exists.

Safety rules you should always observe:

1. Think the job out beforehand and stick to your plan.
2. Plan an escape route at 45° angle opposite the direction of tree fall.
3. Wear a hard hat if there is any chance of timber or branches falling from above.
4. Don't wear loose-fitting clothing. It could become caught in the chain saw or falling limbs. Always wear work gloves.
5. If your job collects a crowd, stop. Keep bystanders, especially children, clear of your cutting site and area of tree fall.
6. Work only with a sharp saw chain.

# Look what you can make from metal tubing

By WALTER E. BURTON

**Tubing of brass, copper, steel or aluminum can be made into all kinds of unusual and useful objects. It is easy to work with, requiring few sophisticated or expensive tools to produce handsome products**

**SOME METAL TUBING** can be bent satisfactorily simply by wrapping it around grooved pulley wheel (sheave). Here, ⅜-in. aluminum tubing is bent this way.

MANY USEFUL OBJECTS can be made from aluminum, copper, brass or steel tubing. Metal tubing is cut with a hacksaw, tubing cutter or lathe. Cut ends are file-finished, or smoothed in a lathe. For smooth surfaces, abrasive cloth or a flap-type sanding wheel is used and a final luster is given with metal polish. Tubing can be joined by soldering, brazing, welding—or even using epoxy or plugs (either metal or wood) and

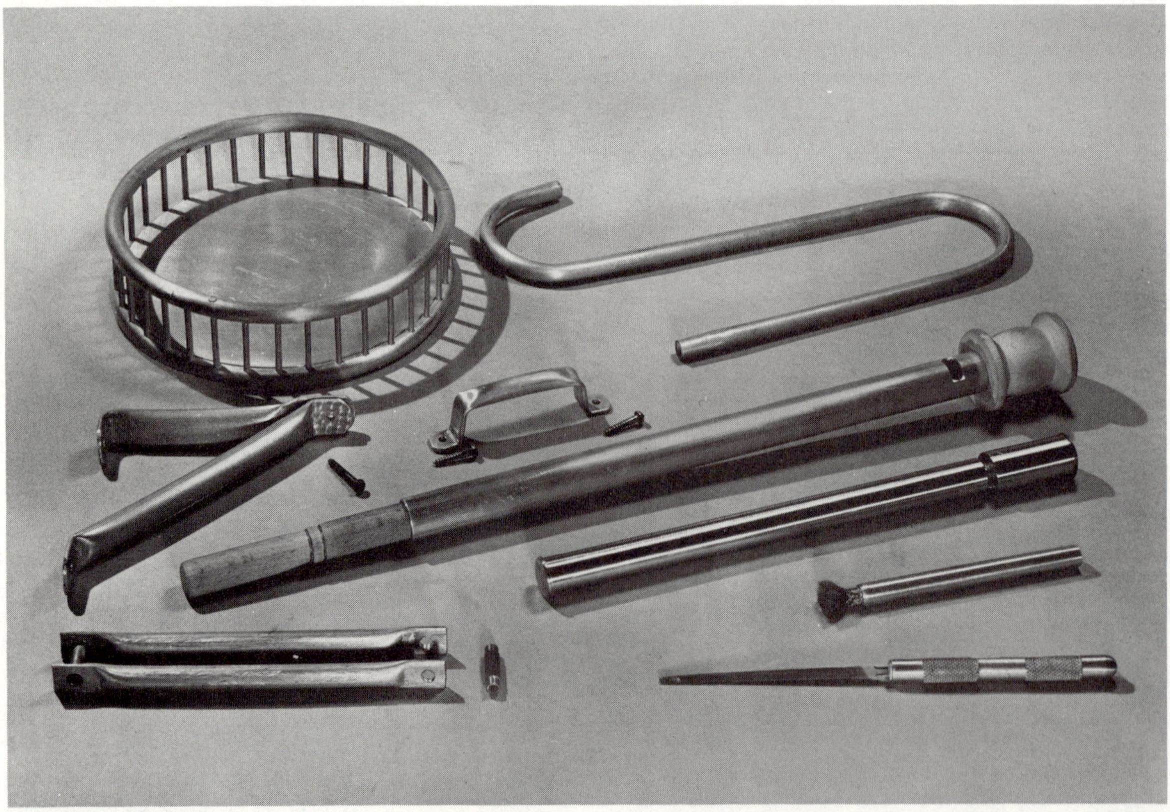

**VARIOUS ITEMS** that can be made from metal tubing include 1) ring basket or tray, 2) siphon, 3) shelf bracket, 4) drawer or door pull, 5) slide whistle, 6) metal tubing with ends flattened, connected by peened spacers, 7) adjustable shelf post/bookend, 8) spacer, 9) brush handle and 10) file handle.

SEE ALSO

**Bookends . . . Gifts, Christmas . . . Racks, book . . . Shelves . . . Tools, hand . . . Toys**

**SPACER** with the diameter of the ends reduced connects the flattened ends of the larger tubing. Here, the spacer ends are peened to hold ends together.

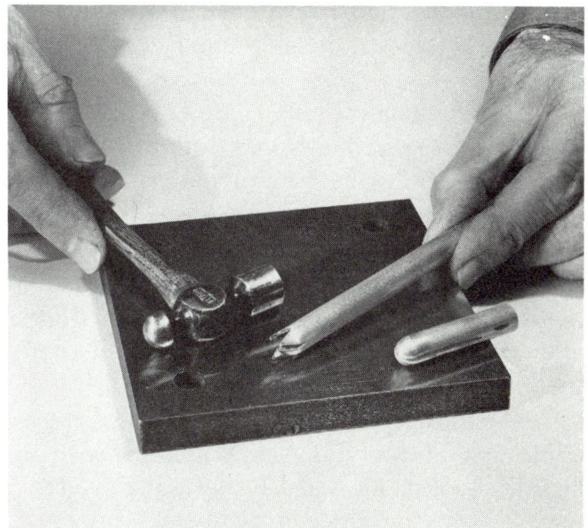

**ALUMINUM TUBING** can be closed and rounded by first cutting it as shown. Then, use a hammer to lightly tap the cut ends until it is round.

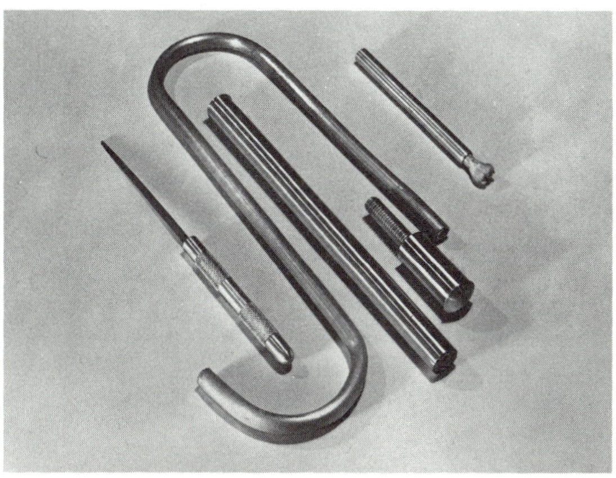

**TOOL HANDLES** and siphon made from ⅜-in. aluminum tube; post bookend from ¾ and ⅝-in. copper tubes.

**ADJUSTABLE BOOKSHELF POST** serves as a bookend and as an added support for the upper shelf.

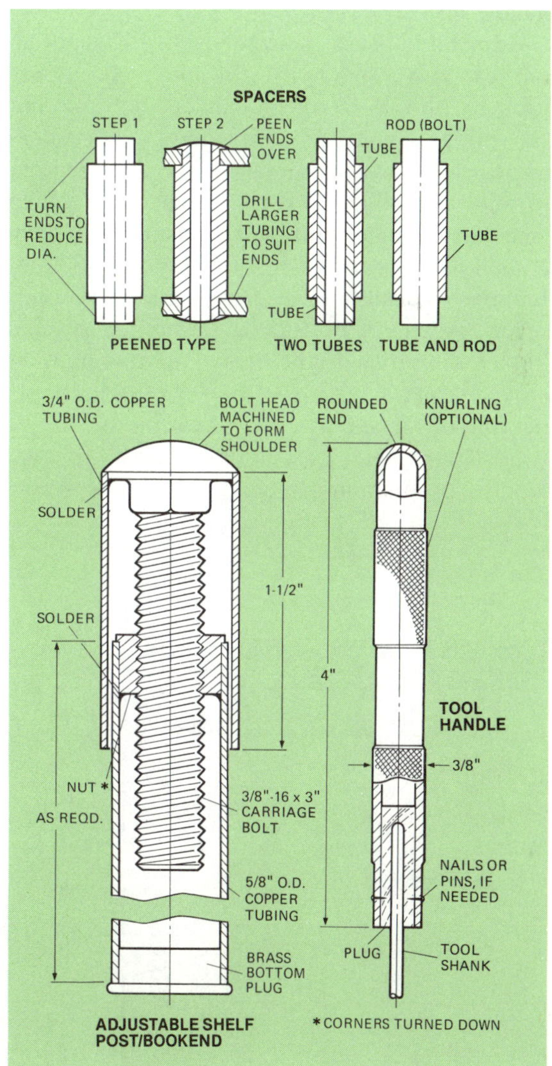

screws, pins or nails. Bending can be done with coil-spring sleeves or the method shown in the photo.

Details on six metal tubing projects follow. All sizes of tubing given refer to outside dimensions.

**Spacers.** Short lengths of tubing are often used as spacers between two plates, strips or other elements of a mechanism. One type of spacer is made from a single tube, with the ends turned or filed down to form shoulders and peened over after installation. A tube, rod or bolt within a tube might also be used.

**Tool handles.** Improvised tool handles can be made easily from tubing. A common way to anchor the tool shank is to drive a wood dowel into the tube and drill a hole in the dowel for the tool. The relatively new "plastic-metal" preparations or an epoxy filler could also be used. Outer end of the handle can be left open, plugged or closed by using the method shown or by spinning or bending the metal. Light knurling makes a handle less slippery.

**Adjustable shelf post/bookend.** This dual-purpose item is made from ⅝ and ¾-in. copper tubing with a ⅜-16 x 3-in. carriage bolt and nut providing the adjustable movement. Nut corners are turned down for about 5/6 of their length, forming a shoulder to rest on end of ⅝-in. tubing (see drawing). The bolt head is machined to form a shallow shoulder to rest on the end of ¾-in. tubing. Nut and bolt head are soldered to their respective tubes by fluxing the joints, placing bits of solder inside the tubes and heating over stove burner. Plug at bottom of post prevents denting of the shelf.

**Shelf bracket.** By flattening ends of two lengths of aluminum tubing and drilling screw

**SHELF BRACKET** is made from ½-in. aluminum tubing; whistle from ¾-in. aluminum tubing, dowel and spool.

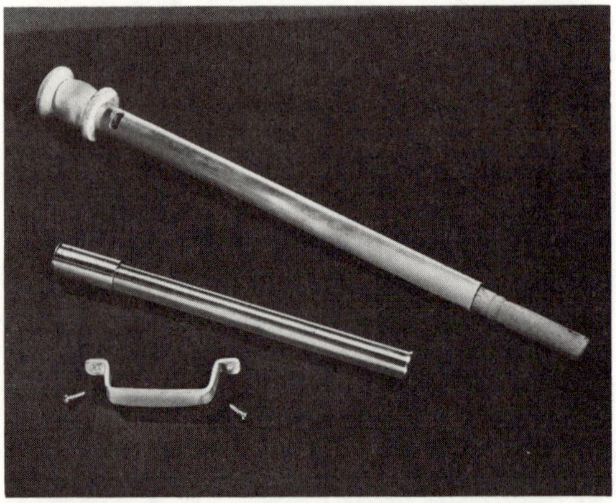

**FROM TOP:** assembled slide whistle, adjustable bookshelf post, drawer pull from ⅜-in. aluminum tubing.

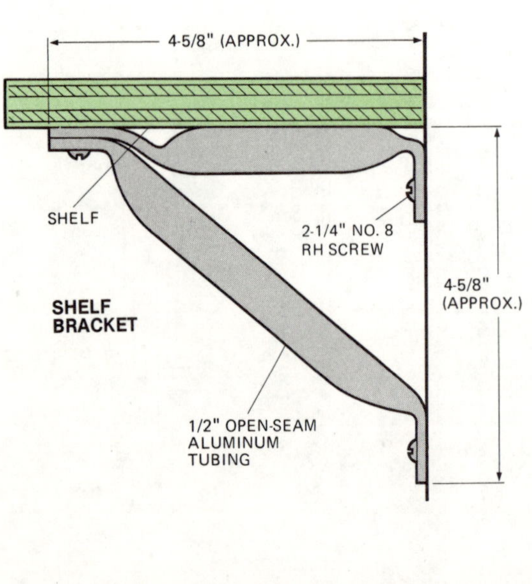


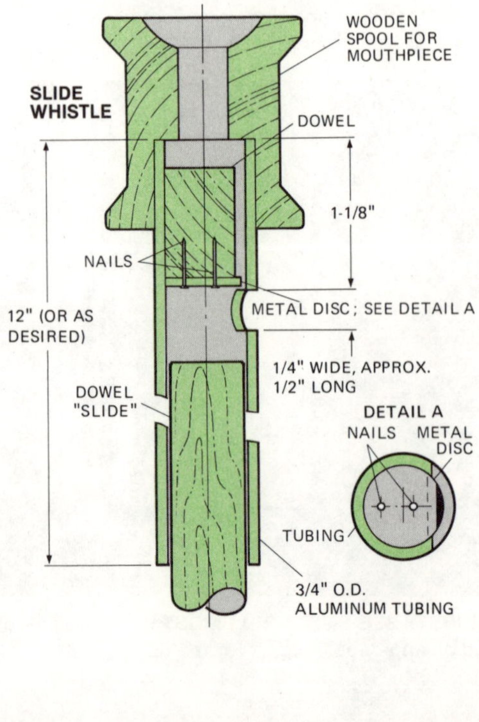

**NAILS IN** clamped wood hold metal ring in place for drilling holes in center of rim to receive "side rods."

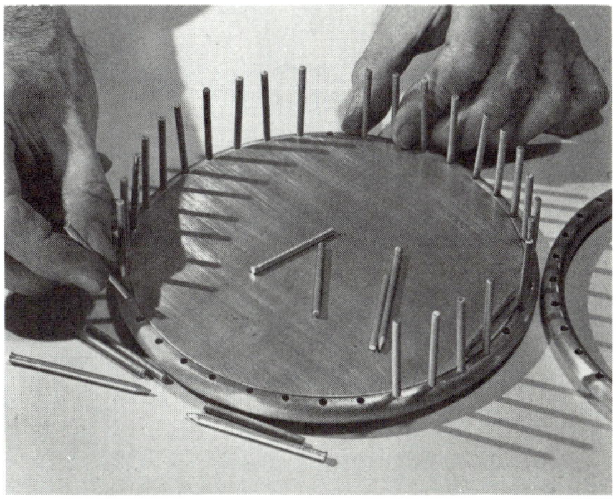

**"SIDE RODS"** (nails with heads cut off) are inserted in bottom ring holes; sheet aluminum bottom fits inside.

**BASKET** made from ⅜-in. seamless aluminum tubing and aluminum nails makes attractive server.

holes in them, a handy shelf bracket can be made.

**Slide whistle.** A slot in the tube is made by drilling two ¼-in. holes tangent to one another and filing out intervening metal. The plug is a short piece of dowel; a metal disc with a flat area on its circumference is nailed to one end of the plug and positioned at slot edge. The slide is a free-moving length of dowel, the mouthpiece, a wood spool.

**Ring basket.** Two lengths of metal tubing are bent to form two circles with 7-in. outside diameters. Ends of each circle are joined by inserting a maple plug and nailing through tubing into plug. The circles are joined with 36 "side rods" made by cutting heads from ⅛-in.-dia. aluminum nails. A total of 33 "rods" engage holes drilled through one side of each ring; the other three are longer and extend through rings with their ends peened. The bottom piece is sheet aluminum cut from siding scrap and glued in place with epoxy cement.

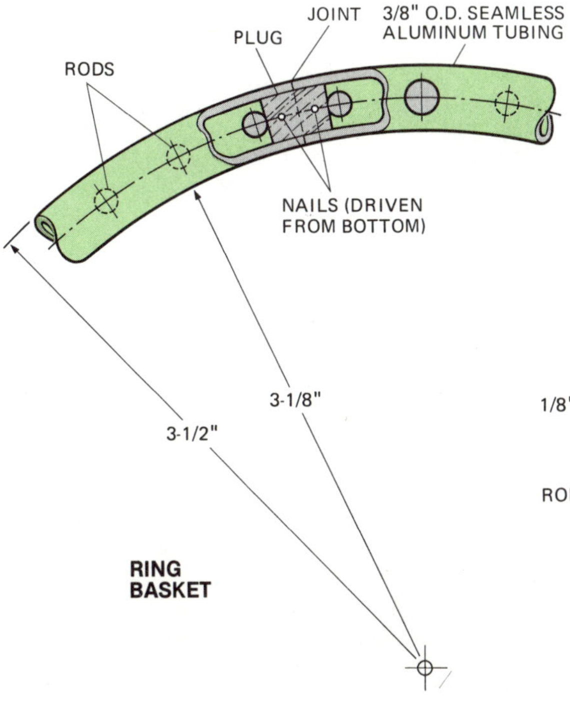


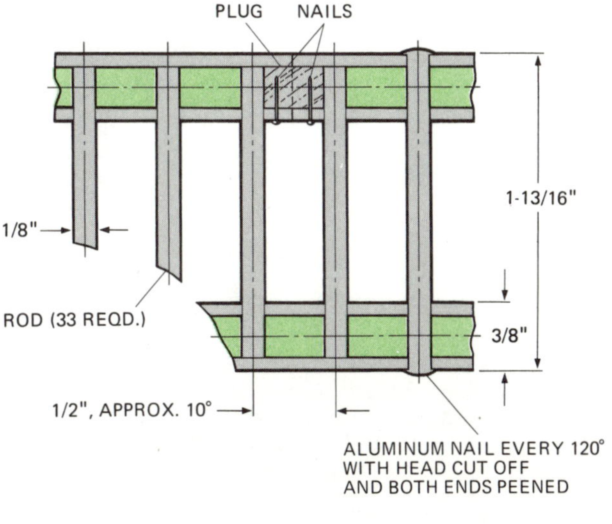

# A basic course in engine tune-up

By MORT SCHULTZ

**A complete tune-up goes well beyond the slap-dash treatment you may get down the street. It's more thorough— and far more important. Here's the step-by-step approach to use**

■ TUNE-UP KEEPS AN engine running smoothly and economically. It helps curb pollution and uncovers hidden problems. And it's called for at least every 12,000 miles or 12 months, whichever comes first. The sequence of services we suggest here will help you be sure you're touching all the bases.

In the procedure we suggest, some tools are named that you may consider exotic or expensive. But, with the modern automobile, they're necessary. And when you spread their cost across all the jobs you'll be able to do for yourself, their real cost is comparatively low. Besides, the right tools and instruments make the work simple.

Some jobs, however, will require costly professional tools. And they may well require the touch of a professional mechanic. We include them, nevertheless. Even procedures that you decide you can't handle should be understood. When you turn some part of the job over to a professional, you may get better work if you know what his job will entail.

We have two purposes, then: To help you handle all the maintenance and service that's reasonable for a do-it-yourselfer. And to make you knowledgeable enough that you can see when a mechanic's work is done properly—or improperly.

SEE ALSO

**Auto batteries . . . Carburetors, auto . . . Differentials, auto . . . Distributors, auto . . . Emissions controls . . . Engines, auto . . . Ignition systems, auto . . . Lubrication, auto . . . Sparkplugs . . . Transmissions, auto**

**compression test**

The best tune-up won't be able to compensate for the inefficient performance that comes from low or uneven compression. If the engine idles roughly because of a sticky valve, that idle can't be smoothed out by other tune-up procedures. So, if you have any doubt, you should rule out these problems with a compression test on each cylinder.

This calls for a compression gauge. Like the other tools and supplies we mention here, one is available from your auto parts and accessories dealer. You'll press the end of the gauge stem into each spark-plug port while the piston travels up and down a few times. The gauge reading will indicate the pressure built up inside the combustion chamber.

The first step in a compression test is to warm up the engine so the choke plate is wide open. Then disconnect all the ignition leads from spark plugs. Don't pull the leads themselves, however; pull and twist the *boot* around the contact at the end of each plug. Ignition leads aren't designed for great physical strength; their role is to conduct high voltage. Pulling directly on a lead can damage its insulation or separate the lead from its terminal. You may well disrupt the current flow or cause more misfiring—perhaps the very illness you're hoping to cure.

Be sure plug leads are marked so you can restore them to the proper plugs, also numbered, or you'll mess up the firing sequence. (Masking tape works well. Traditionally, cylinders are numbered from front to rear. Number plugs and leads the same way. When you take plug leads from the distributor cap, use the same numbering system on distributor cap towers—with an L or R to distinguish left-bank connections from the right.)

Blow debris from the well around each plug port—a rubber ear syringe or an ordinary soda straw works nicely. Then remove the plugs. If yours have metal gaskets, save them. You'll

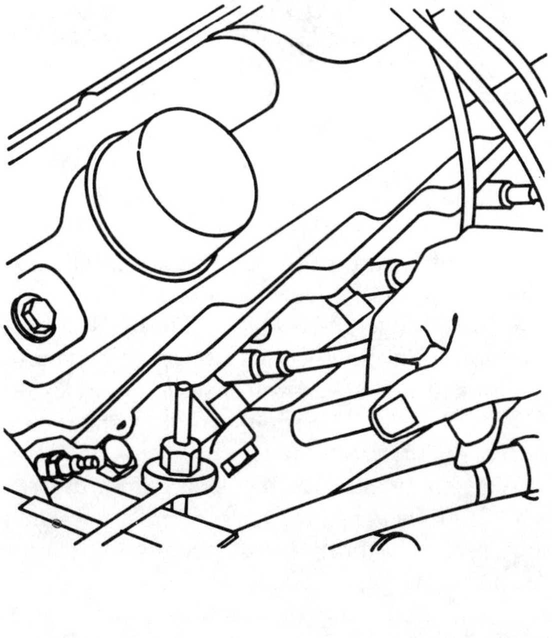

need them for any plugs you return to service.

For the actual test, you'll have to be sure the choke and throttle plates don't close. Open the throttle with the throttle lever. Unless you have a co-worker inside the car who will hold the accelerator pedal to the floor, reach for a screwdriver. Extend it carefully down the carburetor throat past the choke plate to hold the throttle wide open.

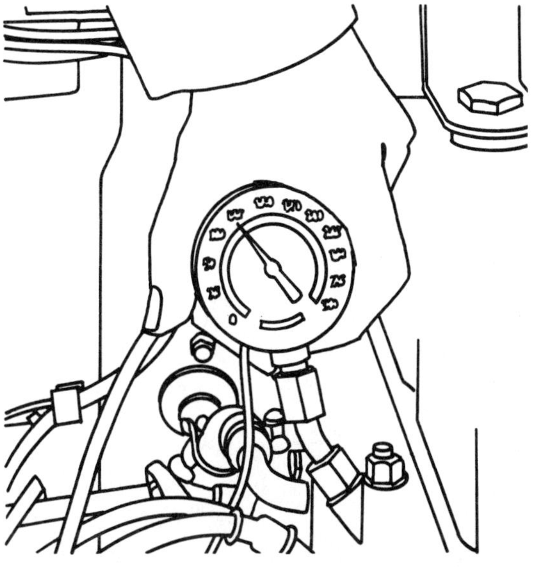

**the test itself**

For the test, hold the end of the gauge firmly in a plug port while someone uses the starter motor to crank the engine a few revolutions. Note the highest reading you get for that cylinder and move on to the next for the same procedure.

You'll quickly have all the data collected. The next question: How does one interpret it?

You needn't be particularly surprised if compression readings vary somewhat from cylinder to cylinder. It would be much more surprising if every cylinder, from end to end, maintained new-car compression for several years.

The *amount* of variation is what's significant. The lowest compression should be no less than 80 percent of the highest. Cylinders with too little compression alert you to problems beyond the scope of a tune-up—but they're problems that you'll need to know about as soon as possible.

A cylinder that can't build up enough compression may have a valve sticking so it doesn't close as fast as it should. Or a valve that's burned, so it can't seal tightly. Or piston rings that are seriously worn. The condition of the end of the spark plug and any engine tendency to burn oil will go a long way toward confirming that last failing.

Compression specifications for your car are in the car's service manual. You'll also find them in general automotive references such as *Motor's Auto Repair Manual,* usually available in public libraries. As you become adept, you may want to get a copy for yourself. Or you may be able to get specs from the service department of a dealer that sells your make of car. Perhaps even by telephone.

To avoid wear on the points, it's a good idea to disconnect the coil-to-distributor primary wire from the coil before you crank the engine with the starter motor. This is the thin wire from the side of the distributor to the coil.

**sparkplug service**

New sparkplugs are recommended every 12,000 miles, but you may be able to get lots more wear out of them. If they aren't damaged or badly worn, they're well worth checking and servicing.

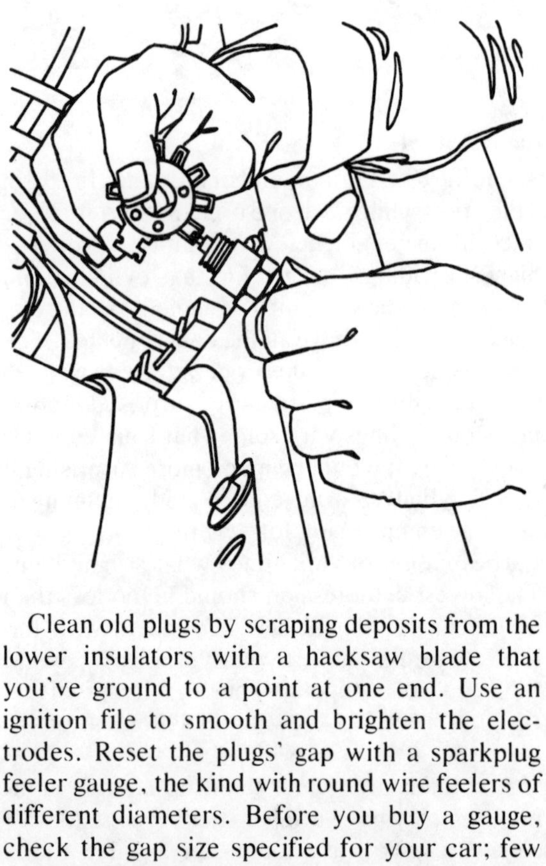

Clean old plugs by scraping deposits from the lower insulators with a hacksaw blade that you've ground to a point at one end. Use an ignition file to smooth and brighten the electrodes. Reset the plugs' gap with a sparkplug feeler gauge, the kind with round wire feelers of different diameters. Before you buy a gauge, check the gap size specified for your car; few gauges will have enough elements to check *every* possible plug gap exactly.

Your owner's manual will specify the right plug gap. So will the emission-control label mounted on or near the radiator.

Your plug gauge should include a bending tool to bend the outer or ground electrode. Don't use pliers and don't try to bend the center electrode. Either approach can easily ruin the plug.

Remember that you'll have to gap new plugs properly before installing them. They aren't necessarily gapped for your car when new.

Carefully clean the threads in the spark plug port. The best tool is a small wire brush that has been coated with grease. That will help it pick up any deposits. A little grease getting into the combustion chamber isn't serious. It will burn away quickly.

Name-brand plugs—and most others—come with metal gaskets. Unless the seats for your plugs are tapered, you'll need to use the gaskets with new plugs. If you re-use old plugs, be sure you've saved their gaskets to reinstall with the plugs.

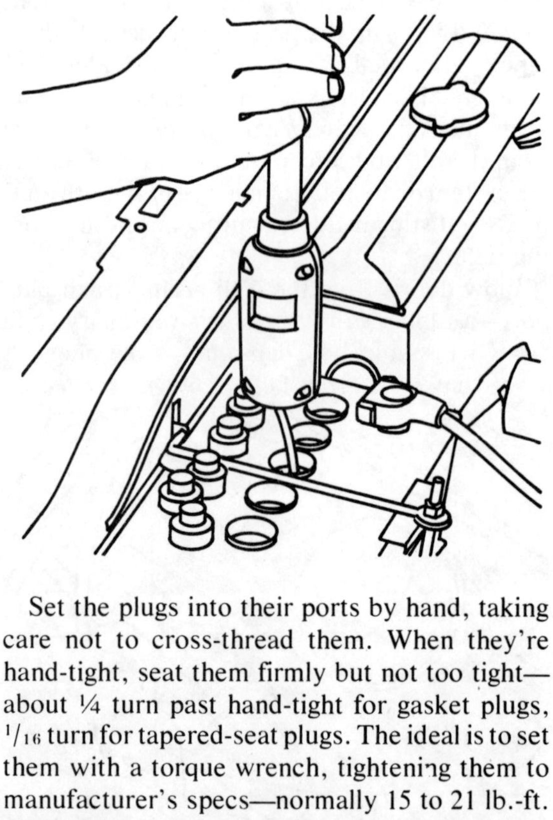

Set the plugs into their ports by hand, taking care not to cross-thread them. When they're hand-tight, seat them firmly but not too tight—about ¼ turn past hand-tight for gasket plugs, $^{1}/_{16}$ turn for tapered-seat plugs. The ideal is to set them with a torque wrench, tightening them to manufacturer's specs—normally 15 to 21 lb.-ft. (20 to 28.5 Nm). Check the shop manual or a dealer for the exact specs.

Wipe the ignition leads clean with a dry rag and check them and the boots. Replace any that are cracked or brittle. Push the wire terminals firmly on the plugs when you finish.

**battery service**

Use a hydrometer to test battery specific gravity; it tells the proportion of sulfuric acid in the electrolyte. The procedure is simple: Draw some electrolyte from one cell into a clean hydrometer tube. Record the reading, return the electrolyte to its cell, and draw another sample from the next one.

Before taking your reading, let the electrolyte set for a minute while the instrument stabilizes. Be sure the float is riding free of the tube's sides, then hold the hydrometer at eye-level to take your reading.

Many low-cost hydrometers are available. The best have a built-in temperature compensator, a useful characteristic since temperature affects specific gravity to some degree.

Specific gravity of a fully charged battery is between 1.260 and 1.280. If the overall reading isn't above 1.230, charge the battery—as slowly as possible. If that doesn't bring the reading up, your battery is about shot.

A cell or cells with specific gravity readings as much as .050 below the others is weak. It may continue to serve you for months, but frequent checking is called for lest you get stuck with a dead battery.

**clean the battery**

Keeping the battery clean is hardly complicated. And it will pay off in promoting longer battery life and in preventing discharging.

To clean it, remove it from the car. First take off the ground cable (usually the negative one) then the "hot" one. A battery terminal puller does the best job of removing the cables and it avoids the danger you might damage posts with a screwdriver or pliers.

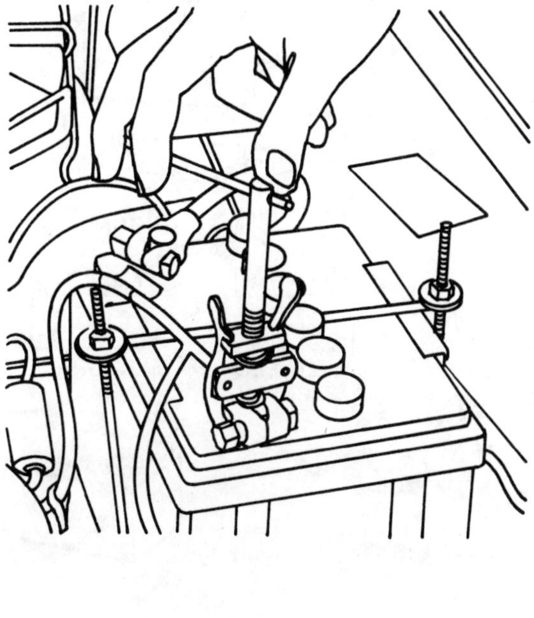

Take the battery out, tighten the vent caps, and cover the vents with masking tape so the cleaning solution (a base) doesn't contaminate—and begin to neutralize—the acid. Scrub the case with an ammonia-water or baking-soda-water solution, then rinse it with plain water. Keep repeating the process until the cleaning agent no longer fizzles.

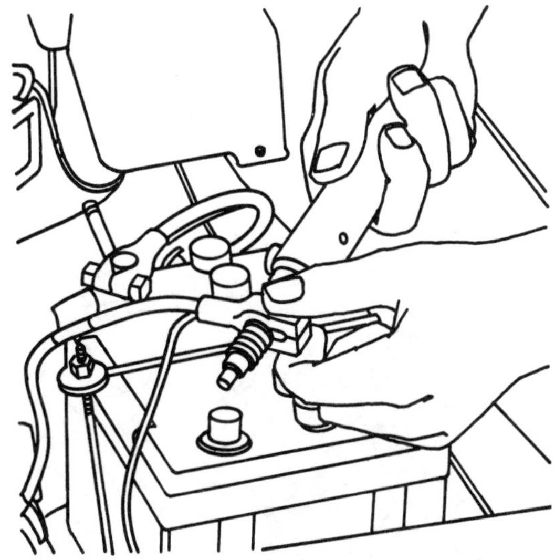

Wash the battery pan with solution, too, and check the battery cables. If they're damaged, replace them. Clean any corrosion from the cable terminals as well as the battery posts with the wire-brush elements of a battery cleaning tool. Only then should you replace the battery.

Reconnect the "hot" cable first, then the ground. Draw the terminal clamps up tight on the posts. A light coat of petroleum jelly over the entire connection will help to retard corrosion.

**ignition service**

Start your ignition servicing at the distributor. Remove sparkplug wires from distributor-cap towers and mark the towers for identification, just as you did for the compression test. Each wire must go back into its own tower.

Now remove the distributor cap, wipe it clean, and inspect it closely inside and out. You're looking for hairline cracks, carbon tracks, and burned or corroded terminals. Such damage usually means terminals haven't been making good contact. Current has been arcing across an imperfect connection. If the cap is damaged,

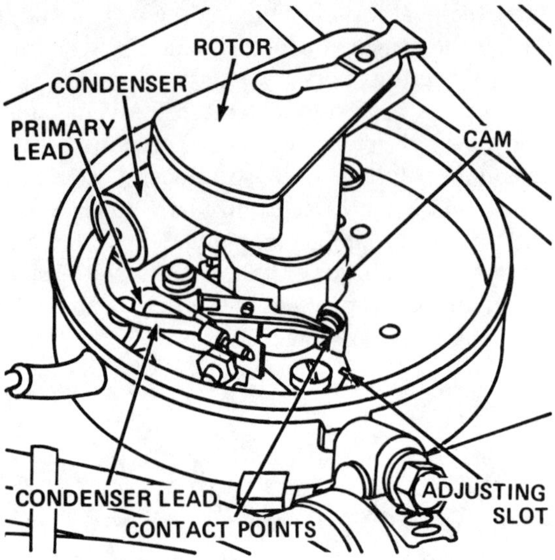


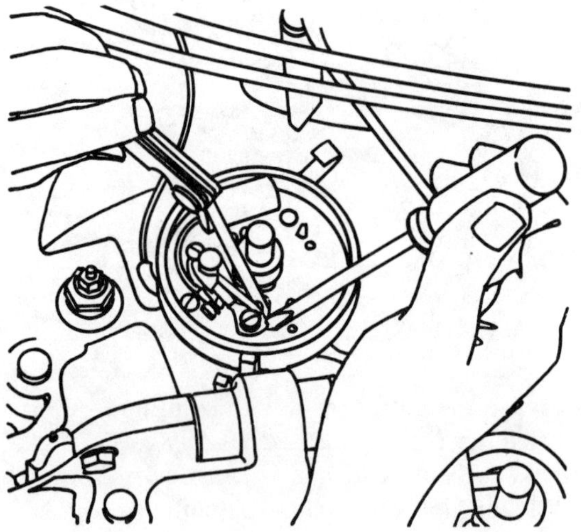

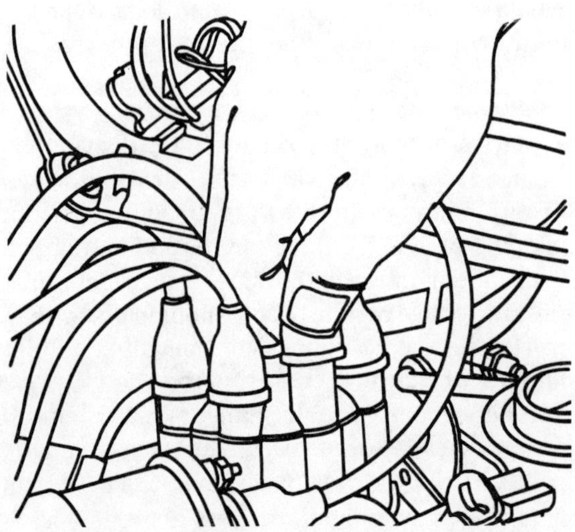

replace it. If not, clean particles of debris from within the towers.

Pull off the rotor and inspect it for cracks or a corroded or broken metal contact. If it's damaged, get a new one.

Then carefully spread apart the distributor contact points and study them. Points with a general gray color, points that are only slightly roughened or pitted, can be kept in use. Certainly those that are badly pitted or burned must be replaced. But it is at least as important to find the reason for their condition and repair it.

Pitted or burned points usually indicate one of about six problems. Most serious are a poorly adjusted or inoperative voltage regulator or ballast resistor, or a defective or incorrect condenser, or high condenser-circuit resistance. Less serious are oil or vapor in the distributor because of a clogged engine breather, excessive distributor-cam lubricant picked up by the points, a weakened contact-point spring, or points improperly gapped.

**servicing points**

If points are in good shape, clean off scale by passing a clean, fine-cut point file between them a couple of times. Don't use emery cloth or sandpaper; loose grit will foul things.

Set the breaker-arm rubbing block on the high

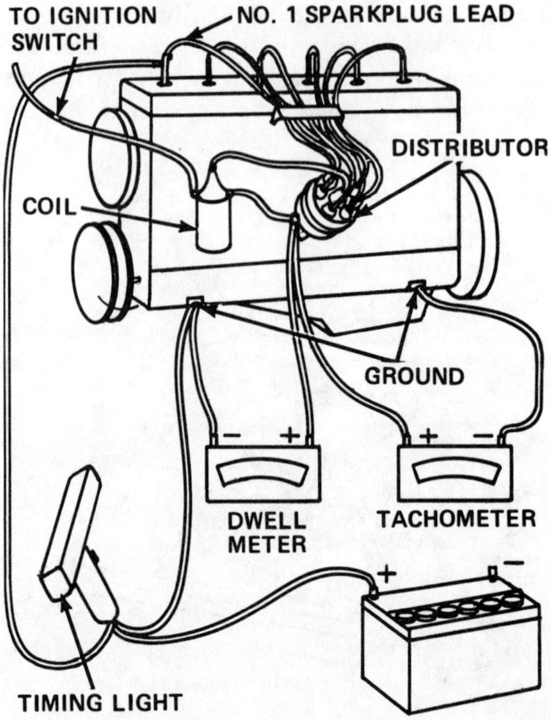

point of a cam lobe and adjust the point gap with a flat feeler gauge. Find proper gap setting on the vehicle-emission-control label or in the owner's manual or shop manual.

If your distributor has a wick-type cam lubricator, replace it. If there's no built-in cam lubricator, apply cam lube yourself. A single drop, about the size of a match head, goes on one cam lobe only.

Reinstall the rotor and distributor cap and seat each plug wire firmly into its tower by pushing down on the boot while squeezing it to release any trapped air.

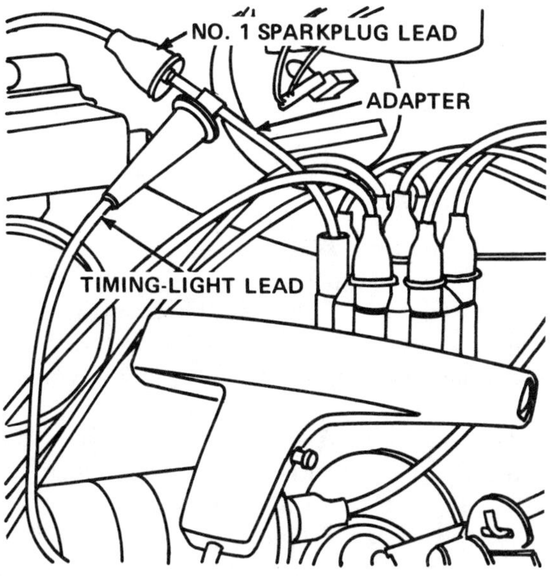


Clean out the high-tension-lead tower of the ignition coil and make sure the high-tension lead is seated firmly in the tower. Also tighten the ignition primary wire connections on the coil.

If you have a dwellmeter, set the contact-point dwell angle to specifications. Without a dwellmeter, you can make an approximate dwell adjustment by ear if the distributor cap has an access cover. Let the engine idle. Raise the access cover and turn the point adjusting screw until the engine barely starts to misfire. Then back the screw up half a turn. When you finish, be sure the access cover is tightly closed so dirt doesn't get into the distributor.

**ignition timing**

Timing the ignition comes next. You'll need a stroboscopic timing light and a tachometer. Like other tune-up specs, the proper timing specifications are on the emission control label and in the standard service books.

Warm up the engine. Hook up the tachometer, leaving it where you can see it as you work on the engine. Hook the timing light into the No. 1 sparkplug circuit—but *not* by puncturing the plug lead insulation for a good contact. If you use one of the new induction lights, you'll need only to place an induction coil segment around the plug wire. Otherwise contact will be by way of an adapter that goes between the plug and its cable. Some go at the distributor end of the plug cable.

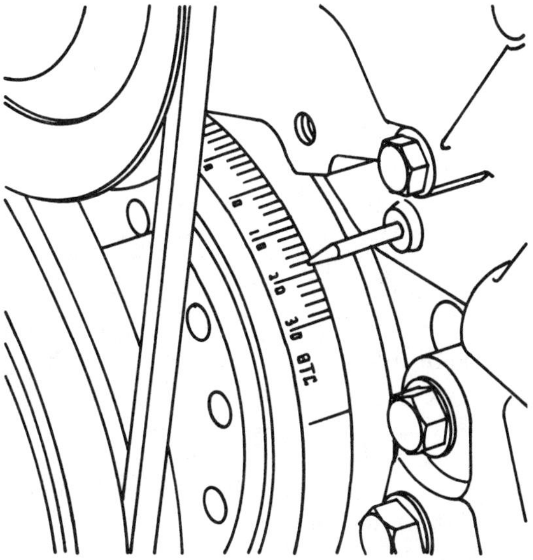

Disconnect the hose from the vacuum-advance control unit on the distributor and plug the end of the hose with a pencil. Any vacuum leak would throw the timing out of whack. Once the engine is warmed and idling at the specified speed, aim the timing light at the timing mark and pointer. Sight straight down along the beam and don't tilt the light or you can throw the reading off.

You can save yourself lots of frustration by checking a manual ahead of time for the location of your car's timing marks. Locate them, and even daub a bit of white paint on them. Everything will be easier.

The engine is properly timed when the light's flashes seem to freeze the mark in the right relationship to the pointer. You shouldn't see the timing marks appearing to shift.

If timing has drifted away from specifications, loosen the bolt that holds the distributor housing. Rotate the distributor until the timing marks line up properly and hold steady. If moving the distributor in one direction doesn't bring the timing marks closer to position, move it the other way. Then tighten the distributor housing.

Don't neglect to recheck the timing after you've tightened the distributor. It's an irritating fact of life that, in many cases, the mechanic finds the timing has, unaccountably, shifted slightly—after he thought he was all through. The right response: Loosen the distributor housing again and readjust the timing.

**vacuum advance timing**

Now test the performance of the vacuum advance unit by shifting the timing light from the No. 1 cylinder to the alternate-firing one. On a V8, that will be the fifth in the firing order; on a Six, it will be the third. Check your service data for the firing order to identify the cylinder—and ignition circuit—you're looking for.

Then check the timing again. There's likely to be some difference between timing at No. 1 and timing when hooked to its alternate. But that difference shouldn't exceed 3°. If it does, the distributor is worn and needs repair.

Now hold the vacuum hose near its connection on the vacuum-advance unit. Keep the light aimed at the timing marks. While a co-worker behind the wheel gradually increases engine speed, push the hose onto its connection, then pull it off. The timing mark should continue seeming to shift quickly back and forth. If it doesn't or if movement is sluggish, the vacuum advance diaphragm has ruptured. The unit will have to be replaced.

**fuel system service**

If the fuel system sends a badly proportioned air-fuel mix to the combustion chambers, your car will be hard to start. It will miss and stall. And it will use more gas than necessary. Service of the fuel system is basic to a healthy car.

Begin by checking the carburetor air filter. Follow the owner's manual recommendations about replacing its element.

On the chance that the fuel filter has gathered foreign matter that's impeding fuel flow, manufacturers generally recommend a new fuel filter at tune-up time. You'll have either an integral filter where the fuel line enters the carburetor fuel bowl or an external one in the line from the fuel pump to the carb.

Remove the external filter by slipping clamps off the line. To get at the spring-loaded integral filter, remove the fuel line at the carb. But be careful not to lose the spring; you'll need to re-use it.

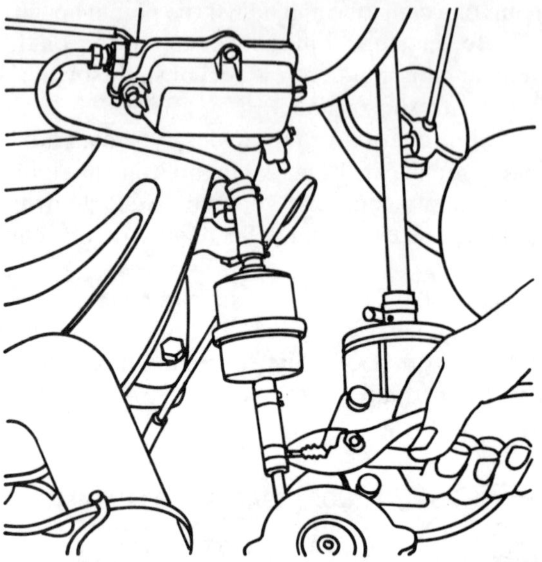

After servicing those filters, it's time to check the choke. Press the accelerator to the floor once; the choke plate should close across the carburetor throat. Then start the engine. The plate should open gradually and be wide open by the time the engine reaches running temperature.

Dirt around parts of the choke linkage or the butterfly plate's pivots can prevent smooth operation. If your choke doesn't operate well, clean the linkage and pivots with choke cleaner. Don't use any lubricant; it will just collect more dirt—and cause the choke to stick.

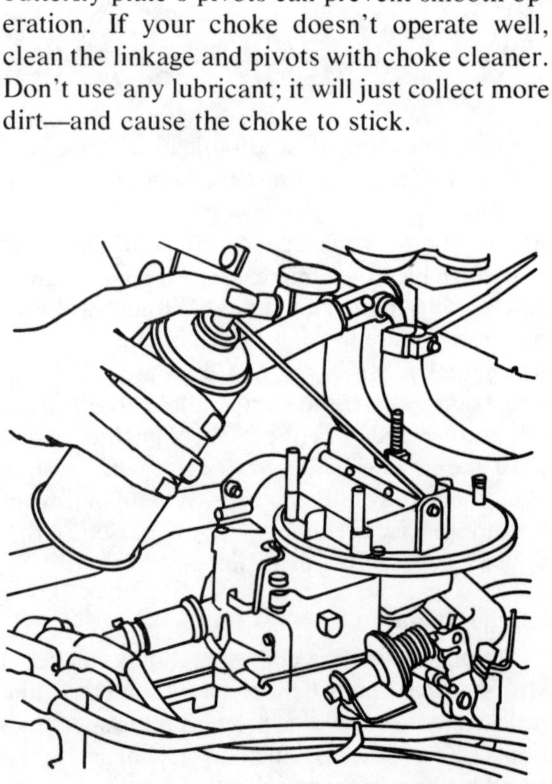

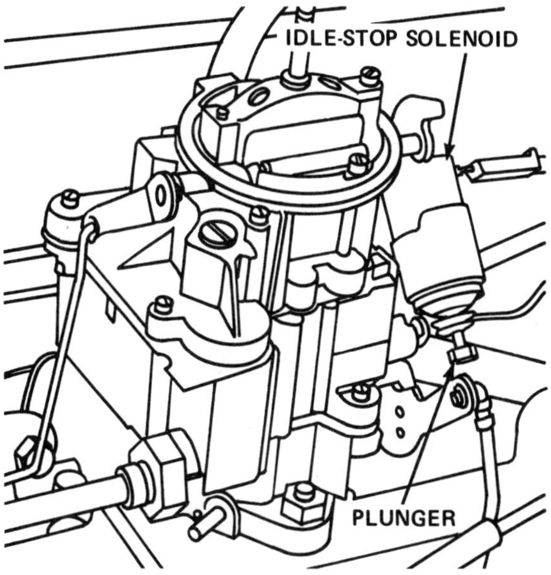


Now recheck the choke's closing and opening. If cleaning didn't help, the thermostatic spring, or choke piston, or electric choke-assist element has weakened and should be replaced.

**idle-speed controls**

Today's carburetors are generally equipped with an idle-stop solenoid that prevents engine run-on by letting the throttle close completely as soon as you shut off the engine. That tendency of an engine to keep chugging on is also called "dieseling."

To see whether you have trouble here, check whether the solenoid's plunger rests against the throttle-plate lever as the engine idles. Then see whether, as the engine is shut off, that plunger retracts to let the throttle valve close. If not, the smart step is to replace the solenoid.

On such a carburetor, you set the idle speed by turning the plunger until a tachometer reaches the specified idle speed. Older-style carburetors rely on an idle-speed adjusting screw to correct the speed.

In any case, the engine should be warm to set the idle speed. The hand brake must be set. A manual transmission must be in *Neutral*; separate idle-speed specs are established for automatic-transmission cars according to whether the gear box is in *Neutral* or *Drive*. Take your choice.

Federal emission standards require factory-set idle speeds, with little chance for you to modify it, on post-1968 cars. Efforts to defeat these restrictions are against the law.

**emission-control gear**

Engines may have three separate systems to combat pollution. Since 1963, all models have been equipped with emission control systems meant to ensure more complete burning of the fuel. A recent addition to this system has been exhaust-gas recirculation, incorporated in 1973 to help cut oxides of nitrogen. (The chemical symbol for this group of pollutants is $NO_x$; hence they're commonly referred to as "*nox*.")

An evaporative-emission-control system, virtually trouble-free, was introduced in 1970 to help trap fuel vapors from such sources as the fuel tank before they get into the air.

• *Crankcase-emission* controls are the place to start servicing. Pull out the PCV (positive crankcase ventilation) valve. On a V8 engine, it's probably in the push-rod cover. On a Six, it's in the rocker-arm cover.

Automatic replacement time for the PCV valve doesn't come until 24,000 miles have passed. Its performance should be checked at every tune-up, however. Just cover the valve with your thumb as the engine idles. If you don't feel a strong pull, replace the valve and check the rest of the system.

Inspect PCV hoses for deterioration. Since 1966 models, there's been a hose from the carburetor air cleaner to the rocker-arm cover. Check it, too.

Many crankcase emission control systems also have a cotton or mesh filter in the air cleaner. Some are filter-and-holder assemblies; others are filters only. If loose dust falls out on tapping or shaking the element, replace it.

• *Exhaust emission controls* include temperature sensors, damper valves and hoses. A large-diameter hose goes to the air-cleaner snorkel. A smaller one leads from the air cleaner's temperature sensor to a source of manifold vacuum.

With the engine cold, look into the snorkel's throat as someone starts the engine. The damper should close fully across the snorkel. As the engine warms, the damper should open gradually until it's fully open when the engine is at normal running temperature.

If it fails, either the temperature sensor or the valve control is faulty. But before repairing these, check the manifold heat-control valve; it has a direct effect on damper-valve operation.

• *Evaporative-emission controls* need nothing beyond replacement of the filter found in the base of a carbon canister. Most cars, especially U.S. production, now have such canisters.

**cooling-system service**

Engines today are designed for their greatest efficiency within a particular—sometimes narrow—temperature range. They should reach that temperature as soon as possible, but shouldn't exceed it from then on. It's the job of the cooling system to hold the engine at that temperature. And that's an important job.

Keeping the engine in tune should include, at least during every other annual tune-up, basic cooling system maintenance work. That involves only four general steps: checking for leaks, draining the system, flushing it, and refilling it.

• *Check for leaks* when the engine is off. Look for any dampness or deposits at each end of upper and lower radiator hoses, heater hoses, or other coolant connections. Significant deposits will be either rust-colored or a rather dirty white. This is the time to check the radiator cap, thermostat, drive belt surface and tension, and water pump, as well.

• *Drain the system* with the engine at running temperature and the heater turned *On*. For a complete drain job, remove engine plugs, too. They are in the lower block, but may not be easy to locate. Sixes normally have one and V8s, two.

• *Flush the system* after closing the drain valve and reinstalling the drain plugs—securely. Fill the system with water plus a commercial fast-flush cooling-system solution. Methods vary somewhat with such solutions; follow the directions on the can. You'll keep scale from accumulating.

• *Refill* your system with a coolant mix. A standard-brand ethylene glycol antifreeze should be mixed with water in proportions to meet the lowest temperature you expect. The directions on the container will show how to get the right mix. Even if your system is perfectly tight and operating flawlessly, you should replace this antifreeze every other winter. Check

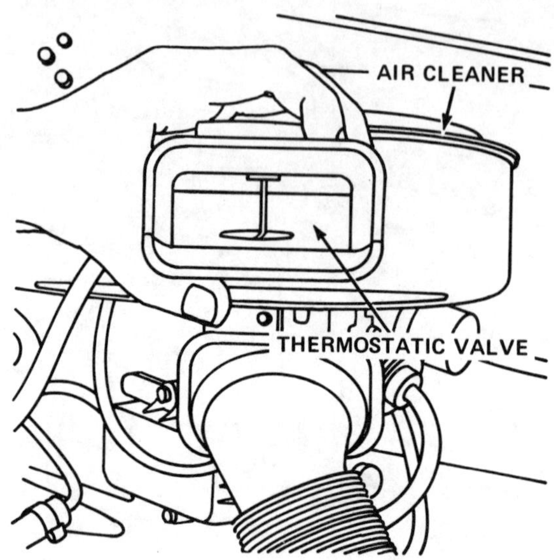


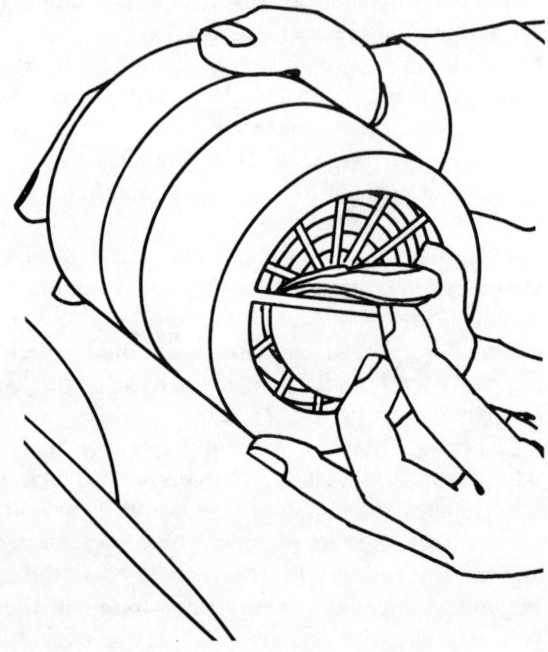

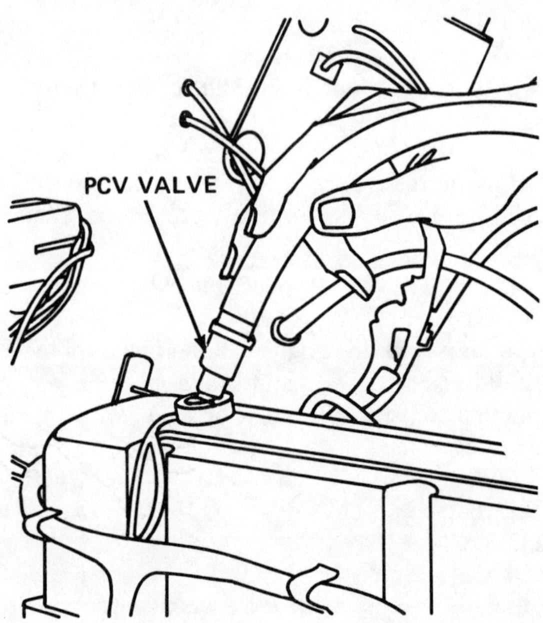

its potency every winter using a hydrometer.

You should also check the temperature warning light among the "idiot lights" likely to be in your instrument panel. When you turn on the car's switch, it should go *On*, too. As soon as the engine starts, the light should go *Out*. If it doesn't, the fuse or bulb have given up or the circuit has otherwise failed. It deserves a prompt fix.

**other tune-up services**

• That *manifold heat-control valve*, in the exhaust manifold, helps warm up a cold engine by closing off the manifold and trapping hot exhaust gases. It's thermostatically controlled to open as the engine warms. That releases these hot gases to prevent overheated and blistered spark plugs.

Not every engine has such a valve. But if there is one in your exhaust manifold, its counterweight will be under the manifold. You can check by feeling under there for the counterweight.

If that counterweight can't be moved easily by hand, the valve isn't working. Lubricate its pivot well with graphite or a special lubricant and, if necessary, rap the counterweight with a mallet. If that doesn't free the valve, replace it. Lubricate it when you grease the car.

• *Drive belts* should be inspected for wear, damage, and glaze. Replace any bad ones. Check belts for tension, too. The most accurate way is with a drive-belt tension gauge.

If a gauge isn't available, press the belt with your thumb midway between pulleys. If the belt gives no more than ½ in. under heavy pressure, you're OK. If you want to be thorough, check service literature for correct tension and use a gauge. Tension specifications vary.

To tighten drive belts, push against the center of the alternator or air-conditioner compressor, depending on the belt, and tighten the bracket nuts. Be sure both pulleys continue to run in the same plane.

• *Charging system* problems can be many, but often the trouble is nothing more than a loose belt. So, when your idiot light stays lighted or your ammeter shows a slow charging rate, check belts first. Also check for clean and tight battery connections. If your battery needs water more often than usual, the charging rate is probably too fast.

When overcharging is the problem, check the alternator or generator and the voltage regulator.

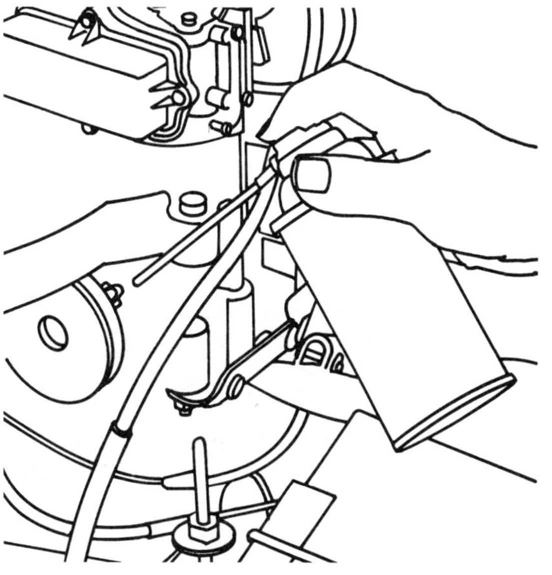

• *Air leaks* at the base of the carburetor or between the intake manifold and head can cause the loss of vacuum that will defeat other tune-up work. Spread heavy oil around these areas and start the engine. If there are leaks, you'll be able to see the oil being sucked into the engine. Tighten all the bolts and try again. If leaks persist, you'll need to replace whichever gasket is appropriate.

• *Road testing* is the moment of truth—the time when you find out how well you actually did. But just taking the car "out for a run" is no real test. To avoid missing anything, you should follow a planned, programmed test schedule. Here's one that makes sense:

Accelerate slowly from a dead stop—several times. Then drive several blocks at constant low speeds. Next, head for the open road. Entering the highway, accelerate briskly from a dead stop—and repeat that several times if you can find safe locations. Accelerate sharply and drop back abruptly from various speeds. Then try accelerating slowly from different road speeds. Finally, try a few miles at a good, constant highway speed.

The odds are strong that your car will perform flawlessly if you've done the tune-up properly. If it doesn't, the engine problems are more than can be cured by a simple tune-up.

Even so, you will have eliminated a host of other malfunctions, many potentially serious. And those are the camouflage that so often confuses even a professional's diagnosis. You're well rid of them.

By PAUL WEISSLER

# Tune-up your four-wheel drive

ALL PLAY and no work can make your 4wd (four-wheel-drive) a dull performer. If you want your 4wd to stay in shape, you've got to get out and get under. Many routine maintenance intervals on a 4wd are much shorter than on a conventional passenger car, and the 4wd requires checks and services the passenger car does not.

Among the important things you can do for your 4wd are cleaning and tightening after off-road excursions.

SEE ALSO
**Gaskets, auto . . . Ignition systems, auto . . .**
**Lubrication, auto . . . Motor oil . . . Noises, auto . . .**
**Power-train noise, auto . . .**
**Steering and suspension, auto . . .**
**Transmissions, auto . . . Winterizing, autos**

**cleaning**

Start by pulling the brake drums and remove any dirt accumulations from brake shoes, backing plates, wheel cylinders and drums. A moderately stiff brush or compressed air is suitable.

Dirt also should be removed from the caliper and shield of a front disc brake. There are openings in the shield through which compressed air can be blown to do the job, so disassembly isn't necessary.

Thorough cleaning of brake parts is important, for dirt, particularly sand, may be very abrasive,

**COMPRESSED AIR** makes it easy to clean the parts of front disc brakes.

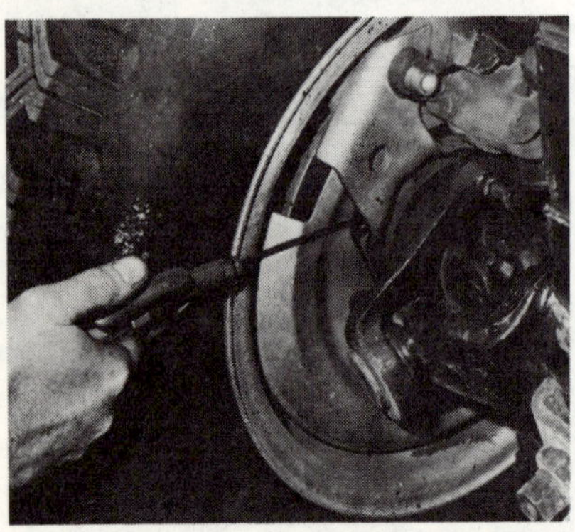

**CLEAR GRASS** that collects between transmission skid and transfer case.

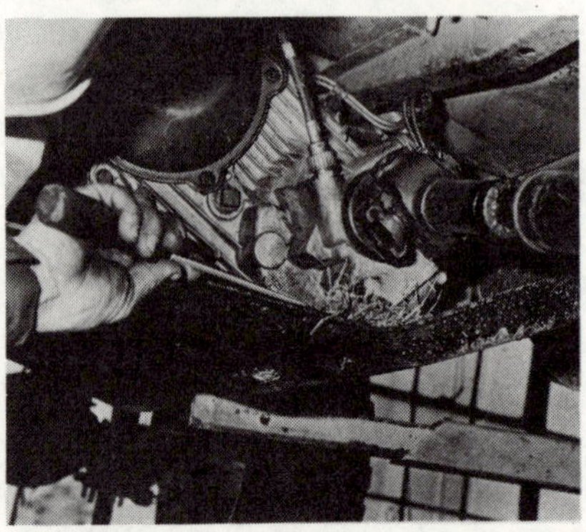

**SPECIAL** grease-gun nozzle is needed for fittings on double-cardan U-joints.

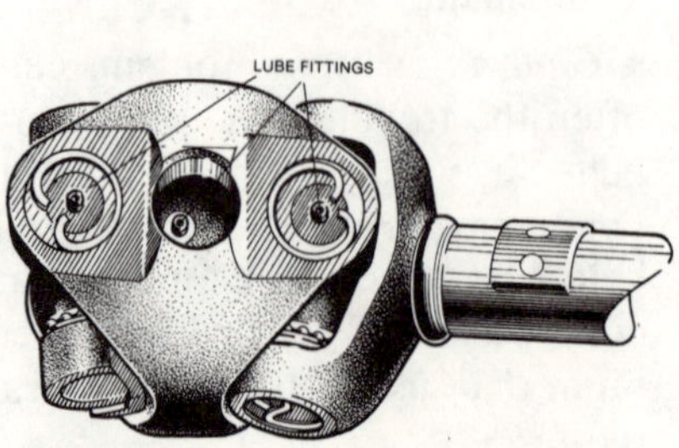

and even small amounts can result in severely gouged drums and linings, and damage to wheel cylinder and caliper dust boots.

**inspect universal joints**

Also inspect the universal joints of the propeller shafts and front axle shafts, and blow out any dirt. If the vehicle has a transmission and/or fuel tank skid plate, dig out any grass or other vegetation that may have accumulated on it, to prevent fire. Dig out stones and pull thorns from the tires. If they are a recurring problem, have a tire dealer inject a sealer into the tires.

Check tightness of the engine oil filter, exhaust system hangers and clamps, shocks, leaf spring brackets, the transmission mount and steering linkage.

**lubrication**

Except for the Subaru, which has packed-for-life joints all around, there may be a lot of work for you and your grease gun. On Jeep, for example, you've got to hit seven or eight fittings on the propeller shafts (number depending on model), three on the steering linkage and another on the steering shaft—and you've got to do it often. On the CJs the recommended intervals are 5000 miles in normal service, 3000 miles or three months in severe service with severe service defined as more than 30 percent of mileage off-road. It's 10,000 miles in normal use, 5000 miles or five months in severe service on other Jeep models.

**special fittings**

On automatic transmission models, three of the fittings are on the front propeller shaft's double-cardan-type rear universal joints, and they pose special requirements: They're the same as the flush fitting on GM full-size cars through 1976, which means you can lube them only with a grease gun equipped with a pencil-type nozzle. This nozzle is available in most auto supply stores and, unless you have small hands, fabulous finger dexterity and a gun with a flex hose, you can't hit more than one of the three fittings with the prop shaft in place on vehicles with a transmission skid plate. Unbolt the shaft from its companion flange at the rear and its U-bolts at the front, remove it from the vehicle and do the job on the bench.

At the same time that you lube, you should check the prop shaft universal joints for wear. Grasp the shaft on each side of the universal joint and try to twist it (one end clockwise, the other counterclockwise). If you feel any real play, the joint must be replaced.

The front axle shaft universal joints are prepacked and have no fittings, but they also must be checked for free play.

**oil changes**

You've probably never changed the differential and transmission oil in your car, but the story on your 4wd may be different.

Ford and Chevy specify semiannual checks of gear-oil level in transmission, front and rear axles and the transfer case, but make no formal drain recommendation. Jeep, however, is very specific on gear oil changes, and its recommendations can be followed by the prudent owner of any 4wd: every 30,000 miles for normal service, a maximum of 30 months for severe service (or 30,000 miles) for front and rear axles, manual transmission and transfer case. On Quadra-Trac, drain the transfer case every 15,000 miles, the transmission itself every 30,000 miles in normal service. If the service is severe, drain case and transmission every 10 months or 10,000 miles, whichever comes first.

**FITTINGS** on double-cardan joints may not be accessible due to skid pan.

**ACCESS** may be easier by removing prop shaft rather than skid pan.

**SLEEVE YOKE** on the front prop shaft of a four-wheel drive needs grease.

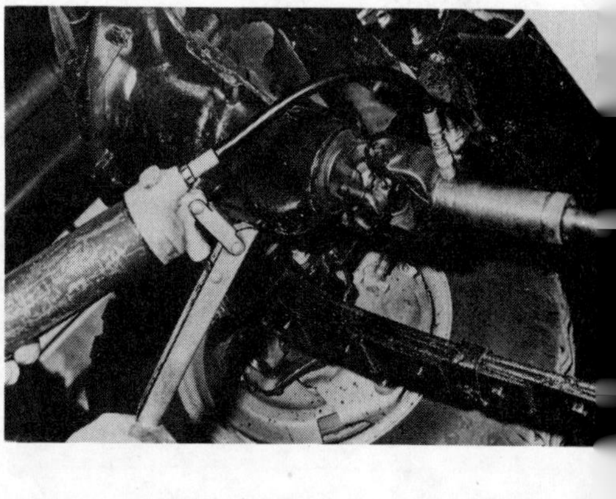

There are drain and refill plugs on transfer case and manual transmission, a drain plug and dipstick tube on automatics. The axle differentials and the Jeep Quadra-Trac reduction unit have only refill plugs (also for checking fluid level).

To properly drain the axle, therefore, pull the cover plate. Discard the old gasket and either install a new one or apply a bead of RTV silicone (make-your-own-gasket paste) to the cover gasket surface. If the axle has no cover plate, siphon old oil out through the filler plug hole.

**remove bolt by Braille**

To change oil on a Quadra-Trac reduction unit, unbolt it from the transfer case. There are five bolts and the top one must be removed strictly by Braille. After the bolts are out, pull the reduction unit out just far enough for the oil to drain, then push it back and refit and tighten the bolts. Full removal and gasket replacement is not advised.

The Quadra-Trac setup does not take ordinary gear oil. Like any limited-slip differential, it requires a special lubricant, available from Jeep dealers. The lube is like that in passenger car limited-slip rear ends, but not interchangeable.

**drop the Jeep pan**

The Jeep automatic is drained and refilled in the conventional way (drop the pan) and takes Dexron II. After you've changed oil on a Quadra-Trac, you must work the transfer case lubricant into the clutches of the limited-slip differential. This is, fortunately, more fun than work. Just take the vehicle to an empty parking lot and do figure 8s for 15 minutes. Hold the steering wheel a half-turn off lock to prevent overheating the power-steering fluid.

In addition to the prescribed oil changes, a Quadra-Trac transfer case may need a drain and refill if it suffers from what shops call "stick-slip," a grunting noise that occurs at low speed, usually when turning a corner or parking.

**wheels and hubs**

Wheels and hubs also require special attention on a 4wd. You must use the same size tires all around and keep them inflated to the same pressures. If one pair of tires is smaller than another pair, it will need more power to travel the same distance. On a part-time 4wd, all wheels always receive the same amount, so the smaller tires would create a force back into the transfer case, resulting in premature wear.

You might think you could get away with variations in the tires on a full-time 4wd system (except obviously when you're in lockup), but you won't. The transfer case differentials would be in the differentiating mode all the time, something for which they're not designed. This is particularly true of the Quadra-Trac, in which clutch wear in the limited-slip differential will rise if there is a variation in tires.

**repack hubs and bearings**

The front hubs and bearings are well-sealed on 4wds, but they still require repacking every 12,-

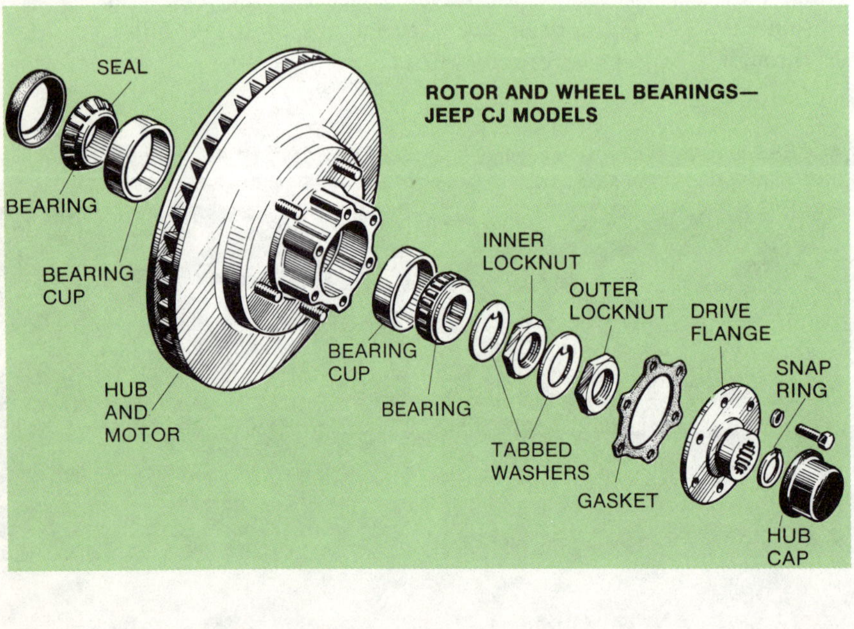


**FRONT HUB** on disc-brake-equipped Jeep CJ shows typical arrangement of parts.

**AXLE-SHAFT** universal joint is quick-checked for free play by wedging a screwdriver against the inboard yoke.

000 miles or one year to 25,000 miles or 25 months (depending on make of 4wd). When you take that run across what seems to be a shallow stream, however, look outside. If the water level gets up to the bearings, you've got to disassemble and repack when you get home. If the water level was up to the wheel bearings, water may also have gotten into the axles, transfer case and transmission (through vents). Remove the fill-plugs, draw out lubricant samples and check for water (or whitish discoloration of the lubricant which would indicate water contamination). If found, drain and refill. Note: Immediately before checking for water contamination, operate the vehicle in 4wd to churn up all lubricants and mix them with any water. If the water is given a chance to settle out and you draw a lubricant sample from lightly contaminated oil, you might not detect the problem.

The typical American 4wd front hub is different from a passenger car setup. The Jeep CJ, for example, has a retaining ring, drive flange, gasket and two locknuts. If you have free-wheeling hubs, there is a clutch in place of the drive flange.

**clean bearings in solvent**

You can't just take off the outer part of the hub and outer bearing. The caliper and disc also must be removed so you can get to the inner wheel bearing as well. Clean the bearings in solvent, allow them to air-dry, then pack them with wheel bearing grease (not chassis grease). Install a new grease seal. After reassembly, tighten the inner locknut to 50 ft.-lb. (30 ft.-lb. on Scout, the one exception) while spinning the wheel forward, to seat the bearings. Think of the wrench handle as a clock hand, and back it off (turn counterclockwise) to specifications (up to three hours on Bronco, four on Jeep and Scout, four and a half on Blazer), so the disc turns freely, but without any in-and-out looseness. Install and tighten the outer locknut, also to 50 ft.-lb. (125 ft.-lb. on Scout) against the tabbed washer and inner locknut. Bend the tabs of the washer against the flats of the outer locknut.

**don't use grease**

If you have free-wheeling hubs, lube them with gear oil, not grease (except Scout, on which Lithium 12 Hydroxy Stearate EP grease should be used). The hub clutch and cap rarely give trouble, but if you have trouble turning the knob, remove the cap, inspect for burrs on the clutch and cap teeth, and if you find any, remove with fine crocus cloth. Then oil the teeth and reassemble the hub.

If your vehicle doesn't have free-wheeling hubs, you can retrofit them yourself to any part-time American 4wd. A kit is available for $50 to $75 and no major disassembly is required. Just take off the dust cap, retaining ring, drive flange and gasket, install the clutch assembly on the axle shaft, refit the retaining ring and bolt on the special cap, which contains a knob-controlled cam and toothed lock. Tab washers are supplied with the kit, and only these should be used under the cap bolts. After tightening down the bolts, bend up the tabs.

**QUADRA-TRAC** reduction units on Jeep four-wheel-drive models require periodic fluid change.

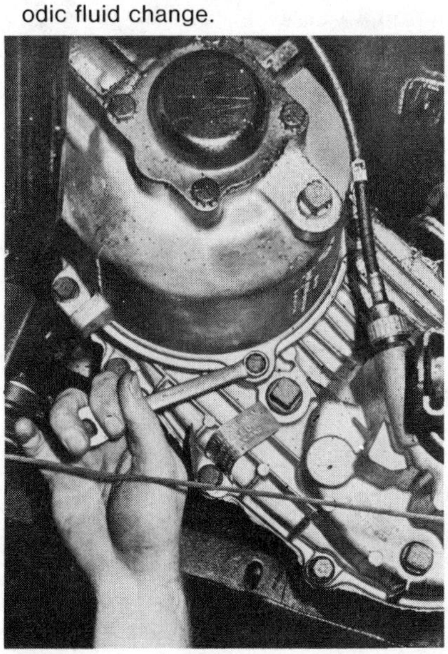

**FOUR-WHEEL-DRIVE** standard front hub and freewheeling-type hub are shown above and at left, respectively. Gear oil is used to lubricate hub as shown at left. Clutch and cap above convert standard hub to freewheeling.

# Tune-up your bicycle

By EUGENE A. SLOANE

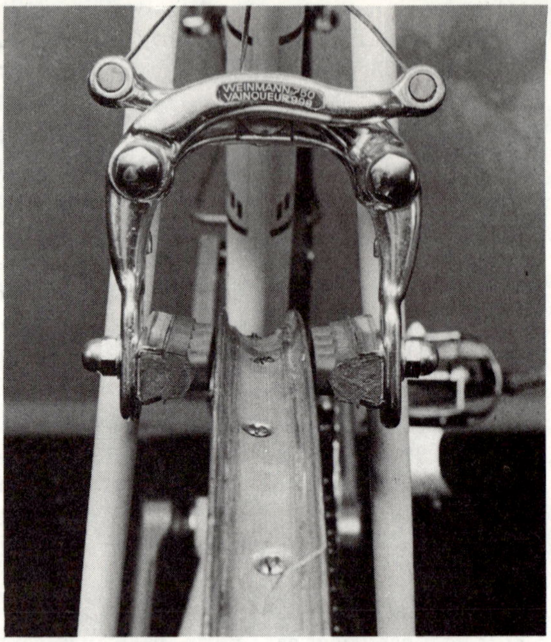
BRAKE SHOES should be 3/16 in. maximum from rim. Front of shoes should be slightly tilted inward.

WHETHER YOU ARE planning an extended bike tour or nothing more than around-town jaunts, check your favorite steed. Here's what to look for:

## brakes

Before you adjust brakes, wheel rims must be true so brake shoes will grab evenly on both sides. Spin wheels, check especially for side-to-side out-of-roundness. True up rims by adjusting spokes, tightening to pull rim to one side, loosening to pull rim to the other side.

If brakes have an adjustment barrel (on levers or brakes) tighten the barrel so the cables are as loose as possible. Gripping brake calipers with a "third hand" tool, loosen cable attachment, pull up all cable slack and retighten cable holder. Brake shoes should be no more than 3/16 inch from rim, with front of shoes tilted inward slightly.

Check brake shoes for particles and wear. Replace worn shoes, making sure closed end of shoe holder points forward. Check frayed or worn cables and replace if necessary. Squirt light oil down brake cables, or coat new cables with light grease before installation.

## tires

Check tires for wear, foreign particles that could cause a flat, cuts and sidewall bruises from ruts and jumping curbs. Replace tires if necessary.

SEE ALSO

Bicycles . . . Minibikes

## chain

If you have a couple thousand miles on the chain, it's time to replace it. Otherwise, remove the chain, dunk it in turpentine or other solvent to remove old grease and road dirt, reinstall and spray with Chainlube from a bike or motorcycle shop. Or clean the chain on the bike, being careful not to get solvent or Chainlube on the tires.

## derailleurs

Push both levers all the way forward. Check for cable slack and remove slack by pulling excess through derailleur cable stops. Run through the gears and make sure the rear derailleur is adjusted so the chain does not overrun high or low gears and will shift to them smoothly. Adjust the front derailleur so the cage just clears the largest chainwheel and is parallel to it; also that the chain does not override either chainwheel.

Eyeball rear derailleur cage to check alignment parallel to rear gears; adjust by bending derailleur body with an adjustable wrench *carefully.* Clean derailleurs with solvent and lube moving points with light motor oil.

## bottom bracket

Grip cranks at pedal location and rock gently back and forth to check for play. Remove chain, spin and check for tightness. Adjust as necessary. If the bottom bracket spindle has not been ser-

**ADJUST** the derailleur limit screws so that the chain does not override the gears.

**FOR SAFETY,** make sure the stem extends several inches inside the head tube.

viced for two years, disassemble, clean and regrease using Lubriplate all-purpose grease; then reassemble. Eyeball chainwheel alignment. If wavy or bent, true up by bending with an adjustable wrench, using cloth to prevent marking aluminum chainwheels. Check chainwheel binder bolts for tightness, using special tools for your make crankset from a bike shop.

**steering head**

Grip handlebars firmly, lock frontwheel brake, rock the bike to check steering head looseness. A loose set of cones means up-and-down pounding as you bike. This can easily flatten bearings, even ruin your headset. Adjust to take out any play. Lift front wheel, move bars to check for tightness; adjust if needed. Be sure the stem has at least 2½ inches inside steering head for safety.

**wheels**

Pull wheels from side to side to check for bearing looseness. Remove wheels and twist spindles between thumb and forefingers to check for tightness. Adjust hub cones as needed. When you spin spindles, feel for roughness indicating sand or grit in wheel bearings. If necessary, disassemble hub, clean bearings and races, repack with Lubriplate grease and reassemble. Check axle when out; roll it on a flat surface or use a straightedge. Replace bent axles.

**pedals**

Twist or move pedals in and out to check for bearing play, spin to check for bearing tightness. Adjust the pedal cone by removing the cap, loosening the locknut and adjusting the cone nut with a screwdriver. If pedals have not been lubricated for two years, disassemble, clean, repack with Lubriplate and reassemble.

**finish**

With matching spray paint, go over all nicks and scratches. Wait five days, then clean and wax the frame. Check it for gouges, dents and alignment of all frame members. Clean and polish all chrome, hubs, rims and spokes.

**saddle**

Check saddle height by measuring the distance from the top of the saddle down to the centerline of the pedal axle. This should equal your inseam measurement (in stocking feet) plus nine percent. Make sure the seat post extends at least two inches into the seat tube for safety. The saddle should have its nose tilted slightly downward for all-day comfort. Take swayback out of a leather saddle by adjusting at the saddle nose fixture.

**carrier**

If you have a carrier over the rear wheel to support bike bags, check for tightness of holding bolts and nuts.

# How to sharpen twist drills

By FRED W. SCHULETER
MASTER MACHINIST, FORMERLY OF STEVENS INSTITUTE OF TECHNOLOGY

**Different materials need different drill points. Here's how to give your drills the right ones**

IT TAKES A PRO just a few deft strokes on a grinding wheel to sharpen a twist drill, but his know-how just didn't happen. He, too, was once told the importance of maintaining equal lips.

This is the cardinal rule to follow when grinding a twist drill, since it's the perfectness of the lips that determines the roundness of the hole.

Upon examining a new drill you will note the angle is rather blunt. This is fine for drilling hard materials like alloy steels, but it doesn't work as well when drilling soft materials like aluminum, brass and plastics. The standard blunt end just doesn't work for all materials. Here is where it's worthwhile to know how to alter the original shape to produce clean, burrless holes in any material.

While lip clearance is not critical, and the angle can be anywhere from 5° to 15°, the degree of angle *must* be the same on each side. If you have normal vision, it's fairly easy to see when the lips are even, but it's still good practice to check them with a drill scale. If you find one side has been ground lower than the other, take a little off the high side.

It takes practice and a certain deftness to do this freehand. First you hold the drill with both hands, as in the photo on the next page, and gently touch the lip of the drill to the flat of the wheel. At the same time you give the drill an upward sweep with a rotating motion as shown in the drawing. Do this several times to each side while holding the drill at a 15 to 30° angle. Dip

**FIVE VARYING DRILL SHAPES,** left to right, are the normal, wingtip, masonry, recessed, and flat. Each is ground to suit the material.

**THE DRAWING** and photo illustrate the proper way to hold and grind a shape best for steel.

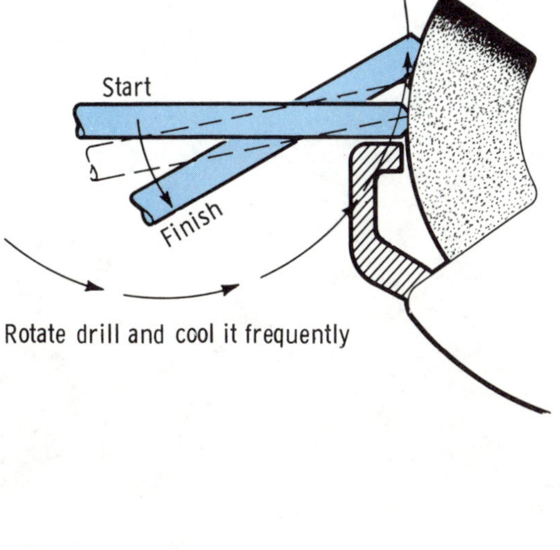


the tip in water or oil occasionally so it doesn't overheat and turn blue. You'll wind up with an extremely sharp cutting edge which will go through the toughest of materials, including stainless steel.

To drill soft materials you need a bit which has the same lip clearance as for steel but a recess ground on the face of the lip. The recess prevents sudden catching of the drill in the work—which often results in breakage—and produces a clean, burrless hole upon breakthrough. To grind the recess, you hold the drill vertically at a 45° angle with the point down as shown in the upper left-hand photo on the next page. Then, with just slight pressure against the edge of the wheel, let the contour of the lip be your guide in a forward motion. As before, it is important to grind both sides so that they will be equally recessed.

A most versatile shape is the wingtip which produces a perfect burrless hole in the thinnest metals. The point acts much like the screw point on an auger bit in locating itself on a centerpunch mark. To grind a wingtip on a bit, place the lip at the right-hand edge of the wheel. Hold it at an opposite 5° angle and follow the same upward motion as used before.

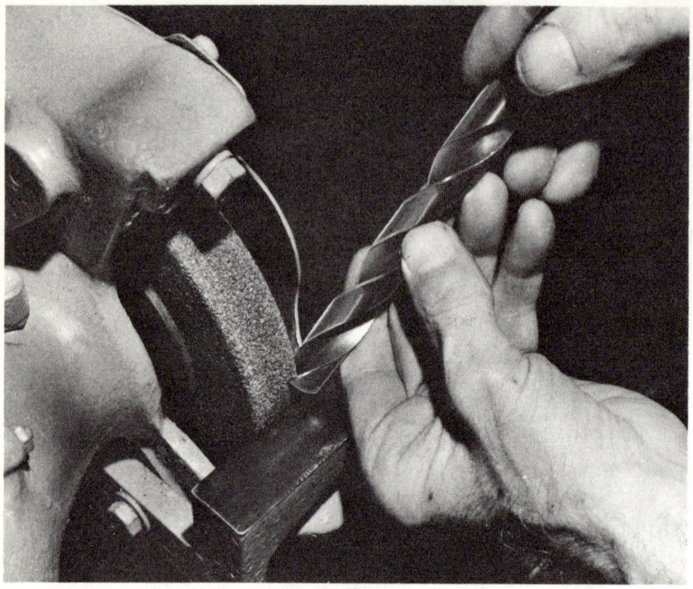

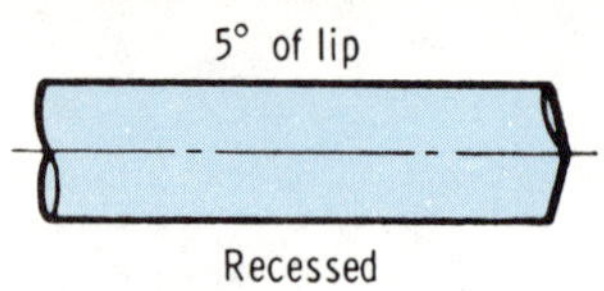


**TO GRIND A RECESSED LIP,** hold a twist drill at the corner of the wheel with the point downward, and at a 45° angle. Touch the wheel lightly and swing the drill up.

Another shape often required is the 60° angle used for drilling masonry, plaster and tile. It's wise to use an old drill on these materials since there's a chance that you may break it, particularly when you're using the bit in a portable electric drill. To grind such a point, you simply hold the drill as before, but at a 60° angle.

By grinding both sides of the drill completely square you can make a bit which will produce a flat-bottom hole. Lip clearance is needed here, but only slightly.

The proper speed is important when drilling and should be determined by the material and the size of the twist drill. A general rule to follow is use a slow speed for hard stock and a fast speed for soft stock. The larger the drill, the slower the speed. The smaller the drill, the higher the speed. In all cases, use normal pressure. Don't force the drill, let it do the work.

When drilling a deep hole, it is good practice to withdraw the drill occasionally to free it of chips. This is particularly important when drilling aluminum and plastic. Also, when you near breakthrough in drilling, ease up on pressure and let the bit slowly sink through. You'll wind up with a neat, clean-cut hole.

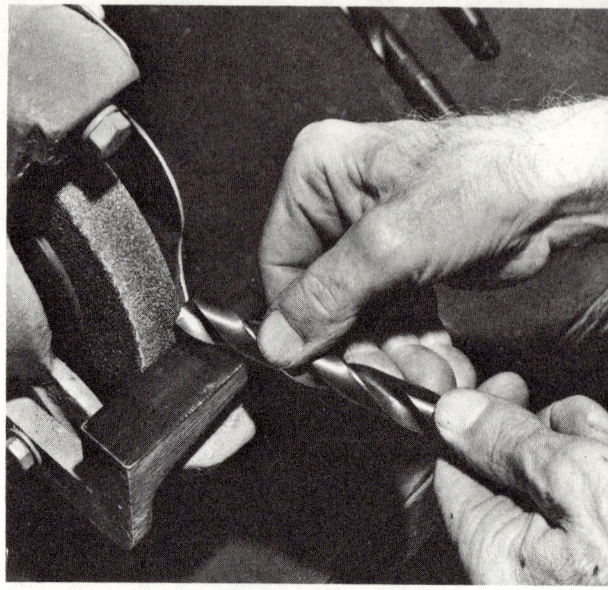

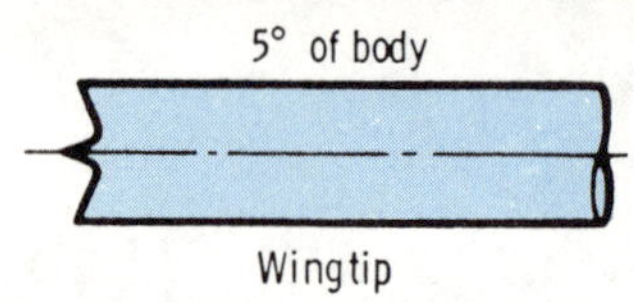


**TO GRIND A WINGTIP,** place the lip against the right-hand corner of the wheel, hold at a 5° angle, and swing drill up. Do it on each side to form a point.

**WHEN GRINDING** a normal or masonry shape, always rotate the twist drill so it won't overheat and turn blue. Dip the end in water occasionally.

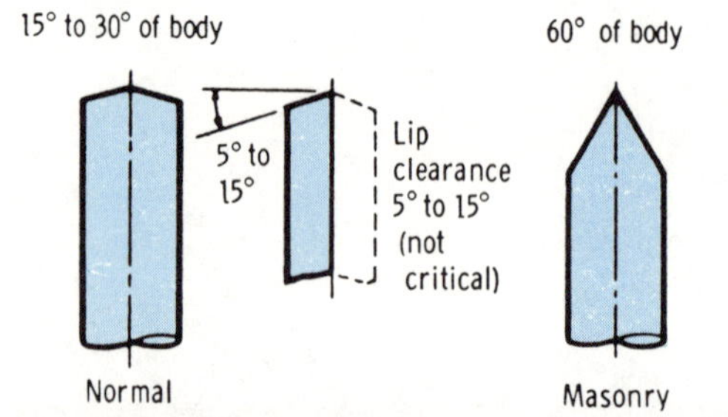


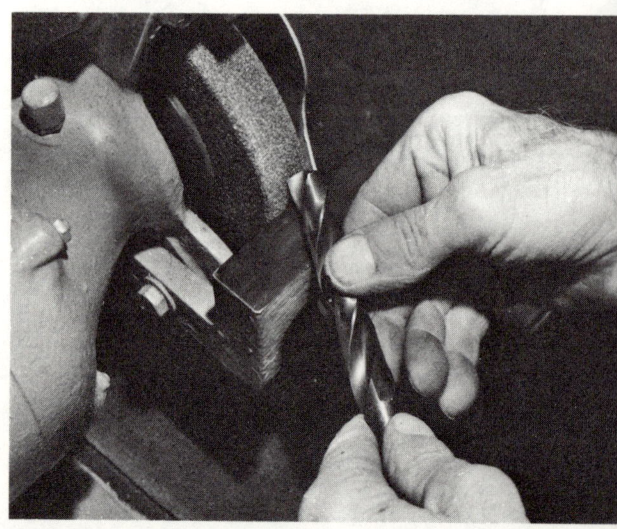

**Kinky handsaw**

*I purchased a handsaw at an auction and, after examining it closely, discovered there is a kink, or sharp bend, about midway along the length of the blade. It's not possible to use it in this condition. I've thought I might heat the blade to straighten it, but am told this won't do. How can I straighten it?—A.N., Tex.*

Don't heat the blade. The heat may "draw" the temper, even warp the blade. I doubt if the saw is worth saving for use, but if the tool appeals to you especially then this may be worth trying. Lay the blade flat on a smooth surface—a length of hardwood is just the thing—with the bend, or kink, up. Then hammer the blade lightly with a soft hammer (not a nail hammer). Tap lightly around the raised portion, working inward to the center. It will take some time and considerable tapping to straighten the kink so that the saw will not bind in the kerf.

**Old alarm clock?**

*I have an old shelf clock and inside the case, at the left of the bell, gong, or whatever—the thing on which it strikes the hours—is what appears to be another striking affair with a key winder and a small bell. A neighbor tells me this is an alarm mechanism. Can he be right about so old a clock? And if so, how does it work?—G.R., La.*

He is right. Alarm clocks are nothing new. There will be an opening in the center of the dial and in this is a disc having the same numerals as those on the dial. Suppose, for example, you want the alarm to let go at 6:00 a.m. Any time after 6:00 p.m. turn this small dial until the numeral "6" or "VI" is directly under the hour hand. Then wind the alarm mechanism until the spring is fairly tight. If the mechanism is in working order and properly connected to the setting dial just back of the hands, the alarm will ring at 6:00 a.m. the following morning.

**Locating furring strips**

*I need to locate furring strips under soft-board paneling. But how? Tapping with a hammer doesn't indicate any change of sound, as it does on other types of walls.—Gene Tomey, Topeka, Kans.*

Use an ordinary pin. It can be pressed through the softboard without leaving a large, unsightly hole. Once you have located one or two strips the others should be easily found by measurement, assuming they are on 16 or 24-in. centers. If necessary, the pinholes can be filled with a spackling compound to match.

**Sticky wallpaper**

*I moved recently and want to remove the paper on the upper part of the bathroom walls. I can't get it off with any amount of soaking with a sponge. I want to paint the walls, but how do I get the old paper off without damaging the plaster?—O.T., Md.*

You refer to the present covering as "paper," so I assume that's what it is, and not some other covering. Many of the newer wallpapers have a plastic coating that is so very nearly waterproof it is difficult to remove by sponging. One way to break the plastic coating sufficiently to permit water to penetrate it and soften the paste is to tack a strip of coarse sandpaper to a 2x4 block about 6 in. long and then go over the surface lightly, overlapping the strokes a trifle. Don't bear down unduly or you may cut through the wallpaper and scratch the plaster. Once over should do it.

For somewhat faster removal, you can rent a steamer from your local wallcovering or paint dealer. Lift a corner of each sheet of the old paper so that you can direct the steam jet to the underside. Once you get the feel of this procedure, you can unhang the old paper fast with comparatively little effort.

Wash the walls to remove all traces of old paste before applying paint or enamel.

**Low heat**

*I live in a recently acquired, older home, equipped with hot-water heating. Originally coal-fired, the boiler is now fitted with an oil burner and room thermostat controls, but I don't keep warm in cold weather. I'd like to do something about it before another winter. But what?—A.E., N.D.*

The answers to two questions may provide a solution or at least point the way. Is your heating system controlled by one or more than one room thermostat and where are they located? And are you reasonably sure the system is of adequate capacity to provide comfortable room temperatures in your locality?

Assuming that your system has adequate capacity, and also that the pipe lines and radiators are in good condition, the remedy could prove to be the relocation of the thermostat, or 'stats. Often, and especially in older converted installations, thermostatic controls are placed where there is inadequate air circulation or they may be affected by a nearby radiator. This possibility should be checked by someone who is acquainted with your particular heating system.

*by W. Clyde Lammey*

# The fascinating world of underwater photography

By DICK JACOBY

**A fast-growing sport almost as popular as skin and scuba diving, marine photography is easier than ever with scads of new equipment**

SEE ALSO
**Boat photography . . . Camera care . . . Outdoor photography . . . Photo hints . . . Photography . . . Skin diving . . . Sports, water**

I HELD THE CAMERA against my mask, staring at a million silver anchovies that schooled in front of the viewfinder. The sight was amazing, but even more amazing was that I could photograph it.

Back on the boat, off Andros Island in the Bahamas, I carefully unsnapped the latches that held my camera in its plastic housing. The camera was dry, protected from the seawater by a tough Lexan housing sealed with O-rings. A week later my pictures were processed, and they, too, came out well. The ocean's irridescent blue actually helped my picture taking because it contrasted with the silver of the anchovies.

Underwater photography is popular because it's challenging, and because the results sometimes are fantastic.

Only skin and scuba divers know the incredible range of brilliant colors in the creatures that dwell in the coral reefs—and in the reefs themselves. And only a photograph can bring a record of this fantastic world to the surface.

To take photographs underwater it isn't necessary to be 1) a professional photographer, 2) a super swimmer, 3) a super scuba diver, or 4) rich.

The key to shooting good pictures underwater is to get as close to your subject as you can. Five feet usually is considered the outside limit, because at greater distances sea water dulls your pictures. In fact, water is 800 times denser than air and contains tiny bits of matter that scatter light. Even in the Caribbean, trying to photograph something 20 feet away is a little like putting the bottom of a coke bottle in front of your lens.

Getting close to fish underwater isn't difficult, though, because, like most living creatures, they are curious. Move up on them very slowly, pulling yourself along the bottom with your fingers. Should you suddenly descend from above they are sure to swim away, just as you would run if a giant bird flew toward you out of the sky.

Once you reach the place where you saw them, the fish probably will have moved a few feet further away. Don't worry, though; they'll return to within that five-foot shooting distance once they feel that you are safe. You may have to wait a few minutes, but the results will be worth it.

The time to snap a fish's picture is the moment it swims towards the center of the viewfinder. At the same time, the fish should be located just above the coral so that blue water backgrounds him. The resulting portrait will show the fish in clear water, accented by a bit of landscape beneath. You've got to stay low to shoot pictures like this, but the results are really worth it.

"People pictures" are even easier, because your subjects understand what you want to do. Be sure to discuss your plan with them before entering the water, though, so that they don't look at the camera when you shoot. Dress your subject (model) in a simple oval mask—any color but black—and check for flying straps that make divers look like uncoordinated octopuses.

**OCEAN WATER** acts as a giant filter that strains out every color except its own, usually blue-green. The brilliant color bull's-eye at left is shown above at a depth of 60 feet in the available light. Only blues and greens retain their hues.

At the close shooting distances required underwater, plan to photograph just your model's head and upper body. Indeed, there is no prettier picture than a bikini-clad model wearing no scuba equipment at all; snap it just at the moment she dives toward the camera.

In most South Atlantic and Caribbean waters, plenty of sunshine is available to light your pictures just below the surface. And if you're new to underwater photography, it's probably a good idea to wait awhile before getting involved with flash attachments. Because water filters out warm colors such as red and orange first, confine your shots to within the first 10 or 15 feet of depth. Exposure is best there, too.

Use negative film with the resonably priced pocket or Instamatic type cameras. Kodacolor 400 works fine because it responds satisfactorily to low light levels underwater. When used at shallow depth, the film also tends to make people and fish appear slightly redder in the blue water.

With 35-mm and larger format cameras, it's OK to use slide film, such as Eastman Kodachrome or Ektachrome. The more sensitive (faster) films (Ektachrome 200 and Ektachrome 400, for example) are the easiest to use. When you shoot with slide film you must adjust the controls on your camera when exposure conditions change. Example: shooting that bikini-clad girl on a sunny day just below the surface, try Ektachrome 200 film with exposure set at f/8 to f/11 at 1/125 of a second. Increase your exposure to f/5.6 to f/8 when you descend to fifteen feet.

Screw a red filter in front of your lens to make the skin tones of your model appear more natural. A CC30R filter works great, but make sure you stay close to the surface where the water hasn't filtered out too much red and orange. You'll need to change your settings a little, too: use the same f-stops, and set your shutter speed to 1/60 second for the model swimming toward your camera.

Scuba gear lets you turn the underwater world into a photographer's studio. Adjust your buoyancy so that you are a little bit negative on the bottom, but take care not to stir up the silt. Then enjoy the passing parade of fish until you get the pictures you want.

But scuba equipment isn't absolutely necessary for underwater photography if you have a mask, snorkle and fins—and the ability to hold your breath for several seconds. Sink five or ten

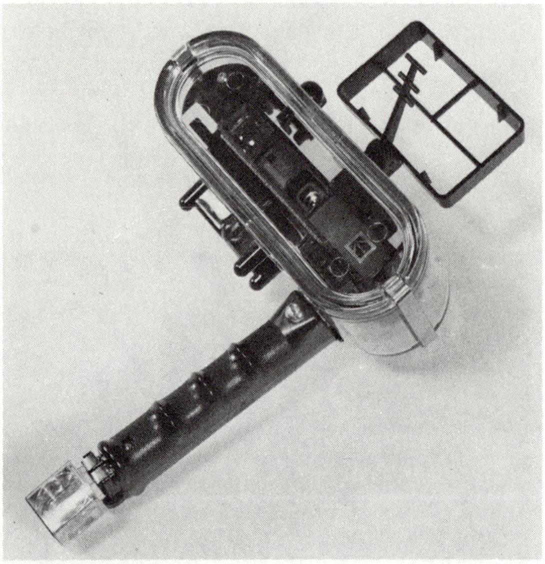

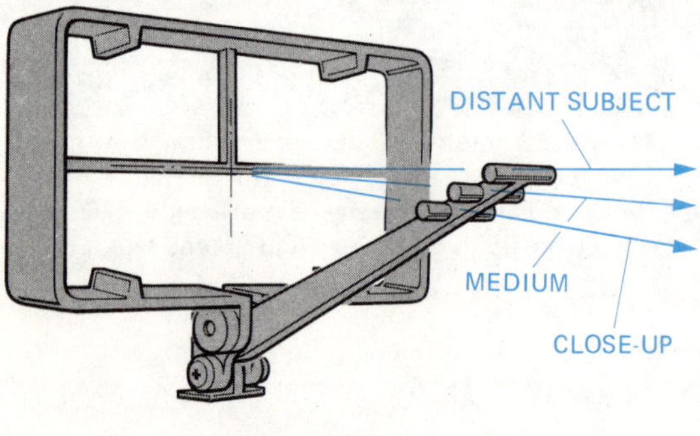


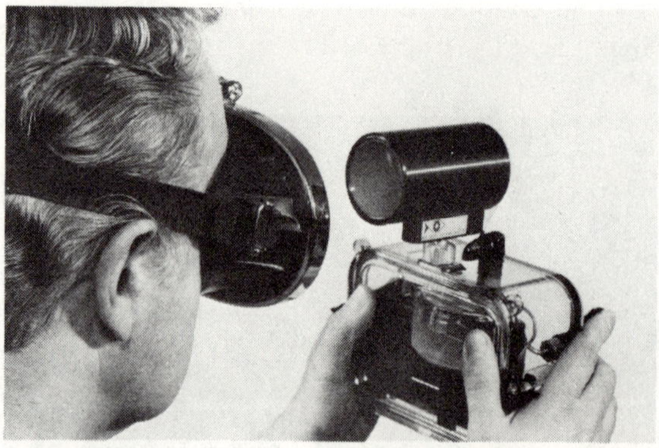

**HOUSING** for 110-series pocket cameras can be used with or without flash. Ikelite, at left, puts its flash on the bottom of the handle. Pointing a camera is difficult under water, and external sportsfinders help considerably. You operate the open sportsfinder at left by aligning the crossbar with various "rungs" on the ladder sight, depending upon the distance to the subject. "Optical" sportsfinders, such as the one above by Seacor, frame the picture area with a series of removable masks; the mask used depends upon the lens.

feet below the surface, grab your picture, and ascend.

Most amateur underwater photographers start with an inexpensive camera that fits into a pressure-proof housing at relatively little expense. The 110 camera series manufactured by Kodak, Canon and Minolta slip easily into molded Lexan housings from Ikelite Underwater Systems. Price: under $50 for the housing.

Ikelite also builds housings priced between $40 and $70 to fit 126 series Instamatic cameras. Indeed, whatever camera you own, there's probably a housing to fit. There's even one for Polaroid's instant SX-70 camera.

Many pocket and Instamatic cameras don't focus closer than three or four feet. The least expensive camera, Kodak's Trimlite 18, doesn't focus closer than five feet, so the camera's inside

**FOR SLR SHOOTERS,** highly sophisticated housings are available. The two shown top center are Ikelite's Lexan housing and Farallon/Oceanic's aluminum model. Ikelite's adapts to several makes of camera, and Farallon/Oceanic's is compatible with top-of-the-line models by Nikon and Canon. Bottom right, Sea Research & Development custom-builds housings to fit user's needs. Lower right, Ikelite even builds a housing for Polaroid's SX-70. As this was written, the cost was about $100.

focusing limit corresponds to the outside limit for underwater pictures. However, the camera still makes underwater photography for an investment of less than $75 for camera and housing combined. (All prices in this article, of course, are subject to change.)

As your experience grows you'll want to move up to more expensive equipment. Several housings are on the market for 35-mm and larger cameras, ranging from clear plastic housings under $200 to aluminum ones for $600 and up. Nikon and Canon systems used with either Ikelite or Farallon/Oceanic housings allow exact through-the-lens viewing so you can see exactly what your picture will look like.

Most viewfinders, though, are separate attachments perched on top of the housing. Viewing through them is a simple matter, but you don't see exactly what you get on film, particularly at distances less than three feet.

There's one special camera on the market that is used with a viewfinder but requires no housing. The Nikonos looks like a regular 35-mm camera with controls for focus, shutter speed and aperture, and it's a tough, all-weather camera topside. The big difference is that it's waterproof, pressure-tested to a depth of 165 feet (50 meters).

Like its topside cousins, the Nikonos accepts different lenses for different purposes, making it extremely versatile. Because of its popularity, specialty manufacturers market all sorts of accessories—trays, handles, meters, brackets, trigger releases, optical wideners, closeup equipment, and flash connectors. Price of the Nikonos III (the third model in the Nikonos series) and 35 mm lens is in the $400 range. Accessories can up your total outlay several hundred dollars more.

Flash cubes work well with pocket and Instamatic cameras, but sooner or later you're going to want electronic flash. Here the price runs from slightly over $100 to ten times that much.

It's great to bring electronic sunshine beneath the surface because it puts all those warm colors back in your subject. However, you don't need flash if you do your picture taking just inside your water wonderland, still near the sun.

Whether you borrow, rent or buy your first underwater photo equipment, be sure to read the instructions carefully. The most common error made is not reading and following instructions.

For catalogs, prices and additional information on underwater photo equipment, write the following manufacturers: Aquacraft, 3280 Kurtz St., San Diego, CA 92110; Dacor Corp., 161 Northfield Rd., Northfield, IL 60093; Farallon/Oceanic, 1333 Old County Rd., Belmont, CA 94002; Glenn Beall Industries, 887 South Route 21, Gurney, IL 60031; Green Things, 5111 Santa Fe, Suite K, San Diego, CA 92109; Hydrophoto,

3909 13th Ave., Seattle, WA 98108; Ikelite Underwater Systems, 3303 North Illinois St., Indianapolis, IN 46208; Ehrenreich Photo-Optical Industries, Inc., 623 Stewart Ave., Garden City, NY 11530; Sekonic, Copal Corporation of America, 5825 Queens Blvd., Woodside, NY 11377; Seacor, Inc., 10575A Roselle St., San Diego, CA 92121; Sea Research & Development, Inc., P.O. Box 589, Bartow, FL 33803; SubSea Products, Inc., 210 Brant Rd., Lake Park, FL; Sunpack, Div., Berkey Marketing, 25-20 Brooklyn Queens Expy. West, Woodside, NY 11377; Toshiba Photo Products Co., Ltd., Elmo Mfg. Corp., 32-10 57th St., Woodside, NY 11377.

Check your local dive shop if you are interested in renting before you buy. One underwater photography rental store that ships anywhere in the U.S. is Helix, Ltd., 325 W. Huron, Chicago, IL 60610. Write for their rental catalog.

**SLEW OF ACCESSORIES** is available for Nikonos. Those at left include light meter, meter mount, handle assembly and trigger, viewfinder, strobe arm and strobe. You can also put topside strobes in pressure housings as shown at right. Don't be confused. The units are posed upside-down on table because they all have cords coming from base.

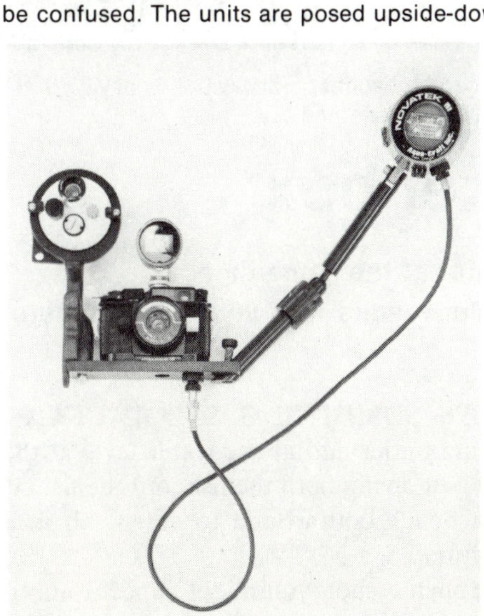

**MERMAIDS, MOTORS,** any kind of marine action just under the surface can be caught on film with this device that provides a sea-level-line outlook for a single-lens reflex camera while housing it safe and dry.

# Build a split-screen snorkel box

**With this secret weapon you can shoot photos over and under water at the same time, the way the professionals do. You can get spectacular results with your own camera**

**By NEIL SANDER**


SEE ALSO

**Boat photography . . . Camera care . . . Cameras . . . Outdoor photography . . . Photography . . . Skin diving . . . Sports, water . . . Used cameras**


THERE'S SOMETHING SPECTACULAR about seeing under and above water level at the same time—showing both the fish and the fisherman, or a boat's bottom and topsides—all in a single picture.

To take such a shot, you might expect to need simply an underwater camera or conventional

**GETTING SET** for the shot at left, photographer Sander focuses on both models above and below the surface. He squats in the water to balance rig and steady himself, then finally shoots (right).

**OVER/ UNDER WATERBOX**

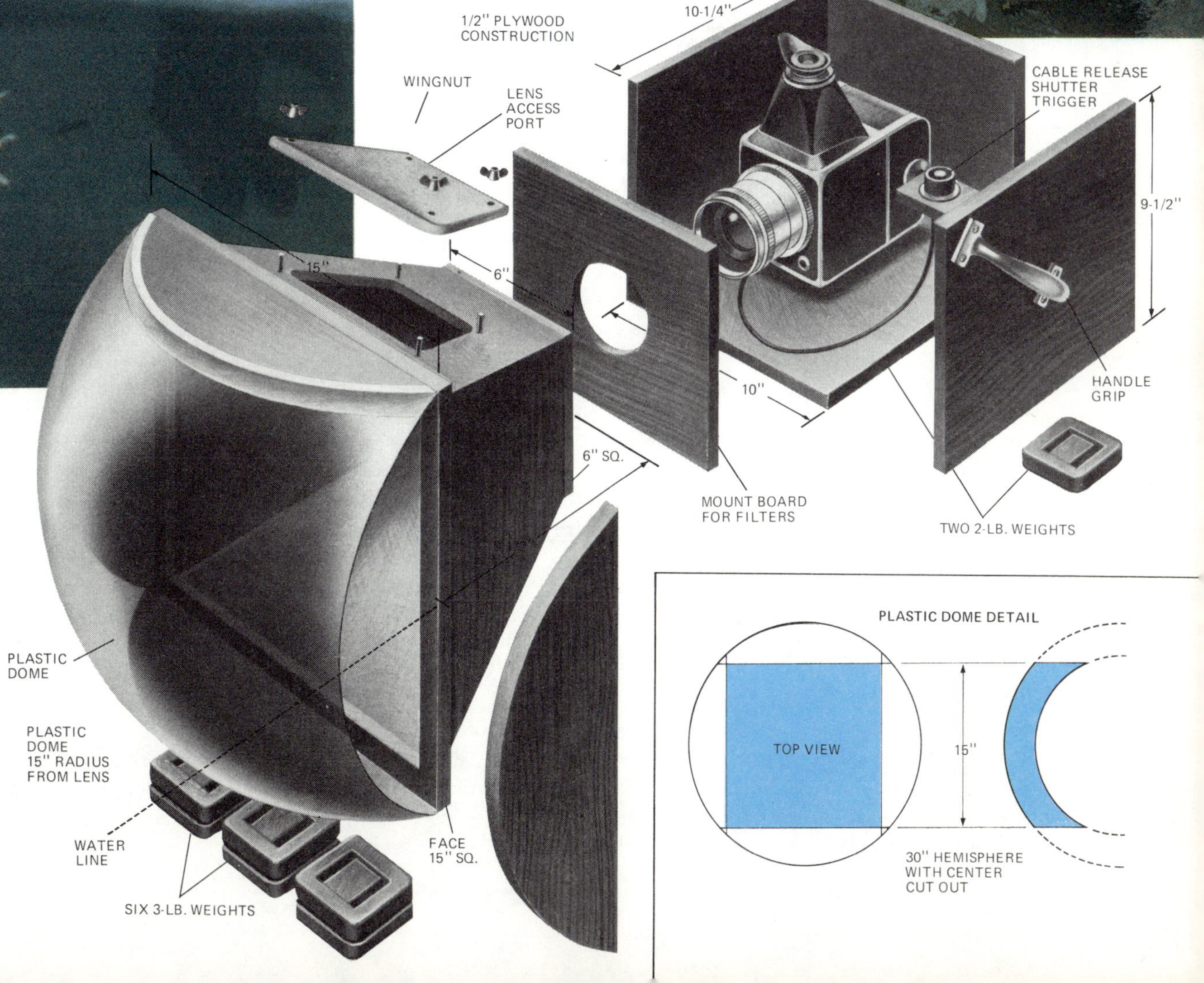

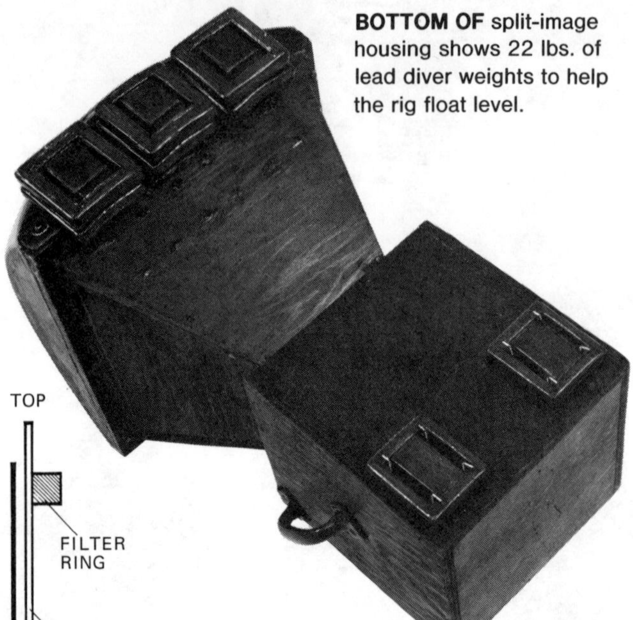

**BOTTOM OF** split-image housing shows 22 lbs. of lead diver weights to help the rig float level.

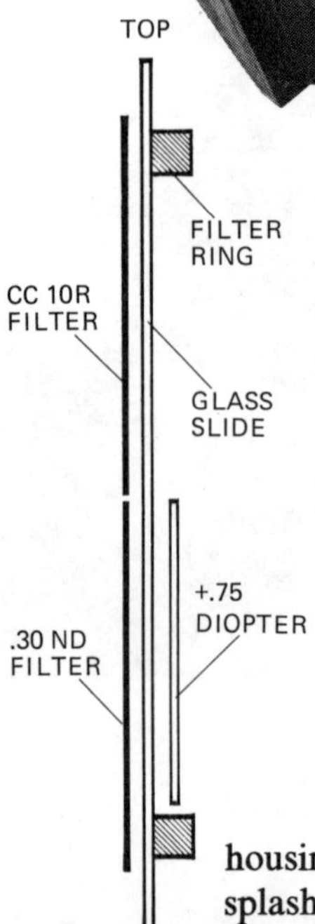


**FILTER RING,** at left, holds a +.75 diopter lens in lower half to make underwater images the same size as above-surface subjects. Taped to glass slide cemented to ring are a gelatin CC 10R over lower half for color correction underwater, a .30 ND filter at top over upper half.

housing for one, but neither is enough. Water splashing against a cover plate immediately next to the lens will be out of focus and confuse the picture. Instead, you need a special enclosure that can give you a distinct waterline. Fortunately, you can build one yourself.

As photographer for Mercury Marine's saltwater test center on the Florida Gulf Coast, I have to record extensive engineering experiments, as well as how our engines and equipment work with a great variety of boats. Sometimes underway reports should show over and underwater performance in the same photo. Since I couldn't find a manufactured over/under housing for my needs, I made my own.

If you build one, dimensions will be different (and smaller) than those shown here if you have a 35-mm, single-lens reflex camera. I wanted to use a 2¼x2¼-inch model for its larger picture size and viewing hood. If your 35-mm SLR does not have an interchangeable hood for right-angle focusing, you can get a right-angle viewing accessory. Spiratone, 135-06 Northern Blvd., Flushing, NY 11354, is one mail-order source.

With my camera; I use a motor drive for convenience and a medium wide-angle 50-mm lens (a 35-mm focal length lens on a 35-mm camera gives about the same field of view). The wide angle allows working closer to the subject for an improved underwater image and less chance of diffusion from the water. Pick the clearest, calmest water you can find for a sharp picture with a distinct division waterline.

For the transparent faceplate, I chose a 30-inch-diameter plastic dome that gives me a 15-inch radius of view from the lens. A 35-mm camera can use a smaller dome and shorter radius. Recreational vehicle and van accessory stores are one source for these hemispheric bubble windows. Four cuts square the dome, as shown in the diagram, by removing 7½ inches from each side to fit a 15-inch-square aperture.

**building the camera housing**

The camera housing, constructed of ½-inch marine plywood, is a box approximately 10 inches square and 9½ inches deep. The front has a circular hole, through which the lens extends into a 9½-inch housing that expands out from a 6-inch square to the 15-incher that mounts the plastic dome. In the top of this lens housing, an access port cover is secured with wingnuts and can be removed to fit and adjust a filter holder on the lens, focus or make diaphragm adjustments. All plywood joints are waterproof-sealed with marine silicone sealant during assembly. All surfaces, inside and out, are painted flat black to reduce reflections.

The result is a very buoyant box and you'll need to add weight to make it easier to hold semisubmerged in the water. For my size housing, I found that six 3-pound lead skindivers' belt-weights under the dome and two 2-pounders at the back of the camera box balanced out the rig, after being attached to the bottom. Hand grips are mounted on each side of the box and a cable-release is positioned near one thumb.

Since water reduces light transmission, changes focus and shifts color balance, I worked out a compensating filter packet. A +.75 diopter lens was cut in half by an eyeglass repair shop and mounted in the lower half of a filter ring. It gives underwater objects the same relative size and focus as above-water subjects. Over it, a Kodak CC 10R color-correcting filter improves color balance, while the top half is a Kodak Wratten .30 ND neutral density gelatin. This arrangement cuts overall light level a full stop, for which either you or your camera must compensate.

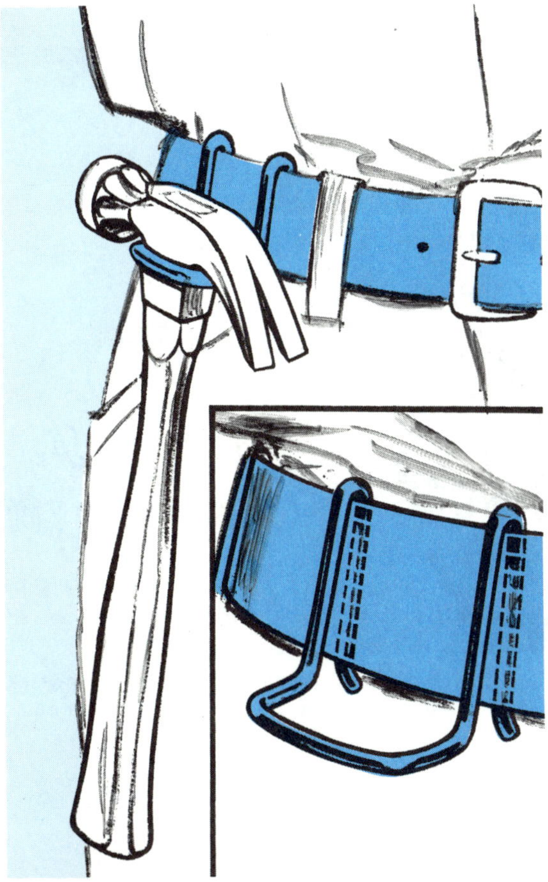

**THIS HAMMER HOLSTER** slips over your belt and holds your hammer when you need your hands free for something else. Make it by bending a length of heavy coat-hanger wire. Round off ends with a file.

**IF YOU'RE A NOVICE** with an ax, one of the safest methods of splitting wood is to prop the log upright inside a couple of old tires. If you should miss the log, the tires will absorb the shock without moving.

**TO PLANT FINE SEEDS** easily and efficiently, use an eye dropper as a seed dispenser. It allows for much better seed spacing than sowing by hand. For smaller seeds plug part of the opening with a toothpick.

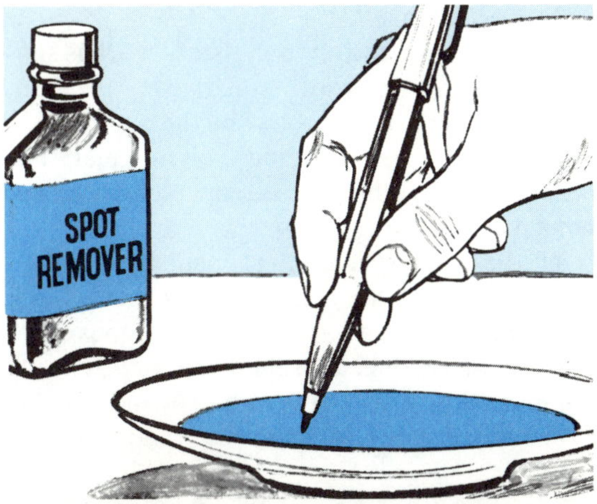


**TO SOFTEN THE TIP** of a felt-tipped marking pen which has hardened after being left uncapped, place a few drops of spot remover in a dish and work the tip around in it. When its soft, wipe the tip.

**Upholstery worn? Springs sagging? Stuffing sticking out? Then reupholstery is for you. Not only can you restore a fine look to your chairs and sofas, but you save a bundle of money**

By LEN HILTS

**THE FIRST STEP** in any reupholstery job is to take off the old fabric. Here a tack lifter and hammer are used to remove the tacks holding the dust cover on a sofa. Using the hammer with the lifter speeds the work.

# A basic course in upholstery

YOU CAN SAVE $200 or more by reupholstering your own sofa. And you can save up to $100 by reupholstering an old chair. Substantial savings like this are good reasons why you should find out how to do your own upholstery work. It is one kind of do-it-yourself activity that truly pays for itself.

To begin with, most reupholstery work is simple and straightforward, so it is easy to learn. You don't need many tools, and the ones you do need are not expensive. And tools and materials are readily available all over the country in upholstery and fabric shops.

The best way to learn to reupholster is to find an old chair or two and practice on them. Look for chairs that are simple in design—ones without special pleating, unusual shapes or obviously complicated covering jobs. Later, you'll be able to do work like this, but for now, practice on jobs that aren't complex. Buy some inexpensive cover fabric and rework these chairs from the frame out. By the time you have finished them, you'll have gained both experience and confidence. Then you'll be ready to work with fabrics which cost $20 a yard and more, and be able to do a creditable job on your good furniture. You'll work your way out of your mistakes—and you'll end up with a couple of useful chairs.

The tools needed are few and inexpensive. You can buy a kit for around $10 at most fabric and upholstery stores. It contains a magnetic tack hammer, a tack lifter, a webbing stretcher and several large sewing needles. Add to this a couple of screwdrivers and a pair of pliers and you have everything you need.

Recently, a lot of upholstery work has been done with staples instead of tacks. Staples offend the traditionalists, who feel that they cheapen the work, but I have found that staples are effective in 90 percent of the work—and in some cases are better than tacks. For example, staples are less likely to split the wood, especially when you drive them near the edge of a seat rail.

SEE ALSO
**Armchairs . . . Caning . . . Chairs . . . Sofa-beds**

The trick in using staples is to use staples that are long enough. Also, use a gun which has enough power to drive the staples completely into the wood. The ideal tool, when you use staples, is an electric staple gun. These are available for about $30 and are a good investment if you intend to do much upholstery work. Buy a gun which can drive staples of different lengths (most will) because you need to be able to choose the size of the staple. When putting on a cambric dust cover, for example, you need a very short staple. But when you must tack through several layers of fabric, you need a staple with legs ½ in. long or more.

You also can staple with a hand gun. The gun should be able to drive staples of different lengths, too, and should be powerful enough to drive them all the way into the wood. Most furniture frames are made of hardwood, which resists staples, and a gun which isn't powerful enough will not drive long staples all the way.

The electric gun is particularly good when you upholster a couch, where you must drive hundreds of staples. With a hand gun, your hand will be aching by the time you finish. With an electric gun, you can do the work quickly and without fatigue.

Upholstering materials—tools, fabric, and padding are easy to find. Most professional upholstery shops will sell you what you need, and fabric shops today carry a full line of upholstery goods.

**CORNERS ON UPHOLSTERY** work should be firm and square. As you apply the final fabric, use wads of cotton or polyester to shape them.

In many cases, you'll find you can reuse the padding from the piece you are redoing. You can also reuse the springs. You'll need new webbing, perhaps some new padding and, of course, new fabric for the final cover.

**TO FIT THE FABRIC** around leg and arm posts, you must make cuts. Here the fabric is cut to fit around the back posts of a sofa.

**A LONG, SMOOTH STICK** serves as a stuffer to help push the fabric through the slot between the sofa back and seat. Fabric is tacked at the back.

**A TACKING STRIP** with the tacks already embedded in it is handy for making closures. You can buy these strips by the foot at fabric stores.

**ELECTRIC STAPLE DRIVER** is a very handy tool for upholstery work. Look for one which will drive staples of different lengths.

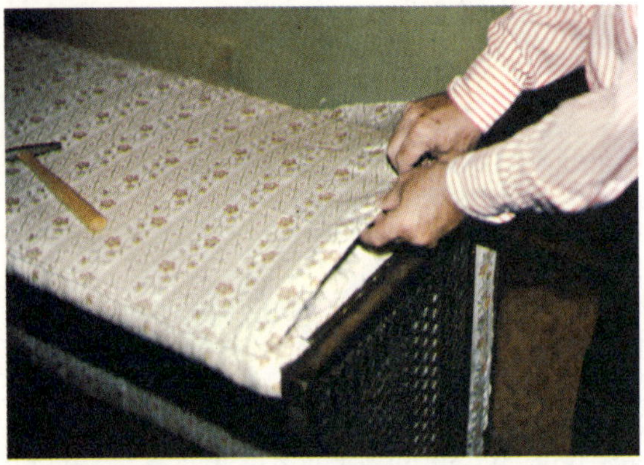

**THE TACKING STRIP** is placed in the folded end of the material, with the tacks pointing down toward the frame. Push the tacks through the material.

**USING PLIERS** to pull the fabric tight, you then drive the tacks into the frame. The tacks are invisible and the result is a neat blind tacking job.

Keep in mind that your first chair is your best textbook in upholstering. Strip the old upholstery from it slowly and with care. Study the chair as you work, noting how the fabric was applied, how the corners were made, where the upholsterer used a needle and thread and where he used tacks. Don't just rip the old cover off, even if it is badly worn, but remove it carefully, a piece at a time. Save each piece of fabric and padding, because these can serve as patterns when you cut and shape the new materials.

Pay special attention to the way the fabric is folded, pleated or tucked at the corners, since corners usually prove to be the biggest mystery for the beginner. If necessary, make notes and sketches in a book for later reference. Watch to see how the material was cut to fit around posts, keeping in mind that when you apply the new cover, you'll want to cut the fabric the same way.

One final equipment note: It is very helpful to have a sewing machine available when you upholster. Almost every upholstering job requires welting or cording, which you must make from the fabric you intend to use as a final cover. Hand sewing of welting can be a long and tedious job. You'll also want a sewing machine for joining pieces of the cover and for sewing stretch tabs of old fabric to your new cover material. This latter gimmick cuts down on the amount of expensive fabric you need, since in using it, you use an old fabric as a pull tab and use the good fabric only in the places where it shows.

Here is some information on the upholstery materials you will need:

***Tacks.*** Upholstery tacks are the standard tacks with which you already are familiar. They come in sizes identified by numbers. No. 1 (1 oz.) tacks are small, used to tack the dust cover on the bottom of furniture. Nos. 3 and 4 are all-purpose tacks, used for tacking on muslin covers, final fabric, and burlap. Most of your work is done with these sizes. No. 6 tacks are larger, used for tacking through folded material and very heavy materials. Nos. 12 and 14 tacks are jumbo-size, for tacking down jute webbing, anchoring seat twine, etc. If you intend to use tacks in your work, buy boxes of these sizes, with emphasis on Nos. 3 and 4.

***Webbing.*** Furniture webbing is made of jute and is used to support the coil springs. It usually is available in a 3½-in. width. You'll use 10 to 12 yds. on a typical chair, and 30 yards or so to do a sofa.

Rubber webbing is used in some chairs (Danish types, for example), but since it deteriorates rapidly, you should think about replacing it with jute webbing. Your final decision may be influenced by the design of the furniture. Chairs with rubber webbing frequently are designed without springs, and depend on the spring of the rubber for comfort.

***Springs.*** There are two basic types of springs used in furniture, the coil and the zig-zag. Unless the springs in your furniture have somehow been broken, there is no need to replace them. Coil springs need to be retied, and zig-zags may need to be reanchored in the chair frame. If you should have to replace a spring, take the broken spring to an upholstery shop. The proprietor can give a replacement of the correct size and tension.

When zig-zag springs come loose from the frame, they must be repositioned by stretching them across the seat opening and renailing them to the frame.

***Thread and twine.*** Use a heavy flax or linen thread for all upholstery work. The thread called *carpet thread* is fine for this work. Use it in conjunction with large sailor's needles, both straight and curved. Twine is used for tying the springs, and the best twine, which has the necessary strength and is slow to deteriorate, is 6-ply hemp, which can be purchased in large balls. Ordinary cotton twine and most packaging twines either break too easily or deteriorate too quickly.

***Burlap.*** Burlap is used to cover the springs after they have been tied, and to cover layers of padding. As a rule, the 12-oz. material is best for most upholstery work.

***Stuffing.*** Three basic types of stuffing or padding are used in upholstery work: fiber, felt and foam.

The fiber stuffings included curled animal hair (the finest); Spanish moss (next best); and excelsior (poorest and cheapest). Usually you can buy sheets of rubberized hair at fabric shops, and may find that this is best to use.

Felt stuffings include cotton, kapok and those consisting of polyester fibers, all of which come

**THE FIRST STEP** in installing new webbing is to lay the webbing on the bottom of the frame and anchor it with four tacks.

**NEXT, FOLD** the end of the webbing back across the first tacks and drive three more. Magnetic tack hammer makes driving tacks easy.

**USING A** webbing stretcher, pull the webbing tight across the frame. As you hold it, drive four tacks, then cut webbing 1½ in. from frame.

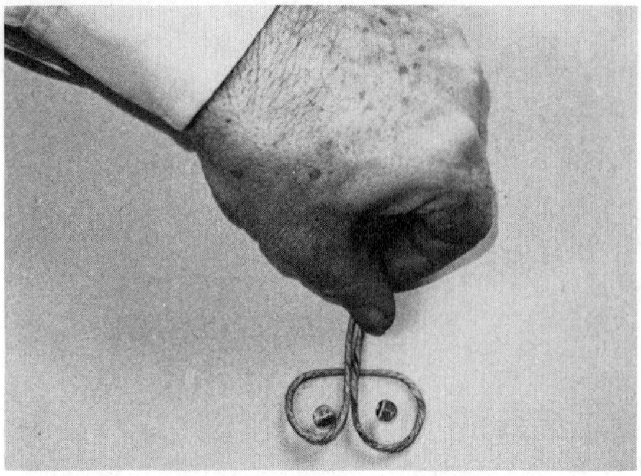

**WHEN TYING SPRINGS,** the tying twine is anchored to the sides of the chair or sofa rails by means of two No. 12 tacks. After looping, drive tacks in.

**SPRINGS ARE TIED** from front to back, then from side to side. Knot is made at each point where the twine crosses a coil. Use strong 6-ply hemp twine.

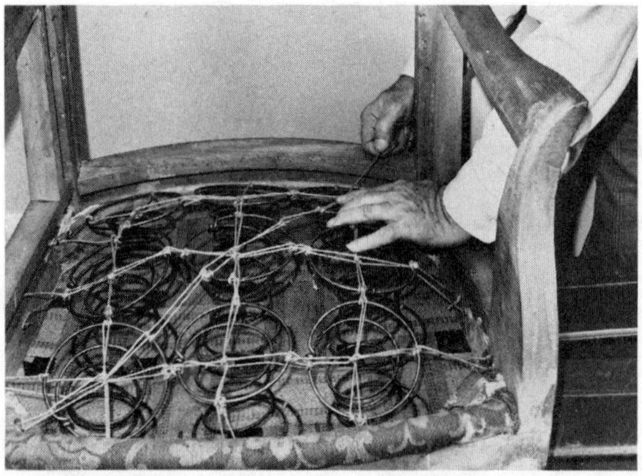

**SEAT IS SHAPED** as you tie the springs. Here, diagonal ties complete the shaping. Springs near the seat rail are compressed to round the seat.

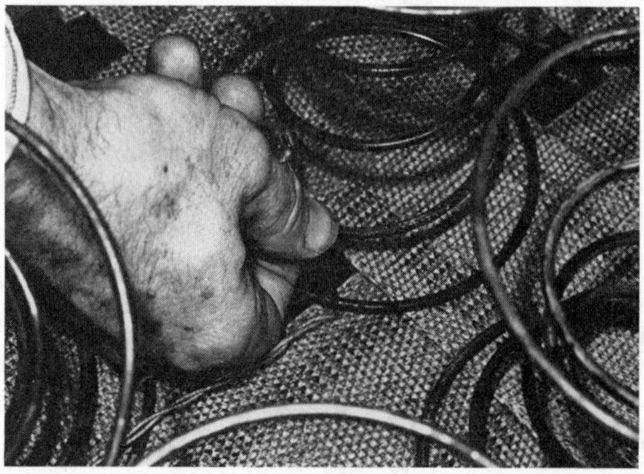

**AFTER REPLACEMENT,** sew springs to the webbing. Each spring is "tacked" to the webbing in four places. Thread is heavyweight carpet type.

in pads. Kapok is the least desirable because it tends to separate into lumps. Cotton is the old standby. But at present, the most available padding is polyester, which is softer and lighter than cotton. It doesn't pack down and it doesn't deteriorate. It is easy to use.

In recent years, a lot of furniture has been padded with foam. The older work was done with foam rubber, but today, much better polyurethane foams have taken over. You can buy this in sheets of different thicknesses, and in preformed cushions and pillows. You can cut this foam easily, and can make pads of different shapes by cementing the pieces together. If you are replacing an old foam padding, simply make new padding pieces the size and shape of the old ones. If you have decided to replace cotton or other padding with foam, use a sharp knife or scissors to shape the foam pieces to fit the chair.

***Edge rolls.*** An edge roll is a type of padding used around the edge of seats and chair backs to both pad and shape the outer contours of the furniture. You can buy them ready-made, or make them yourself by wrapping burlap around rolls of hair, cotton, or polyester. The final edge roll looks like a long sausage from ½ to 1½ in. in diameter, with a tab along one side to be used for tacking it in position. You can save any edge rolls you find on furniture as you string it, and reuse them during reupholstery.

***Tacking Strips.*** A tacking strip is a long strip of cardboard ½ in. wide. You can buy it by the yard or in rolls. It is used in blind tacking, as shown in the photographs. You can also buy tacking strips with large tacks already inserted in the cardboard. These are used in making final closures—as when you tack down the cover fabric on the back of a sofa.

***Cambric.*** Thin black cambric is tacked to the bottom of every upholstered piece to serve as a dust cover.

***Welting.*** Welting is used in most chairs and sofas at those points where fabric pieces meet, to provide a finished look. Welting is made from the fabric you are using as a final cover. You do this by cutting strips of the fabric 2 in. wide and then sewing these strips around welting cord.

Measure the running feet of welting you need for your work, then cut enough strips of fabric 2 in. wide to make this much. You may need 15 to 20 feet for a chair, and three times that amount for a sofa. Begin by sewing all the 2-in strips of fabric you have cut end to end, making one long strip 2 in. wide. Trim any excess fabric from each sewn seam to prevent bulges in the welting. Now wrap the 2-in. strip around the welting cord (which can be purchased at fabric shops) and use the sewing machine to stitch through both layers of fabric right next to the wrapped cord. The finished piece of welting has the fabric wrapped tightly around the welting cord, and two flaps about ¾ in. long for tacking.

***Stripping the old upholstery.*** The best tools for this job are a light hammer and a tack lifter. The easiest way to remove a tack is to place the blades of the tack lifter next to the tack head, and then gently tap the handle of the lifter with the hammer, guiding the blades under the tack head as you tap. The head will lift after several taps.

The first fabric to strip off is the cambric dust cover on the bottom. Turn the chair or sofa over, supporting it on a sawhorse while you work. Lift out the tacks holding the dust cover in place. While the piece is upside down, you can also remove the tacks which secure the final fabric of the seat and back which are tacked to the bottom side of the bottom rails.

Now turn the piece right side up and take off the outside back cover. If this piece has been sewn to the side fabric pieces, cut the thread to remove it—and at the same time, make a note to yourself to sew the new cover on in the same manner.

Now take off the outside arm covers. Observe carefully how these pieces have been attached to the front of the arm, and how the fabric has been cut to fit around the leg and back posts. You may find that the top of the outside arm fabric has been blind tacked, using a tacking strip. Make a note of this.

Now remove the inside back cover, starting by pulling the fabric up through the bottom frame since you have already removed the tacks holding this piece to the bottom rail. Be sure to save each of the old cover pieces to serve as a later reference. Also, as you take off each cover piece lift out the padding under it. Some of this padding may be tacked or sewn in place. Remove the tacks or cut the thread, and save the padding. You may be able to use it again, or at least use it as a pattern for forming new pads.

The next step is to remove the inside arm covers. These also were tacked to the bottom rail. Begin by pulling them up through the frame, then removing the tacks which hold them to the back and front posts of the frame. Once again, observe carefully how these pieces were fitted to the piece. In particular, see how the front of the arm was formed, and how the fabric was fitted around the front and back posts.

Finally, remove the fabric and padding covering the seat. Look to see if the fabric of the seat has been made in two pieces. Frequently, the good final fabric is used to make the forward part of the seat piece (the first 6 to 8 inches), and a heavy muslin or other fabric is sewn to it and used to cover that part of the seat which is under the cushion.

With the cover fabric and padding removed, you now see the burlap covering the springs. You'll also see any roll edges which have been used. Remove the roll edges carefully, since you can reuse them. Take off the burlap, exposing the springs. If the chair hasn't been upholstered in a long time, it is likely that the twine tying the springs has rotted and broken. Cut away all of the old twine.

The springs have been sewn to the webbing in the bottom of the piece. Cut the thread which holds the springs in place, and lift them out. Finally, remove all of the old webbing by turning the piece over again and removing the tacks which hold it in place.

The piece has now been stripped to the bare frame. Before beginning the reupholstery job, examine the frame for damage. Fill any cracks with glue, and clamp them tightly while the glue dries. Replace any wood which cannot be repaired. If you want to refinish visible wood parts, do it now.

***Reupholstering.*** If the piece has coil springs, the first step is to install new webbing across the bottom of the seat. If the piece has zig-zag springs, these will not have been removed during the stripping. Just check to see that all are solidly anchored in the frame. If any have come loose, you'll have to restretch them across the bottom, then renail them to the bottom rail.

Zig-zag springs are stiff and hard to stretch back into place after they have come loose. One way to do it is to set up a leverage situation. Make a loop about 4 in. in dia. of three or four lengths of heavy twine. Place this loop around the second zag from the loose end of the spring. Now insert a lever (use a long-handled hammer, a pry bar, etc.) through the loop. Pull the handle

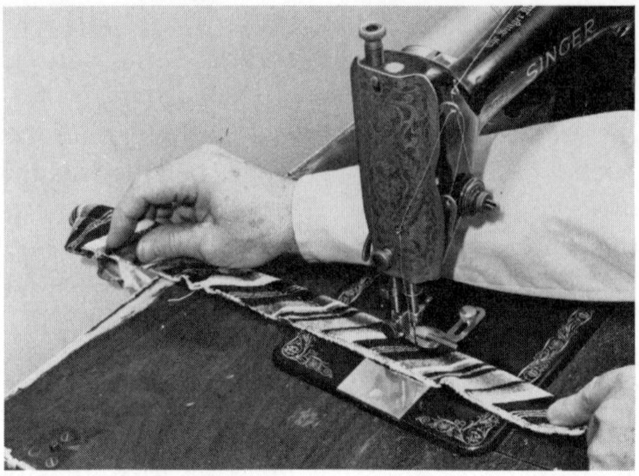

**WELTING** is used on most furniture. Make your own by folding a 2-in. strip of fabric around cording, then sewing close to the base of the cording.

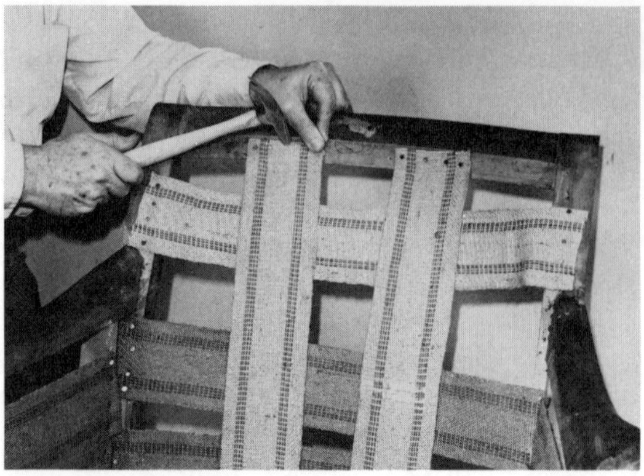

**AFTER COMPLETING** the work on the seat, install any webbing needed to support the arms or back. This webbing should not be stretched in place.

toward the outside of the frame until you can rest it against the outside of the frame. This will stretch the spring almost into position. Now slowly pull the top of the lever, with the bottom of it against the side of the bottom rail. This will pull the end of the spring into position over the rail. While you hold the lever firmly, have someone drive 1-in. nails or heavy staples through the holes in the spring clip into the chair rail.

***To install webbing.*** To install webbing across the bottom of the piece, use a roll of 3½-in. jute webbing and No. 12 tacks. Plan to place strips of webbing just as they were in the original job—usually about 1 in. or less apart, with webbing strips run from front to back and from side to side, interwoven.

Place the first strip with about 1½ in. of the webbing extending beyond the outside of the rail. Drive four tacks to hold the strip in place (see photos), then fold over the extended end of the webbing and drive three more tacks. Now stretch the webbing across the seat opening. You won't be able to stretch it tight enough with your hands, so use a webbing stretcher to pull it as tight as you can. Hold the webbing tight with the stretcher while you drive four tacks to hold it. Now cut the webbing about 1½ in. outside of the rail and fold the cut end back across the rail. Drive three more tacks to complete the job. Install all the front-to-back strips of webbing first, then do the side-to-side strips. Interweave the side-to-side strips as you put them in place.

***Installing the springs.*** Turn the chair right-side up and position the springs on the webbing inside of the seat. They should be spaced evenly and symmetrically. Use carpet thread and a large needle to sew the springs to the webbing. Begin by sewing the spring at one corner of the seat, using a long, continuous length of thread. Sew each spring to the webbing in four places, so that the thread makes a square pattern, then move on to the next spring. When you finish sewing, all springs will be firmly fixed to the webbing.

Next, the springs must be tied, using a 6-ply hemp twine. The twine is anchored to the chair rail by two No. 12 tacks driven at each end of a line of springs. The twine is tied to each spring as it passes over the coil, and as you tie each line of springs, you shape the seat, giving it a smooth, rounded contour. To do this, you compress the springs near the seat rails, and allow the springs to stand a little higher. Run the twine from front to back, then from side to side, tying it tightly to both sides of each spring.

***Arm and back supports.*** In some cases the chair or sofa may have jute webbing as a support for the padding in the back or arms. Install this now by tacking the webbing strips in place. As a rule, this webbing is not stretched.

***Burlap cover.*** Cover the newly tied springs with a layer of burlap, tacking it in place on the side rails. If edge rolls have been used to pad out or square up the front rail of the seat, install these now. Tack them in place, then sew them to the burlap cover.

***Installation of padding.*** Next the padding of the seat is installed. This may be two layers—one of hair and one of cotton, separated by a layer of burlap. Or it may be just one full layer of cotton. Or it may be a shaped pad of polyurethane foam. Whatever the padding is, it should be positioned carefully because the final shape of the seat depends on how the padding is placed.

It is a good idea to anchor the padding in some way. You can tack or staple it to the side rails if it reaches that far, or you can stitch through it into the burlap beneath it in several places. These anchors prevent the possible slipping of the pad-

**USE THE OLD FABRIC** pieces as patterns to guide you in cutting the new fabric. Cut the new pieces slightly larger, then trim as needed.

**HAND SEWING** to join sections of the final cover is easy and makes for a smooth, good-looking job. Sew wherever tacking isn't practical.

ding under the final cover.

***The muslin cover.*** The best furniture has a cover of muslin over the padding, with the final cover fabric applied over the muslin. Because it is very costly (in terms of labor), not much furniture is made this way any more. Instead, the final cover is applied right over the padding. But I recommend that you do it because it makes the application of the final cover much easier and provides some additional protection for the padding.

***The arms and back.*** Now move to the arms. Check the notes you made during the stripping of the piece to see how the padding was positioned and how the fabric was cut and tacked. At this time, simply rebuild each arm as it was before, using muslin as a cover, applying the final cover after the muslin.

When covering the arms, do the insides (that part facing into the seat), and then the outsides. The fabric goes down between the seat and the lower wood part of the arm, and is tacked to the bottom of the bottom rail. The outside arm piece most often is blind-tacked at the top, then stretched down the side and tacked to the bottom side of the bottom rail.

There are two tricky spots to watch for as you cover the arms. The first is cutting the fabric to fit around the arm and back posts. Check the old fabric to see how these cuts were made, and make the new cuts carefully. If you cut too much, you may spoil the fabric and be forced to make a new piece for the arm.

The second tricky place is the front of the arm. There are at least a dozen ways in which the front of the arm may be finished. The best way, until you have become proficient at upholstering, is to remake the arm exactly as it was before. Once again refer to your notes, and observe how the old fabric was cut and tucked or folded the first time. Sometimes the front is only tacked; other times, it may be sewn as well as tacked.

***The inside and outside backs.*** After the arms are finished, proceed to the inside back. Put the padding in place, and anchor it by stitching. Cover it with muslin, and then with the final fabric. The inside back usually is tacked about two inches below the top of the outside of the back rail. It is then stretched over the top of the chair and down the front. At the bottom it is pushed through between the seat cover and the bottom back brace and pulled tight. The bottom edge is tacked to the bottom of the bottom rail.

The outside back now is blind-tacked at the top, pulled down tight across the back, and then tacked to the bottom of the bottom rail. As a rule, the sides of the outside back cover are sewn to the fabric of the sides with tight stitches.

***Welting.*** No mention was made of welting until now because some chairs don't use it. However, if you use it, welting is tacked in place. It may be used, for example, to outline the back. If so, it is tacked in place after the arms and the inside back cover have been installed.

***The dust cover.*** Once the final fabric is on, turn the piece over and tack black cambric to the bottom as a dust cover.

***Protecting the fabric.*** After the upholstering has been finished, purchase a can or two of one of the fabric protector sprays, such as *Scotchgard,* and spray the completed work according to the directions on the can. This will help to protect the fabric from dirt and grease, make it easier to clean, and keep it new looking for a longer period.

Presto! A new piece of furniture!

# How to 'respring' an upholstered chair

By LEN HILTS

**Don't despair when the bottom falls out of your favorite upholstered chair. You can put it back in good order with an hour's work and a $10 bill**

■ WHEN THE BOTTOM drops out of an upholstered chair or sofa, don't panic. The hanging springs and torn webbing may look like a bomb went off inside the upholstery, and the sagging seat may make the job look hopeless, but things aren't really as bad as they appear.

Unless the upholstery fabric itself is badly worn, you aren't faced with a huge bill for a complete reupholstering job. In fact, with a few materials and less than an hour's work, you can restore the piece to better than its original condition. Furthermore, you won't have to touch the upholstery fabric as you work, since all repairs can be made through the bottom.

Start by turning the chair or sofa upside down. Use a hammer and tack lifter to remove the torn dust cover and all of the old webbing. You may be tempted to leave any strands of webbing which aren't broken—but don't do it. Webbing usually breaks because it has rotted with age. If

SEE ALSO
**Armchairs . . . Caning . . . Chairs . . . Sofa-beds**

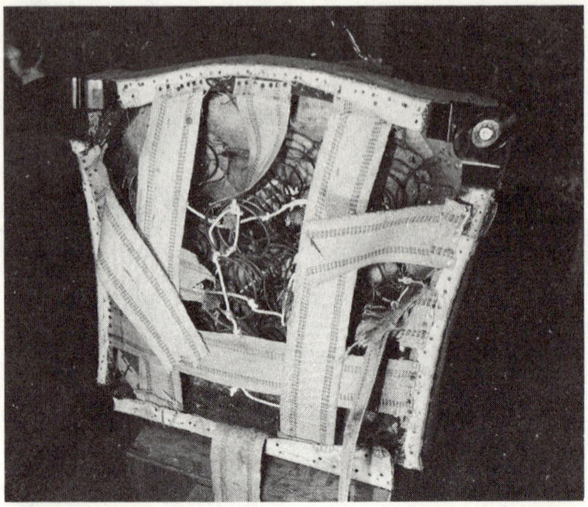

**UNCLE CHARLIE** sat down too hard, but don't blame him. The webbing was old and ready to go. You can see that someone once retied these springs with rope.

**AS THE TYING** progresses, the springs stand up straight and no longer lean. When finished, each spring should have eight knots on its topmost coil.

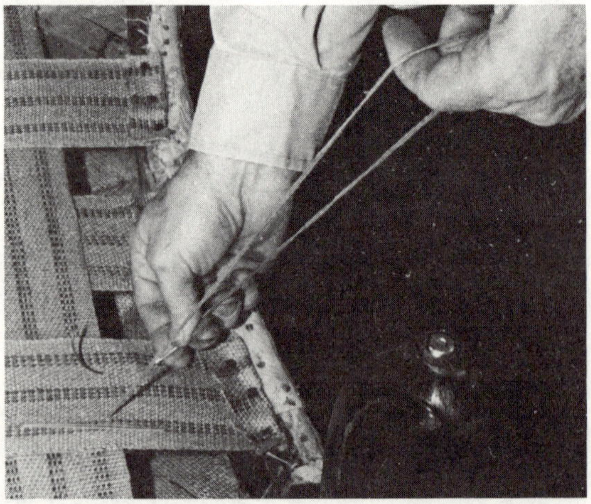

**THE CURVED NEEDLE** makes it easy to sew down through the webbing, around the top wire of the spring, and then back up through the webbing in one stitch.

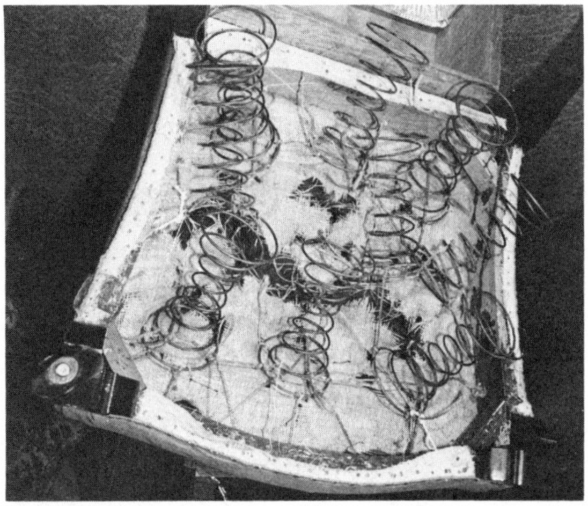

**THE OLD WEBBING** has been stripped away and you can see that the twine holding the springs is loose or missing. The springs are now loose and leaning.

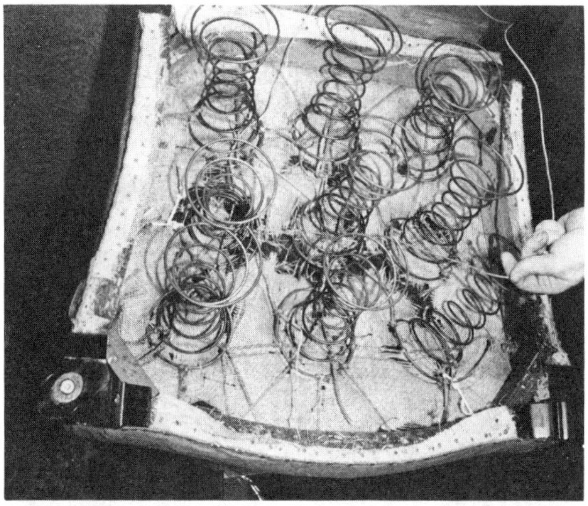

**REACHING UP** through the springs, use heavy twine to retie them. The ties connect the top wire of each coil to the neighboring coils.

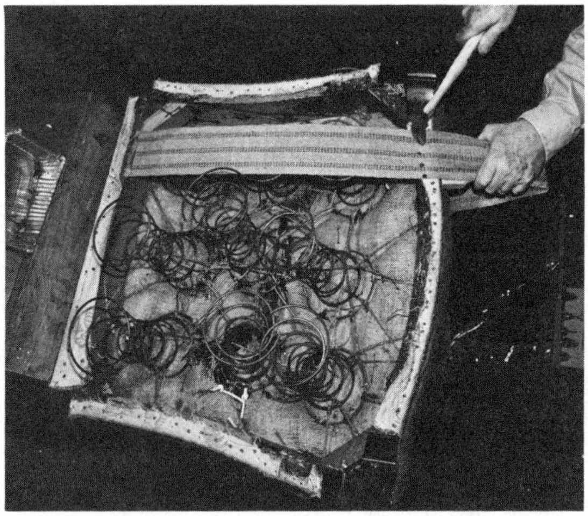

**THE WEBBING** is tacked to the back rail, then stretched taut across the row of springs. Use the webbing stretcher to pull strand as tight as possible.

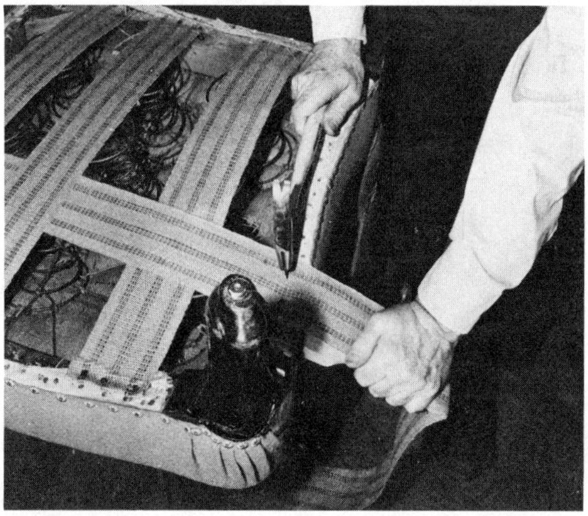

**FOUR TACKS** are driven into webbing. Then the strand is cut about 1½-in. outside of the tacks and the end is folded inward and secured with three tacks.

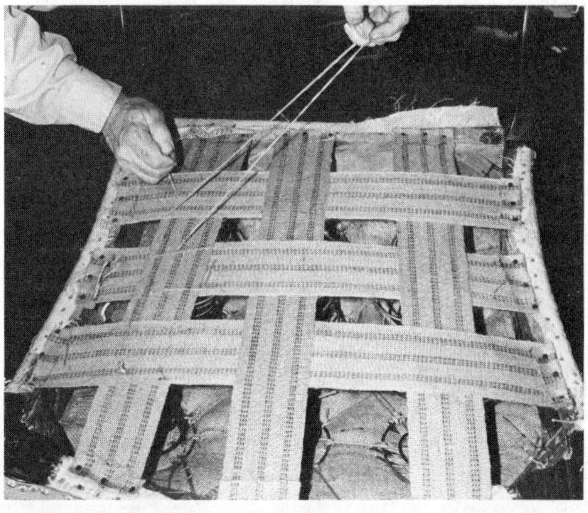

**SEW THROUGH** the webbing four times over each spring, making a square pattern, with the spring sewn to the webbing at each corner of the square.

**AFTER SEWING,** you may want to attach several more strands of webbing to provide additional support for the seat. Here two more strands were tacked in place.

**THE JOB** is completed by tacking or stapling a dust cover of black cambric to the bottom. Note how flat the bottom is because the webbing was stretched tight.

*'respring' a chair, continued*

some of it broke, you can be sure that the rest will go soon, too. Plan to put in all new webbing.

Webbing is made of jute, is 4 in. wide, and you can buy it by the yard at most fabric stores. Count the number of strands used across the chair bottom, and then compute how much you will need, adding a yard or two to allow for stretching. Ten yards is more than enough for most chairs, but you may need 20 yards for a sofa.

In addition to the webbing, you should also buy a webbing stretcher, a magnetic tack hammer, a box of webbing tacks (No. 12s), some heavy thread (the kind used for sewing carpeting), and a large, curved sailmaker's needle. You'll find all of these items available in the upholstery section of large fabric stores. The total cost, including the tools, won't be more than \$10 or \$15. If you already have the tools, you can manage for \$5 or less.

Once the old webbing is off, probe into the seat and check the twine which was used to tie the springs. You'll have to reach up through the springs to get at it, and if any is broken or loose, cut it away and replace it. At the start, each of the springs may be leaning in a different direction. By the time you have finished repairing the ties, each spring should be standing up on its own.

This retying is one of the secrets of this type of repair. If you simply replace the webbing without retying the springs, the seat will be lumpy and uncomfortable.

With the springs tied, apply new strands of webbing. Put one across each row of springs from front to back, then do the same from side to side. To apply each strand, tack one end of the webbing to the frame, using the method shown in the pictures—four tacks, evenly spaced, then fold the end of the webbing over and drive three tacks.

Use your webbing stretcher to pull the strand tight across the row of springs. And I mean *tight*. You are compressing the springs up against the seat, so you'll have to pull the webbing tighter than you would if you were just starting the upholstery job and the springs were not in place. You want to end up with the webbing stretched flat across the bottom of the chair.

You may have to reach under and adjust the springs as you stretch, making sure each spring is upright and in contact with the webbing. Once the webbing is tight, tack the loose end to the frame and go to the next strand.

When you have all the strands of webbing in place both ways across the springs, get out the curved needle and the carpet thread. The curved needle makes it easy to sew through the webbing, around the top wire of each spring. You want to sew each spring to the webbing in four places.

The easiest way is to make a square pattern with the thread over each spring, sewing down through the webbing around the top spring wire at each corner of the square—then moving on to the next spring to begin another square. This sewing is important because it anchors the springs and assures you that they won't shift out of position as the chair is used. If the springs remain unanchored and do shift, the seat will sag or collapse.

You will note that in this method of repair you have not replaced the webbing strand for strand, but have simply installed strands over each row of springs. This is necessary so that the springs are compressed properly. However, you may end up with fewer strands of webbing than were originally used. You may want to install several additional strands after you have finished the sewing of the springs.

Whether you do or not depends on the size of the piece and the strain which will be put on the webbing. In the chair pictured, I added two more strands of webbing because I felt the chair seat needed additional support. As a general rule, there should be no more than 1 in. between strands of webbing to give adequate support.

Finally, tack a dust cover of black cambric in place, and your upholstered piece is as good as new—with only a small outlay of time and money. You'll find it convenient to staple the dust cover in place if you have a stapling gun. The work is quicker and, since the dust cover receives no stress, strength isn't necessary.

**Hints for easier work.** The inside of an upholstered seat can be pretty dusty and dirty. After taking off the old webbing, use one of the tube attachments on your vacuum cleaner to reach in and get rid of the dirt before proceeding.

When you buy jute webbing, get the amount you need in a continuous piece, buying a yard or two more than you know you'll need. Don't cut strips from the webbing roll. Instead, tack the loose end, then stretch the webbing across the seat, and tack it down. Then cut the webbing about 1½-in. beyond the row of tacks you drove. Using this method, you are always sure of having enough webbing available to apply the stretcher.

When retying the springs, keep in mind that they were originally tied eight ways. That is, the twine ran from the front to the back, from side to side, and in both diagonal directions, and was tied to each wire it passed over, making a total of eight ties to each spring.

In retying, you won't be able to run a continuous length of twine in each direction. But you can tie each spring to its neighbor individually and end up with the same eight-way type of tie. Heavy twine ideal for use in spring tying can be purchased in balls at the same time you buy your webbing.

**THE PATTERN** to follow when sewing the springs to the webbing is shown here. By making a square over each spring, the coil can be stitched four times.

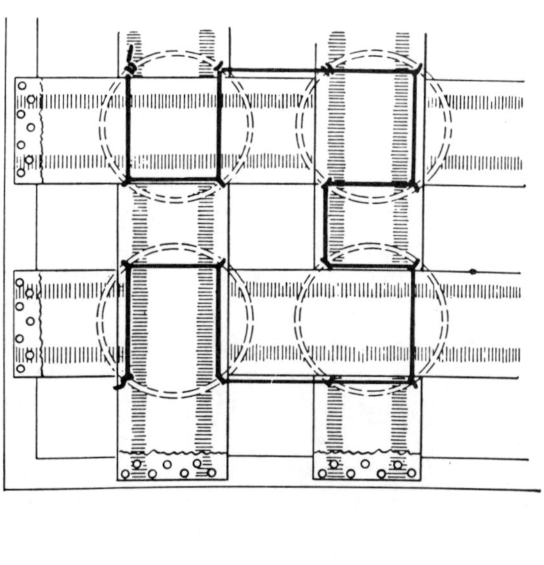

**THE PATTERN** followed in originally tying the springs produces eight ties on each spring. In repairing the seat, use the same number of ties.

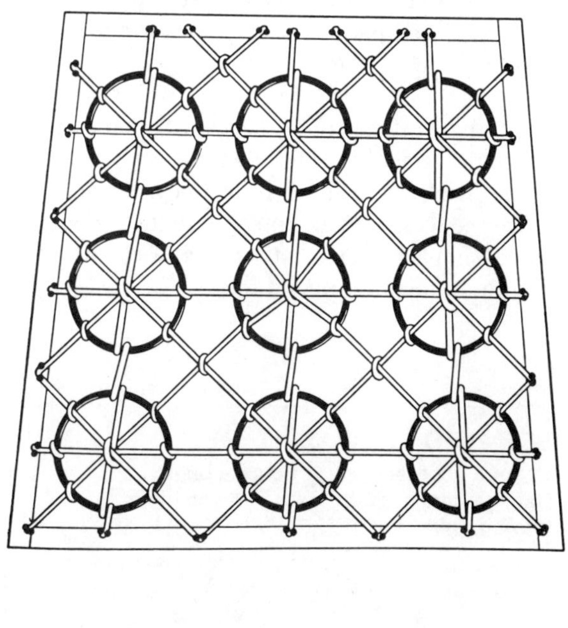

**Want to upgrade your photo equipment at a savings? Then consider buying a good used camera. Make these checks in the store or at home and assure yourself of a good buy**

**By LEN HILTS**

**OPEN THE BACK** of any camera you are considering, hold the unit to the light, and depress the shutter. Check to see that everything works smoothly and easily. Check the operation at different time settings.

# How to buy a good used camera

■ LOOKING FOR A WAY to upgrade the quality of your photography equipment? A very good way to do it inexpensively is to buy used equipment—notably cameras. By shopping carefully, you can own the best camera of its type at a price you can afford.

The trick, of course, is in knowing how to judge the used camera you are buying. Here are some simple checks you can perform to help assure yourself of a good buy:

SEE ALSO
**Camera accessories . . . Camera bags . . . Camera care . . . Cameras . . . Photo hints . . . Photography**

1. Know the kind of camera you want before you start to shop. Even make a decision as to the brand and model, if possible. Then visit several camera stores and make a cursory check. Is the camera you want available used? What is the price range? What is the general condition of the equipment?

This information should lead you to the dealer with the best stock and the best prices, and give you a ''feel'' of the market.

2. Select the most promising dealer and visit him to talk some serious business. Select the camera that seems to fit your situation both in price and in general condition. Now settle down with that camera and perform a thorough inspection.

3. First, the appearance. How does it look? Does it show signs of heavy wear? Look for

**WITH THE BACK** of an SLR camera open, depress the shutter and observe the action of the focal plane shutter. Cock the camera and look again.

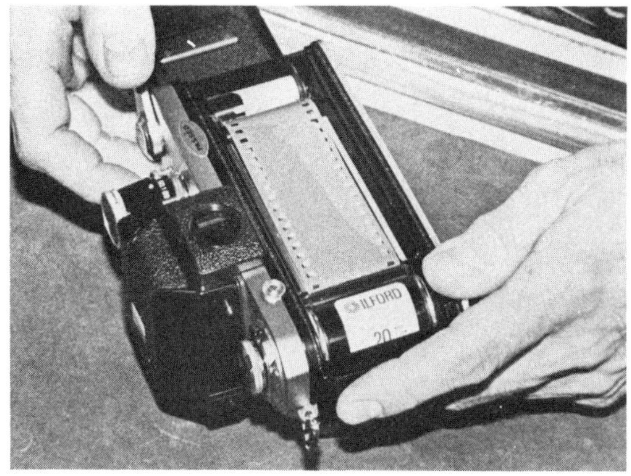


**RUN A ROLL** of exposed or out of date film through the camera, noting the action. All parts should work smoothly with no binding.

**TEST A BUILT-IN METER** by taking a reading from a Kodak gray card. Place the card in a light place and note the reading given by the meter.

**NEXT, TAKE A READING** with a good light meter, using the same gray card and placing the meter in the same position as the camera. Readings should agree.

dents and other clues that it may have been dropped. Look for signs of corrosion, and for evidence of an accumulation of dirt—anything that tells you the camera didn't receive good care. Check the tiny screws that hold it together. If they are burred, suspect that an amateur tried to repair it.

Reject the camera if you suspect it was dropped, was badly cared for, or repaired by an amateur. A well-worn camera can be a good camera—but only if it was cared for.

4. Open the back. Check the serial number, and if it has been deleted, reject the camera. Is the interior clean, showing care? Snap the shutter and advance the film controls. Watch to see that all the controls function smoothly. Look to see that the shutter is absolutely undamaged.

5. Thread a roll of film into the camera to see that all the parts work smoothly. Most camera stores have an exposed roll you can use for this purpose. If not, bring your own, or even invest in a new roll. Remember, you are making a considerable investment.

6. Remove the lens, or, if the lens doesn't come off, open the back of the camera so you can look through it. Put the shutter on "bulb" and hold the lens toward the light. Look for nicks, scratches, discoloration or disfiguration. Ignore small air bubbles, since these appear in most lenses. While the lens is open, move the lens aperture to each of the f-stops. The iris blades should move in unison and form a symmetrical opening (usually hexagonal) at each stop, and each opening should be half (or double) the area of the one next to it.

7. Now, with the lens aperture wide open, close the shutter and run a similar test. With the camera toward the light, cock and fire the shutter at each of its speeds, up and down the scale. It should look and sound consistently faster or

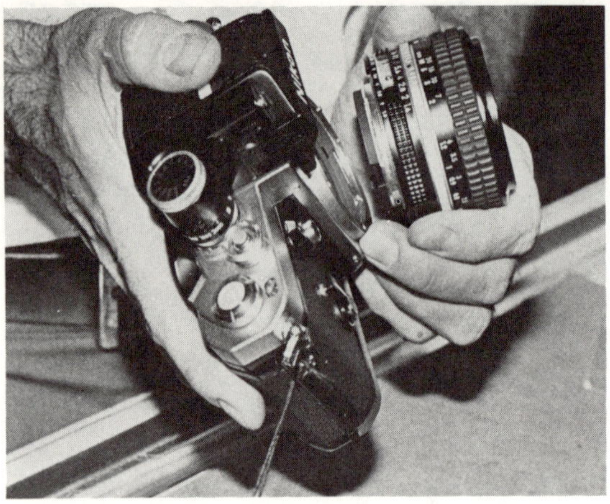

**REMOVE THE LENS** from cameras with interchangeable lenses. Examine the lens threads for damage. Be sure all parts of lens mount are undented.

**TEST SHUTTER** by this test, using an electronic flash gun. Connect the gun to the camera, then place the gun so it fires directly into lens.

*good used camera, continued*

slower than the previous setting. If the blades on either the iris or the shutter stick—or in severe cases flop loose—reject the camera. On a camera with interchangeable lenses, make the shutter and aperture tests separately.

If examining an interchangeable lens, see that the threads are undamaged. Shake it and listen for loose elements. Move the turning rings with your fingers to be sure they move easily but at the same time are snugly in place. Reject the lens if the rings are loose and wobbly.

8. Check the accessories. For example, fit a flash gun into the hot shoe and fire the camera—to be sure the hot shoe contacts are good.

9. If the camera has a built-in exposure meter, check it by borrowing an Eastman gray card from the dealer (he has them in stock). Set the card up in a light place and look at it through the camera, taking a reading from the meter in the camera. Now borrow a good light meter (or bring your own) and make a reading, placing the meter at the same distance from the gray card as the camera was. The two readings should agree. Otherwise you can suspect trouble in the camera's built-in unit.

10. If the camera has a focal plane shutter (a flat cloth shutter which travels from one side to the other, visible when the back is off the camera) examine it to see that there are no holes. You can test it for timing and operation in the following manner: Borrow a small electronic flash unit. Place it on the counter, attached to the camera so that it will fire when you depress the shutter button (use a short connector cord). With

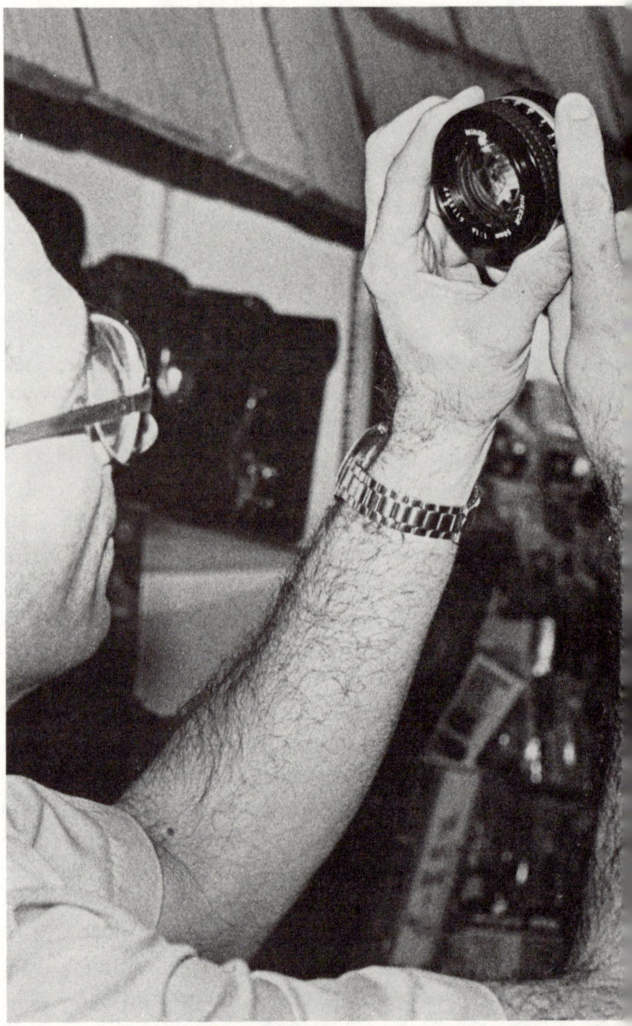

**HOLD THE LENS** up to the light and look through it. Look for scratches, discoloration and other damage. Ignore tiny bubbles, which are in many lenses. Shake the lens and listen for rattle.

**WITH FLASH UNIT** pointing into lens, place piece of paper over shutter. Set camera at 1/60-second, fire flash, and watch rectangle on paper.

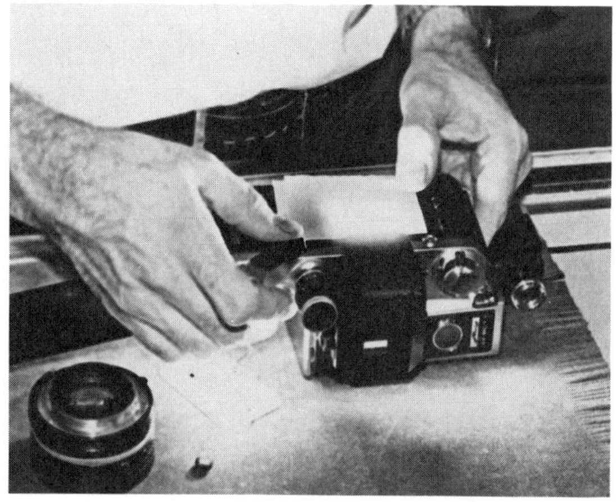

**FULL** rectangular opening of shutter should be visible at 1/60 during flash. About half is visible at 1/125, and a quarter at 1/250 of a second.

the back off the camera so you can see the shutter, place the camera so the flash gun fires directly into the lens. (See accompanying photos.) Place a small sheet of white paper over the shutter and set the time on the camera for flash synchronization, usually 1/60 of a second.

Now keep your eye on the white paper and depress the shutter button. The gun will fire and you should be able to see the entire rectangular shutter opening outlined on the paper. Now set the timer at 1/125-second and repeat. The size of the rectangle you see should be smaller. Make the test at 1/250. By now, when the flash fires, you should be able to see only a small part of the rectangle. At 1/500, you should see none of the rectangle.

This is a good test to indicate whether the shutter timing is functioning and is more or less accurate.

11. Check the focus by looking at objects through the camera. Bring them into sharp focus. Then measure with a tape the distance from the camera to the object. The footage scale on the lens should agree with your measurements.

If these seem like too many tests to perform in a camera store, ask the dealer for a trial period. Most will allow you 10 days. Take the camera home and make the tests at your leisure. Also shoot some test rolls and have them processed. During the tests it is best to use a tripod to assure steady pictures. Otherwise, you may blame the camera for fuzziness when actually it was your own body motion that caused the problem. Shoot some detailed subjects, such as a brick wall, from a distance of six feet. Make an enlargement of the resulting picture and examine it for sharpness of detail. Shoot a sequence of pictures of the same subject, using all the f-stops and a series of different times. Compare these pictures. Look for a sharp fall off of focus from the center to the edges of the pictures. And look for a steady progression of exposures in the series of time pictures.

Ask the dealer about his guarantee. Most good dealers will allow 30 to 90 days on used equipment, depending on the conditions, brand and price asked.

If the camera is in top shape, don't expect too low a price. You should save a fair amount, depending on the age of the unit, but if the price is too low, be suspicious. The camera may have a history of repairs and the dealer may be trying to dump it.

In general, stay away from antiques—cameras more than 15 years old—unless you are a collector. It is also a good idea to avoid off brands when buying used equipment. Don't be surprised if you find some very recent models available in the used market. Often a shutterbug overextends himself for a new camera, then finds he must sell it back to the dealer to get some ready cash. Cameras acquired under these conditions will have very little use, but will be priced close to the new camera figure.

When looking at any camera, use your nose. Check to see if it has a smell of mildew, and look to see if there is evidence that the camera may have been water soaked. If you see any such signs, pass it by.

# 20 tips on buying a used car

NEW CARS COST too much, and so do used lemons. So the trick is to find a used car that's as good as new and a few thousand dollars less expensive. Impossible? Not if you can remove the gamble. And you *can*.

When you begin those treks down used-car row, your best friend is patience. So often people rush into a used-car deal as if there's no tomorrow. Salesmen capitalize on buyer impatience. "Better hurry and decide now," the salesman may tell you, "because there's another customer itching to buy this car." Never let that sort of talk stampede you. If it takes you two weeks to find just the right car—even two months—don't rush yourself.

**1. While you're settling down, think long and hard about what sort of car you really need.** Everyone's talking small cars these days. But if you've got five kids, two dogs, a 15-foot house trailer, and you're a rockhound, it's not likely you'll be totally happy with a used Volkswagen as your family car.

2

Common sense tells you to balance such factors as passenger and carrying capacity, fuel economy, number of doors and so forth against the size of your family (present and future), how long you plan to keep the car, plus cost and availability of repairs.

Make and year of car aren't as important as condition and the candidate's ability to fill your needs. Say you've settled on a particular Dart as your ideal year, size and type of car. Don't look just at that Dart, though. Look too at same-age

3

Novas, Mavericks, Valiants, Hornets, Comets, Apollos, Omegas, Venturas, Volvos and Peugeots. That way you open up a lot more prospects for finding a good, clean low-mileage used compact.

**2. Eyeball the car.** Check for exterior ripples and defects by sighting down all sheet-metal surfaces: fenders, hood, decklid, doors, roof. Ripples mean bodywork, possibly because of an accident or rust holes. Fresh paint and/or paint over-spray might mean the same thing. Remember that light colors tend to hide ripples and blemishes. Always inspect a used car in sunlight, never at dusk (after working hours) or under artificial lamps of any type.

**3. Also look for interior abuse.** The odometer reading should match pedal and carpet wear and seat sag. Be on the lookout for a punctured headliner, ripped seats, scorched fabric, a scuffed package tray, re-dyed carpets or vinyl, new rugs and new pedal pads.

Most used cars have been "detailed," which means the dealer, or a shop that works for him, has tried to cover signs of wear and tear with dye jobs, a new package tray, new trunk mat, respraying the dashboard padding, spraying carpets or replacing worn ones, installing new armrests, even reglazing bull's-eyes in windshields. Be alert for "detail" jobs and try to look beyond them.

**4. Detailing extends to the used car's mechanicals.** Detailers usually steam-clean and then spray-paint the engine, radiator, air-cleaner and the like, and sometimes they replace underhood decals. The purpose again is to make the car look as new as possible, and that's fine, but it masks evidence of the car's previous use and maintenance. A gummy, grease-encrusted engine at least tells you something about the car's history. A detailed engine tells you nothing. Again, you have to look beyond the fresh paint and new decals. Search for areas that have eluded the detailer. Check, for example, the condition of the battery box, fan belts, air-cleaner element, cracked ignition wires, rusty sparkplugs and so forth.

Smoke from the oil filler or breather, especially if it's heavy, can tell you that the running engine is burning or pumping oil. Rusty water spots on the firewall give clues to previous radiator boilovers.

**5. Make sure everything works.** Prospective buyers always try a car's radio (and dealers therefore make sure it's playing), but also note whether gauges are functioning. Roll all windows up and down. Test lights, locks, air-conditioner, heater, all accessories, seat adjustment.

**6. The biggest gamble remover, the best warranty, the greatest lemon protection you can give yourself when you're shopping for a used car is this step: Take every car you're seriously considering buying to a professional mechanic or an auto diagnostic clinic for a thorough check.** Such an inspection usually costs $10 to $12. Make an appointment with the shop or person who'll do the inspecting, and then drive the candidate car to that place of business. Tell the used-car dealer that you'll be doing this, and if he won't let you (he'll say his insurance doesn't cover such events, but that's not so), forget that car.

Professional inspections usually take about 40 minutes and should always include an engine compression check—all cylinders should show amply high and fairly equal readings.

**7. Brakes and front-end alignment.** The mechanic should pull one front wheel or drum to inspect the disc or lining. At the same time he should test the front end for play in the ball joints, steering, links, and suspension components. Front-end maladies can be particularly expensive, and most used-car buyers never test for them before they make their purchase.

**8. While the car is still on the lift, have the mechanic look for frame damage or bent underpinnings that might indicate past collisions.** Also poke around for rust holes, not just in the rockers and floor pan but also in the exhaust system-muffler, pipes, catalytic converter, and so forth. Note condition of all four tires plus springs and especially shocks. And look for telltale leaks from brake cylinders and lines, engine, transmission, rear axle, radiator and gas tank. Any abnormal leaks (a *little* lube leakage is normal) could spell bills soon.

**9. After the diagnostician gets the car back on the ground, let him take it for a short test drive.** Ask him to check transmission operation, noting smoothness of shifting, delay in going into gear, and play in universal joints and rear axle. At some point he should also remove the transmission dipstick and sniff the fluid for the odor of scorching. That simple test can often tell volumes about an automatic transmission's condition.

In cars with manual gearboxes, clutch action should be smooth and positive. Shifts shouldn't demand struggle or guesswork. If the stick ever pops out of gear during acceleration or deceleration, or if you hear growling or rapping sounds from the transmission, be wary.

**10. During a test drive, even if it's only to the shop making your professional inspection, listen for odd noises, rattles and hums.** Mention these to the mechanic. Also check brakes for veer, steering for play, suspension for bounciness or looseness. Accelerate and decelerate sharply to conduct your own test for sloppy U-joints and rear axle.

**11. Try to avoid cars with four-barrel carburetors.** Four barrels almost always take premium fuel. Engines with two-barrel and single-barrel carbs get by on regular gas. It's not the four-barrel carb that makes a car burn premium—it's the higher compression ratio and advanced ignition timing that go along with four-barrels.

**big-car bargains**

**12. Keep in mind that the used-car market has done a complete flipflop since the energy crisis.** It used to be that the full-sized American cars—particularly Fords, Chevys and Plymouths—were hot sellers before the oil embargo.

Today, though, big Detroit sedans and wagons can go begging on used-car lots. You can often pick up a late-model, low-mileage, full-sized Detroiter for a good deal less than a minicar or compact of the same year and mileage.

The popular (thus expensive) used cars nowadays fall into seven specific categories: 1. economy imports like VW, Datsun, Toyota, Opel, Colt and Capri, but also to a lesser extent Mazda, Renault, Peugeot and Subaru; 2. used domestic economy cars, particularly Pinto; 3. used American ponycars, the hottest being Camaro, Mustang and Firebird; 4. used sports cars—Corvette, MG, TR-6, 240-Z and 260-Z, and the big Austin-Healeys; 5. luxury "heavies" such as Cadillacs and Mark IVs; 6. some intermediate-sized U.S. cars like Chevelle and Skylark; and 7. all four-wheel-drive vehicles—Jeep, Blazer, Scout and the like.

**13. When you buy a used car, try to avoid financing if you possibly can.** Pay cash instead. You nearly always up the cost of a used car by a third or so through financing and mandatory insurance.

**shop for best terms**

**14. If you must finance, shop for terms as you shop for the car.** Life insurance and credit union loans are least expensive; dealer and finance-company loans are most expensive, with banks in the middle. Pay off a loan as quickly as possible.

And set a ceiling on what you plan to pay for a car.

**15. You've probably asked yourself whether you should buy from a private party, a used-car dealer, or a new-car dealer who carries used cars.** All three have good and bad points, but experts pretty much agree that you get the best cars from small, clean, neat, independent used-car lots. These dealers often buy the creampuffs of new-car trade-ins. Try to deal with the lot owner directly, not one of his commissioned salesmen.

Buying from a private party can lead to heartaches, especially if something goes grossly wrong with the car or deal. Buying from a new-car dealer usually means paying more than at an independent lot, because the new-car dealer has greater overhead —but you'll usually get some type of warranty on the car, usually 60 to 90 days. These, though, are generalities and don't apply in every situation. You probably ought to shop all three before you decide.

**16. Don't be afraid to dicker, but never get huffy or nasty during price negotiations.** Again, be patient—use time to your advantage. Never panic when the salesman urges you to buy today. Prices don't change or cars vanish that quickly.

**don't trade old car in**

**17. Avoid trading in your present car if possible.** Sell you old car privately before you buy a newer one. Be shopping, though, while you're selling your present car. If you can sell it privately, you'll be more likely to get "retail" for it. As a trade-in, though, you'll never get more than "wholesale." Also, the cash from a private sale will give you a price and financing advantage.

**18. Where do you find out what used cars are worth?** Banks and finance companies can and will lend you used-car price guides—so-called "blue books." These are much more accurate than the ones you can buy on newsstands. Ask one of the bank loan officers to lend you a blue book. Figures shown will let you check asking prices of cars for sale and will also let you put a realistic value on your present car when selling or trading it.

**19. Put no faith in used-car warranties of any sort.** They might or might not prove worth the paper they're written on. Never let a warranty sway you toward a purchase. A used-car dealer's reputation counts for a lot more than any warranty. Remember that you never get any sort of warranty from a private seller; also that your best warranty is the used-car inspection I mentioned in No. 6.

**20. Sign nothing—no sale contract, no power of attorney, no credit application—until you've read it completely and understood every word.** Now that's easy to say and hard to do. If you have questions, let the salesman explain. And if his explanations don't make sense, take a copy of the document to your attorney for interpretation.

All blanks in a contract should be filled in before you sign it. Leave no deposits while test driving a car or having it inspected. Do not let the dealer "park" or drive your car for you if you're not planning to trade it in. Your car might end up being a "hostage" while the dealer wears your patience and resistance by keeping you waiting.

**the best years to look for**

The best used cars are usually from two to four years old, with between 10,000 and 15,000 miles a year on the odometer. The average American car, properly treated and maintained, will give 100,000 miles of service before a major mechanical breakdown. Body longevity varies with locality and depends largely on salt corrosion.

If you keep these 20 points in mind, your chances of finding a good, reliable, trouble-free used car are around 80 percent. Which means there's still a risk. But then there's a risk in buying a new car, too, and considering how much less used cars cost than new ones, their risk factor at 80 percent still makes them more attractive.

# A beautiful home for your holidays

'Super Camp'

NOT EVERYONE with a piece of land wants—or needs—a true vacation home. Young weekenders especially find themselves "camping-out" and enjoying it more than reveling in a spectacular summer-home showcase.

A "super camp" such as this may be the answer. It will keep you dry on rainy afternoons, keep the wind out at night and minimize the need to pack up your outing equipment and bring it home.

The shelter fulfills three important requirements—it can be locked securely to discourage pranksters and vandals; it provides over 400 sq. ft. of enclosed living area, and perhaps most

SEE ALSO
**Decks . . . House additions . . .
House purchasing . . . Winterizing, homes**

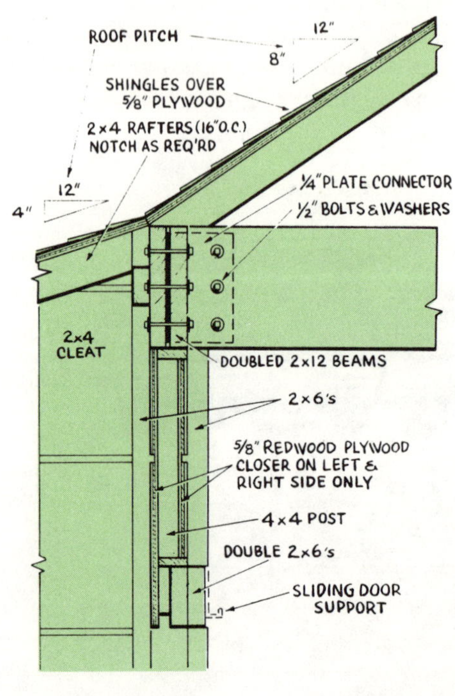

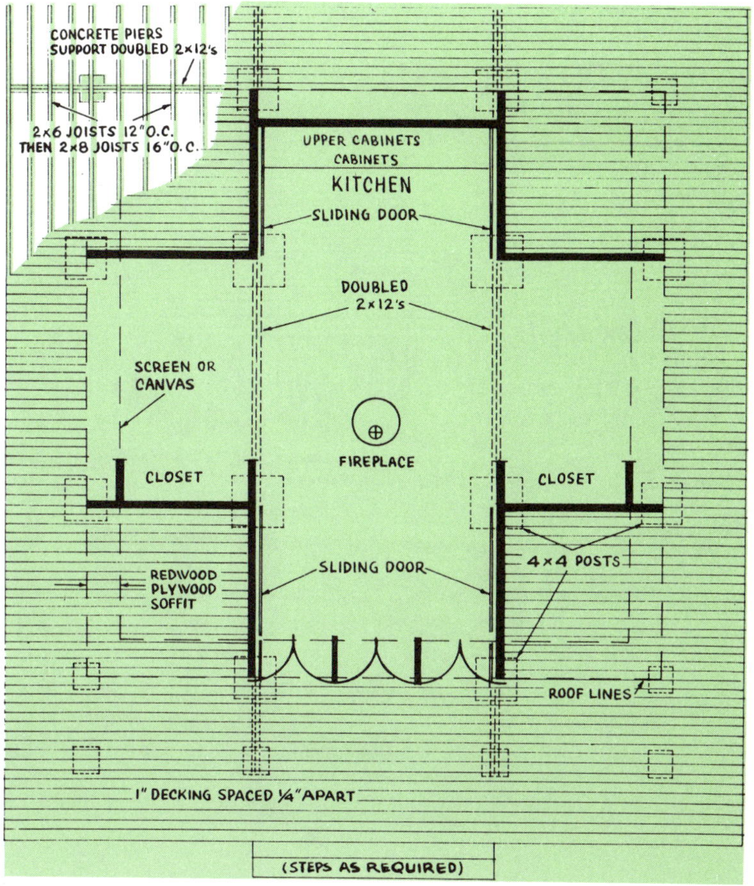


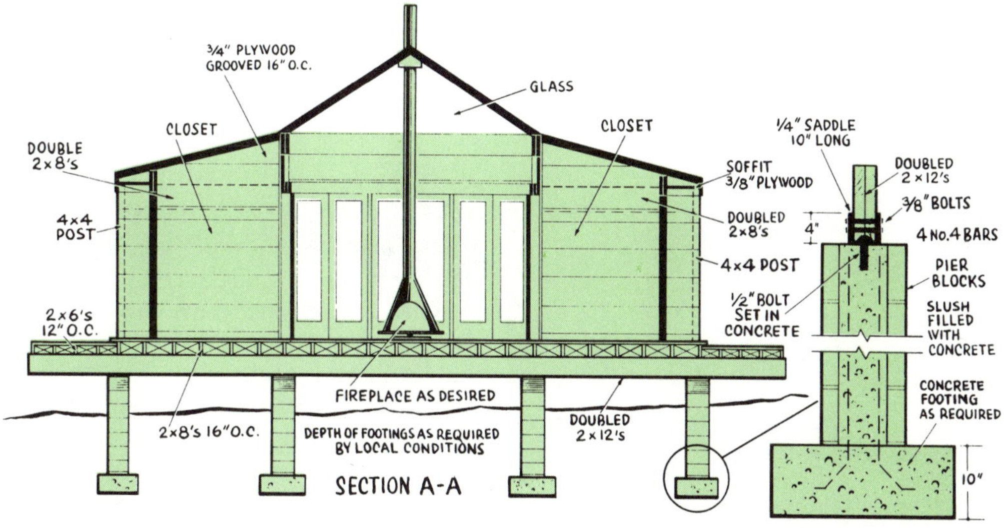


important, it is a stylish structure with a pleasing appearance.

The clerestory above the entrance dramatizes the roofline and also provides good interior illumination. Similarly, a prefabricated fireplace adds interest to the center of the shelter, while providing a source of heat. Functionally, the closets and kitchen cabinets make "roughing it" a bit easier, and the sliding doors allow you to lock up the "camp" in a matter of minutes.

On following pages you'll find plans for other vacation cabins.

## Octagonal house—modern design with complete livability

THIS HIGH-STYLE HOME adapts easily to beach, lakeshore or mountainside to provide a panoramic view of the surrounding territory.

What's more, since the house is shown here in three different sizes, it can fit a variety of needs and lot sizes. Just study the floor plans and pick the one that suits you best.

The smallest version of the octagonal house is basically a comfortable combination of a living-sleeping-dining area with separate bath and kitchen divisions, all built into a 309-sq.-ft. area. The next largest plan has a similar layout, but increases the total area to 483 sq. ft.

The largest of the three plans offers 768 sq. ft. and can be built as either a one-bedroom or two-bedroom house.

A roomy deck edges five of the eight sides of the house, adding spaciousness and guaranteeing a place to sun any time of the day.

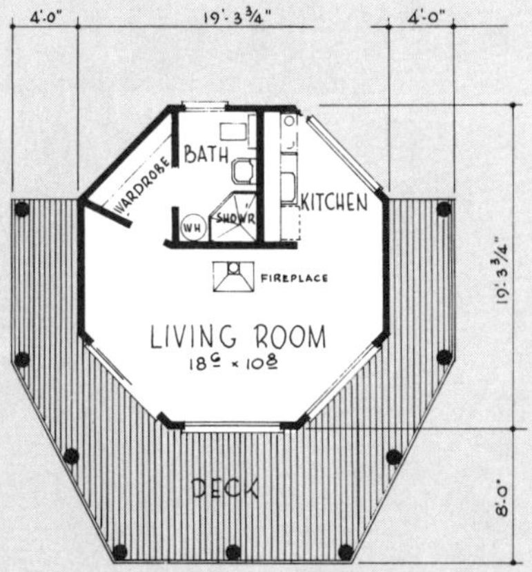


**A BACHELOR** with a small wooded site high in the mountains would be unlikely to find a better plan for a vacation home. It's comfortable and laid out for convenience, but has flair.

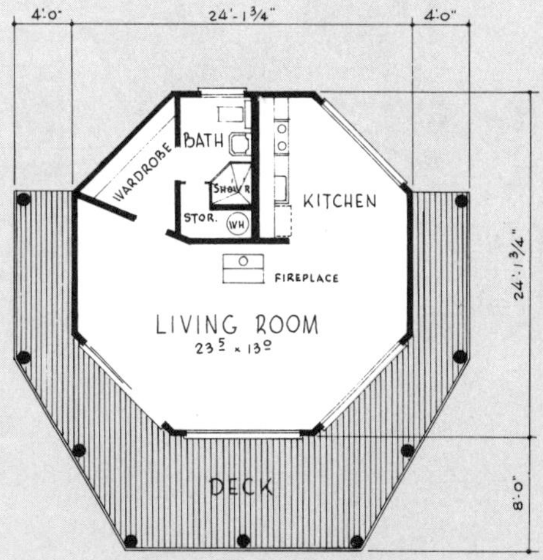


**A LARGER VERSION** of the octagonal design, this plan requires an additional five feet (in length and width) over the smaller version, yet has half again as much available living space.

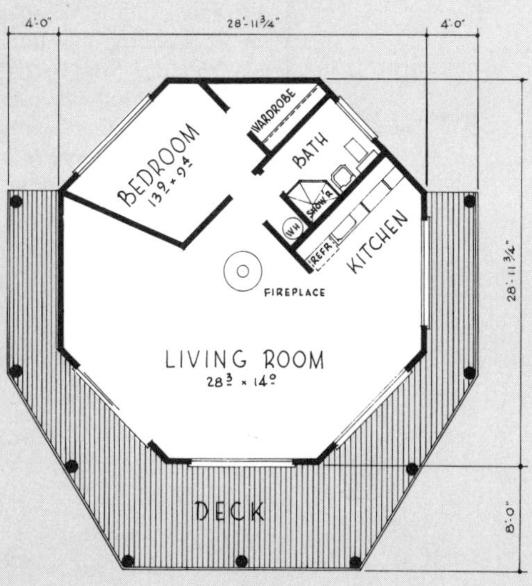


**"A HOME AWAY FROM HOME"** best describes this one-bedroom version of the eight-sided design. Although the deck rings five of the eight sides, amount of deck can be increased or decreased.

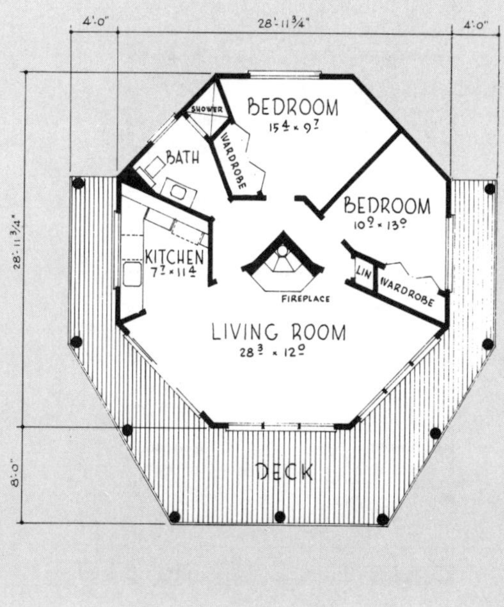


**AS A YEAR-ROUND** vacation home or a retreat solely for warm months, this two-bedroom version leaves little to be desired. Measurements shown in these plans are taken from extreme corners.

## A-frame updated for comfort

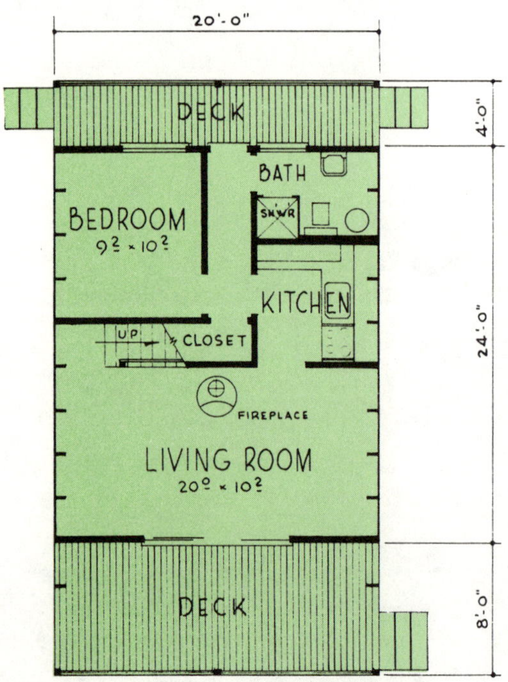


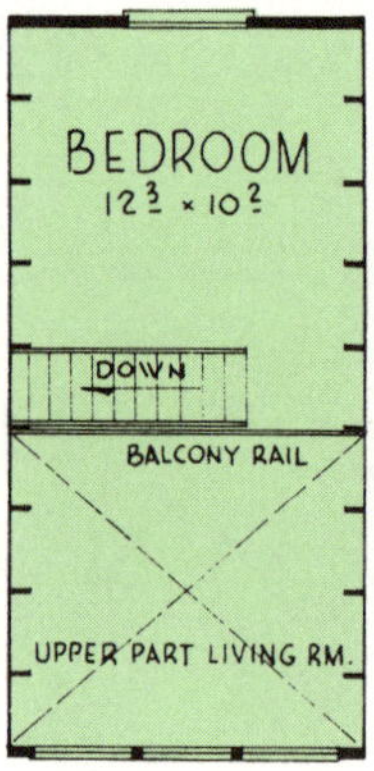


**PRACTICAL** layout of the A-frame is highly suitable for weekending the full year round. A front wall of glass allows full view of scenery and lets in plenty of daylight. Adding a rear door improves the traffic pattern.

■ ONCE CONSIDERED a radical design innovation, the A-frame has become a classic among vacation home styles. The adaptability of the A-frame has much to do with its popularity, since it can be built on most any site and customized to reflect the owner's individuality.

The plan utilizes a large expanse of glass on the front to add spaciousness to the 645-sq.-ft. home (480 sq. ft. on lower floor, 165 sq. ft. on upper level), and includes an often-needed back door.

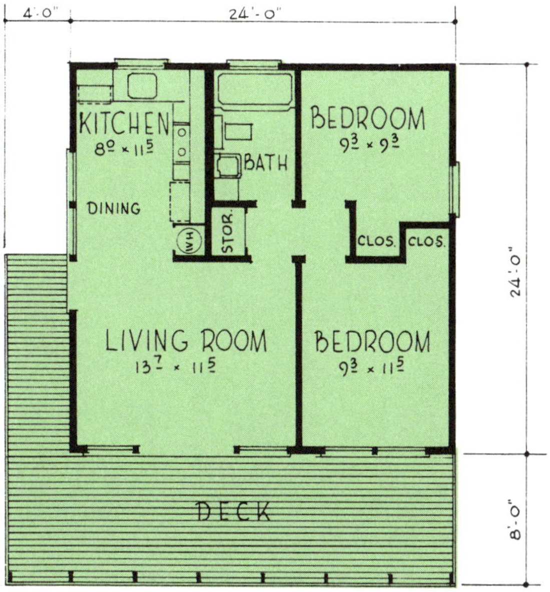


## Sloping roof adds eye appeal

THE WEATHER-WORTHY shed roof has proven itself to be strong, durable and highly practical—and too often, extremely ugly.

However, thoughtful planning in the design stage has made the shed roofline appear clean and contemporary in this plan. Modestly sized, the house offers 576 sq. ft. of enclosed living space, an additional 272 sq. ft. of deck space, and an exterior that's fronted with supporting posts angled to break both the vertical and horizontal lines of the structure.

Inside, both bedrooms have a separate closet, and provision for a hot-water heater is made at one end of the kitchen.

# Attractive vacation-home plans

By LEONARD E. SABAL

SPORTSMAN, family man, banker man, thief—all need a hideaway to get away from it all. Only nowadays, it's got to be a hideout big enough for the rest of the gang.

And, when you consider that it also must be inexpensive, comfortable, trouble-free and adaptable to any location, the obvious solution is a vacation home—preferably one you can build with a minimum of time, skill and cash outlay.

SEE ALSO
**Additions, house . . . House purchasing . . . Winterizing, homes**

With these points in mind, we took a good look at the vacation-home market, or as some prefer, the second-home industry. The result is this collection of five homes you can build *now* and enjoy later, while the last house is presented for what it is—a brand new idea in stylized retreats.

Complete plans for each of the five are available from the American Plywood Assn., 1119 A St., Tacoma, WA 98401. An important part of each set of plans is a detailed bill of materials listing plumbing and electrical supplies, as well as lumber, miscellaneous hardware and foundation materials.

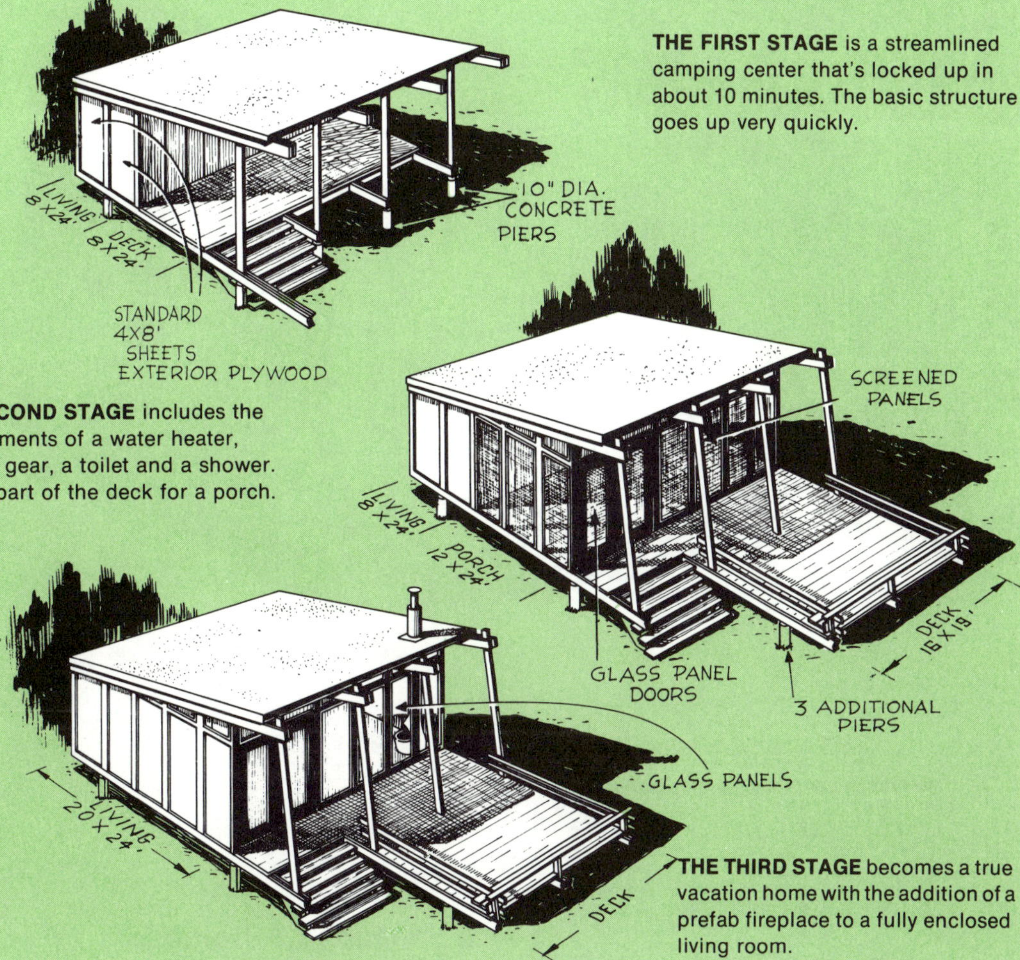


**3-stage expandable home—it will grow with your family**

**THE FIRST STAGE** is a streamlined camping center that's locked up in about 10 minutes. The basic structure goes up very quickly.

**THE SECOND STAGE** includes the improvements of a water heater, cooking gear, a toilet and a shower. Screen part of the deck for a porch.

**THE THIRD STAGE** becomes a true vacation home with the addition of a prefab fireplace to a fully enclosed living room.

**THIRD STAGE FLOOR PLAN**

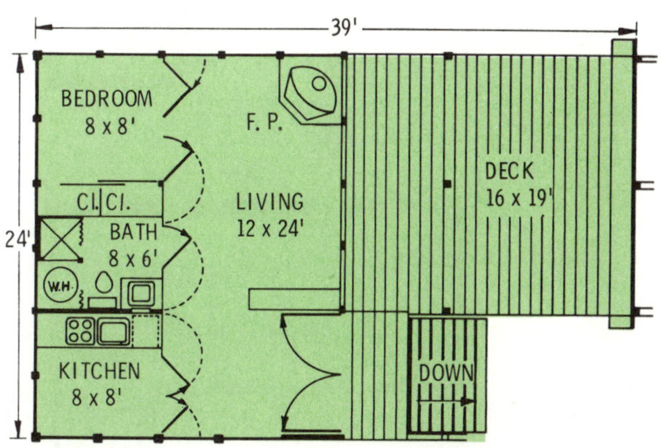


The first home, as shown on these two pages, is a three-stage affair that can be built quickly in first-stage form, then expanded as the need arises. You could, however, complete all three stages at once, because the house is designed around the 4x8-ft. modular concept, and therefore requires a minimum of cutting during the actual construction.

The first stage basically is a simple shelter that doubles as a camping center. Add a cooking unit, water heater, shower, toilet and more deck area to convert the basic module into an easy-to-live-in cabin. To complete the third stage, enclose the living area, install a prefab fireplace, insulate if desired, and add those personal touches that makes a home.

continued

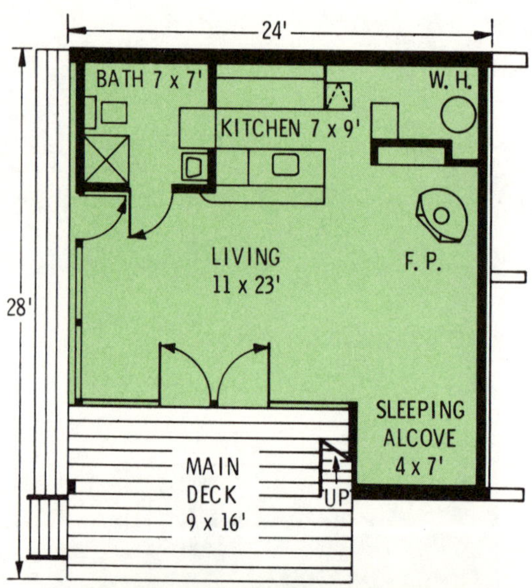


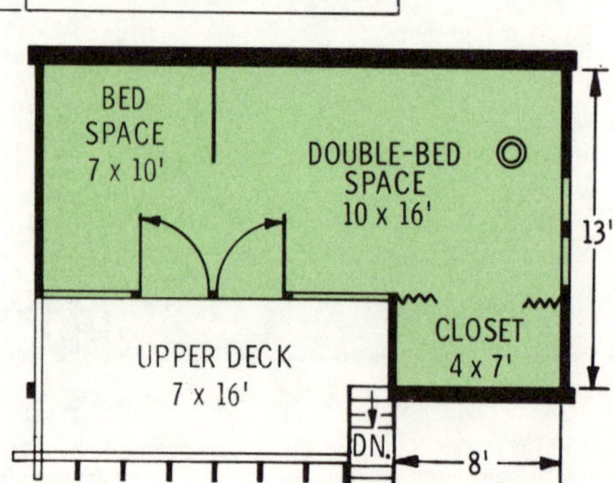


## Stepped A-frame for split-level convenience

■ WELL-PROPORTIONED and inviting, this double-deck A-frame integrates the desirable features of upstairs bedrooms with spacious living areas to provide the privacy and appeal of a split-level home.

The dual-deck arrangement also contributes to this split-level effect while simultaneously providing a natural borderline for the upper and lower walls of windows and doors. The end result is an interior that's always bright, airy and cheerful.

Should the upper bedrooms prove large enough for the members of your family, the lower sleeping alcove can easily be converted to a convenient 4x7-ft. closet like that on the upper level.

The structure rests on nine concrete pilings, while panels of Texture 1-11 act as both roof and walls to provide the lateral rigidity required for an A-frame.

## Rigid-frame cabin for remote homesites

THIS CABIN would make an ideal vacation home for your family or, if you are a hunter, a hunting lodge for you and some friends.

Its rigid-frame construction offers two distinct advantages. First, the cabin goes up in a hurry because all the framing members are identical and, thus, can be prefabricated before the actual erection. Second, the absence of load-bearing interior walls means the floor plan can be varied to suit any requirements without affecting the strength and rigidity of the cabin.

Although normal spacing of frame members is 2 ft. on centers, you could double up on each and space them 4 ft. o.c. for larger sidewall openings. Inside the cabin, the large frames can be left uncovered for a handsome "exposed beam" look. However, if you're already planning on next season's hunting, you can add insulation between the frames and then panel the interior with decorative plywood.

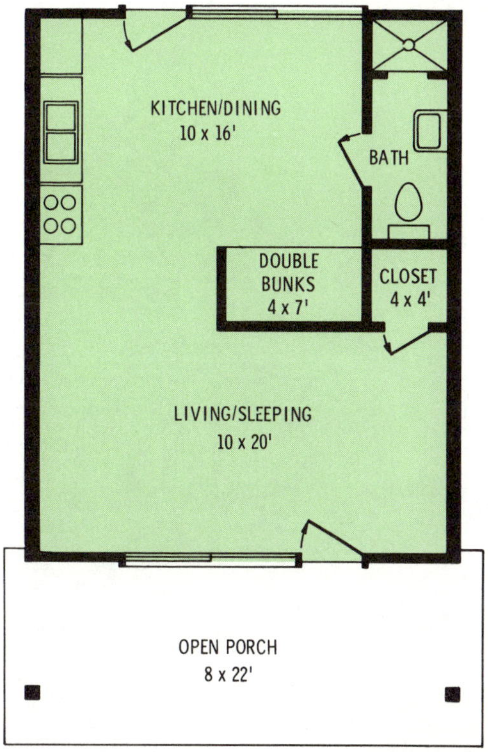


please turn the page

## Palatial hideaway for peaceful afternoons

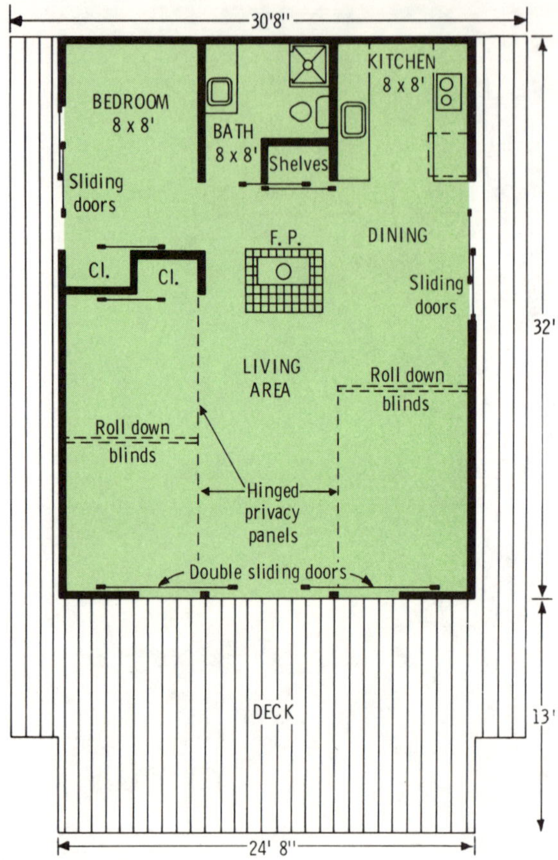


■ DESIGNED for easy building on remote sites, this luxurious retreat can be put together in a week, using preframed plywood panels and precut lumber.

When you're through, you have a vacation palace—a true second home—with 770 sq. ft. of enclosed living space and another 700 sq. ft. of outdoor deck space.

The attractive clerestory arrangement in the roof not only adds to the appearance of the house, but it also serves a utilitarian purpose by flooding the interior with light, even on cloudy days.

Another unusual feature is found in the living room, where hinged privacy panels drop from the ceiling to create three separate sleeping areas for weekend guests. Yet even when the panels are lowered, there's still plenty of space remaining around the fireplace for informal entertaining and relaxing. Using sliding doors throughout also adds a touch of casual elegance.

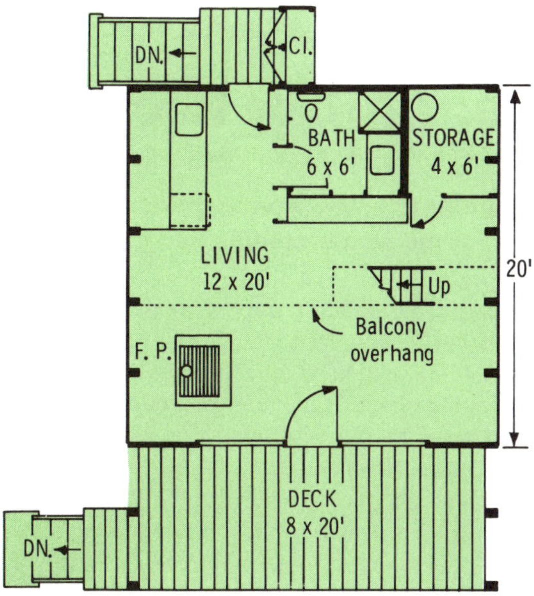

## Spartan A-frame for rugged vacationers

■ NESTED ATOP a rocky mountain, this striking A-frame withstands gusting winter winds as well as sudden summer storms to make it an ideal weekend refuge.

To relieve the bare A-frame lines, an extra pair of frames and a canvas canopy extend over the deck to form a shelter from sun, rain and snow. Inside, a neat plastic skylight provides natural illumination, while the front wall of windows and door takes full advantage of the view.

The living room contains 240 sq. ft. of space with a prefabricated corner fireplace that's perfect for warming up after a hard day's skiing. The 144 sq.-ft. sleeping balcony overlooks the living area and is accessible via a shiptype stairway. The rear of the A-frame has a second entry (into the kitchen) on the lower level, while cool summer night breezes can enter the balcony area through a pair of swinging windows.

As with all the homes designed for the American Plywood Assn., it's best to lay the foundation *in strict accordance with the plans* before the delivery of the other construction materials.

# How to close up your vacation home

**A vacation home can be a lot of fun, but there's also work involved. Here are some tips to help you prepare your home for the winter months**

WHEN THE END of summer approaches the time comes to think about "battening down the hatches" at a vacation home which will be unattended during the winter months.

Many of the closing-down chores are things you've done year after year, and most of the items listed on these pages are simply common sense. But, if you make up a list and assign each member of your family specific tasks, the closing-down will go a lot faster—without a chance of missing any important items.

You can usually hire a local resident who, for a nominal fee, will keep an eye on your place during your absence. To avoid misunderstandings, agree upon his fee and what services he is expected to perform.

Finally, check your homeowner's insurance policy to see if any conditions must be met to assure your policy remains in full force during your absence.

**Start with inspection** of house exterior and grounds. Look for, and remove, broken or dead tree limbs or trees which may be leaning dangerously toward your house. Your "check-list" tour should include the following:

1. Clean out gutters and leaders.
2. Repair any loose roof shingles.
3. Point up any loose chimney bricks.
4. Clear *all* accumulation from the crawl-space area.
5. See that garbage cans have properly fitting covers. Scrub the cans with disinfectant and soap and water. When dry, store them out of the weather. Throw out damaged and uncovered cans.
6. Keep out vermin by covering chimney flues with a galvanized sheet-metal cap, securely fastened. *Immediately, upon fastening flue cover,* go inside and put a *big sign* on the fireplace to assure you *uncover flues* prior to use next season.

If possible, your boat should be drydocked. This may be: 1) at the local marina, 2) at your year-round home after a trailer tow or 3) stored on your vacation-home property. Items 1 and 2 simplify your task considerably. If you elect to do your own storing, follow these simple guidelines: Pick an area near the house on the opposite side from prevailing winds. A small boat can be inverted and stored on sawhorses; just make certain it is lashed down securely with a stout cord. With boat stowed, check your dock, mooring lines and accessories for any loose gear which may be stored in and lashed to the boat.

**Grounds, dock and boat check**

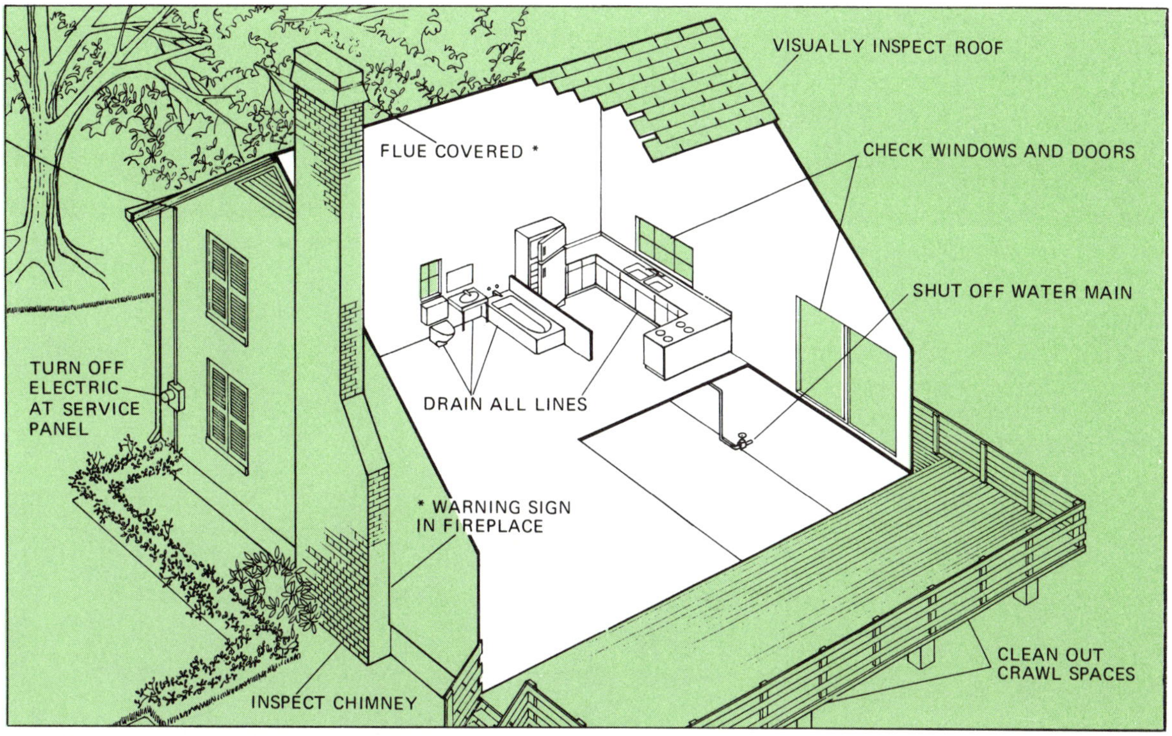


**There's work to be done inside too**

**Scatter a liberal number of mothballs** around the house, in each room. Mothballs will be easier to gather than flakes next spring. Also place mothballs between mattresses and springs. Since camphor evaporates when exposed to air, you may wish to have your "caretaker" replenish the supply every six weeks or so. *Do not set rodent traps.* Decomposition over the winter can cause an odor that will be difficult to eliminate. A strong camphor odor will deter most rodents from entering the house.

**Clean out all foodstuffs.** Food packed in cardboard containers (cereals, flour and the like) will attract rodents and other vermin. Foods packaged in cans and bottles may be subject to below-freezing temperatures and stand a good chance of exploding. At best, they will probably outlive their shelf lives if left behind. Your best bet is to remove all food from your vacation home before leaving. For economy, of course, bring home what you can. Add what you decide isn't worth packing to the pile of trash that is to be hauled to the dump.

Before locking the front door, make a final check to assure that all combustible materials—paints, solvents, cleaning fluids, matches and the like—are removed from the house. Turn the heater switch to off, shut off the gas supply at the main and pull the main electric fuse (or trip the breaker). Finally, check screens, windows and doors to make certain they are firmly secured.

**Shut off water-supply main** and drain *all* water-supply lines. Open valves on fixtures, drain fittings at their lowest points and leave valves open. A small amount of water may remain in the valves. To remove it, rig a section of hose to the pressure side (outlet) of your vacuum cleaner and blow out the fixtures. If your summer home is closed while the climate is still moderate, small amounts of water remaining in valves and lines left open will evaporate prior to freezing weather. Drain or siphon water from the toilet-bowl tank and remove the last bit with a sponge. Pour about a cup of permanent-type antifreeze in every trap. (Don't forget, the bathtub drain has a trap too.) Pour *two* cups of antifreeze in the toilet bowl. Waterpump and well-point systems vary depending upon the type installation. Here, it is best to have your plumber show you what to do the first-time around. Write down what he tells you for use next year. (You may have a foot-valve type point, a flexible submersible point, or other: "Breaking" the vacuum by needless loosening of fittings can shorten the life of the fitting.)

**Final points:** Make certain your washed-down refrigerator is propped open. Also, it is worth the few dollars more your caretaker will charge to have him clear the driveway after each snowfall. In the event that fire should break out while the house is closed, a clear access could spell the difference between minimal damage and total loss.

SEE ALSO

**Boating, storage . . . Caulking . . . Insulation . . . Plumbing . . . Roofs . . . Winterizing, homes**

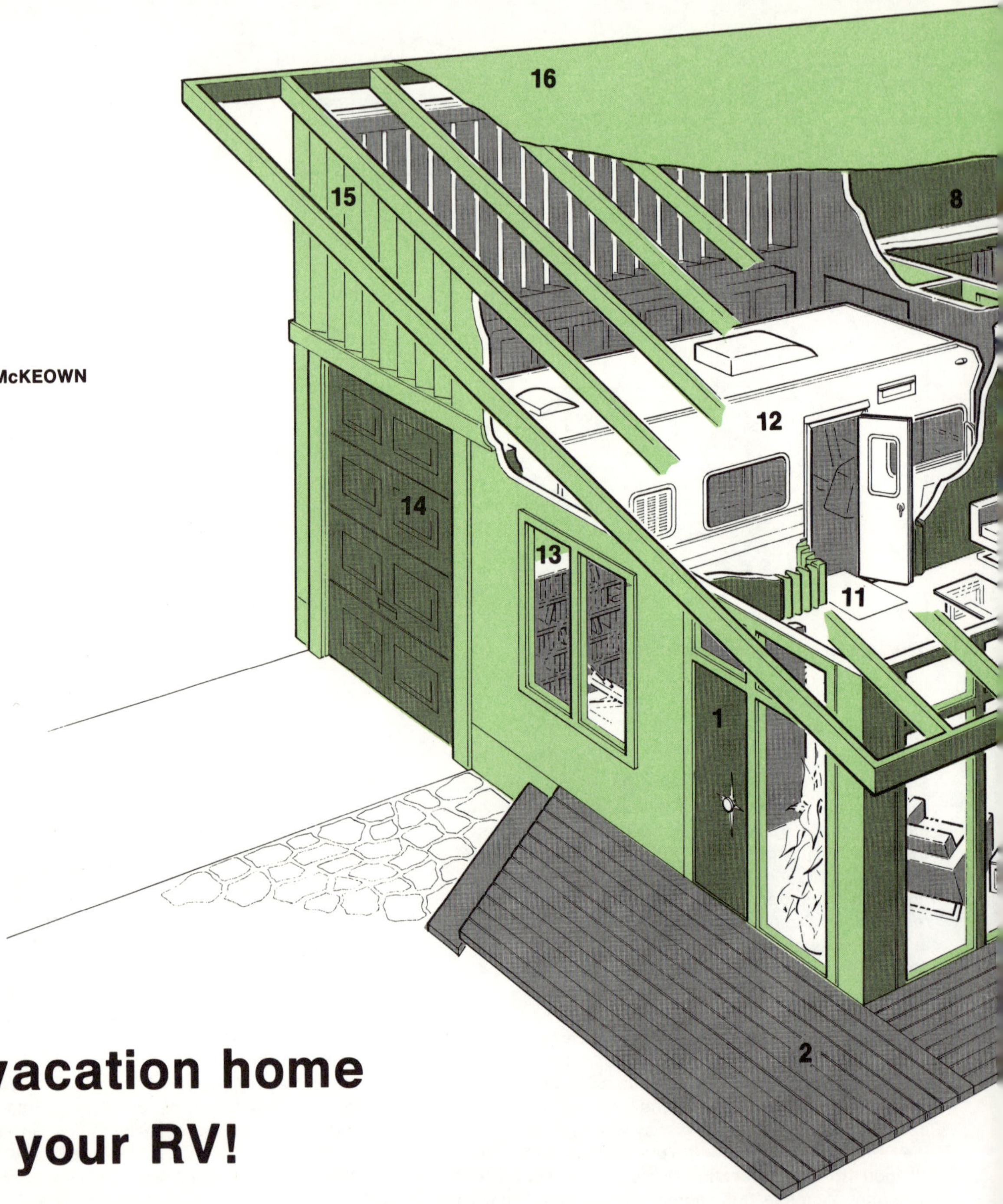


By BILL McKEOWN

# A vacation home for your RV!

**A recreational vehicle can form the nucleus of a more spacious and comfortable permanent vacation home. Rudimentary at first, the shelter can be developed gradually over the years until it contains all the comforts of a regular house**

SEE ALSO
**Campers . . . House additions . . .
House purchasing . . . Recreational vehicles . . .
Trailers, tent**

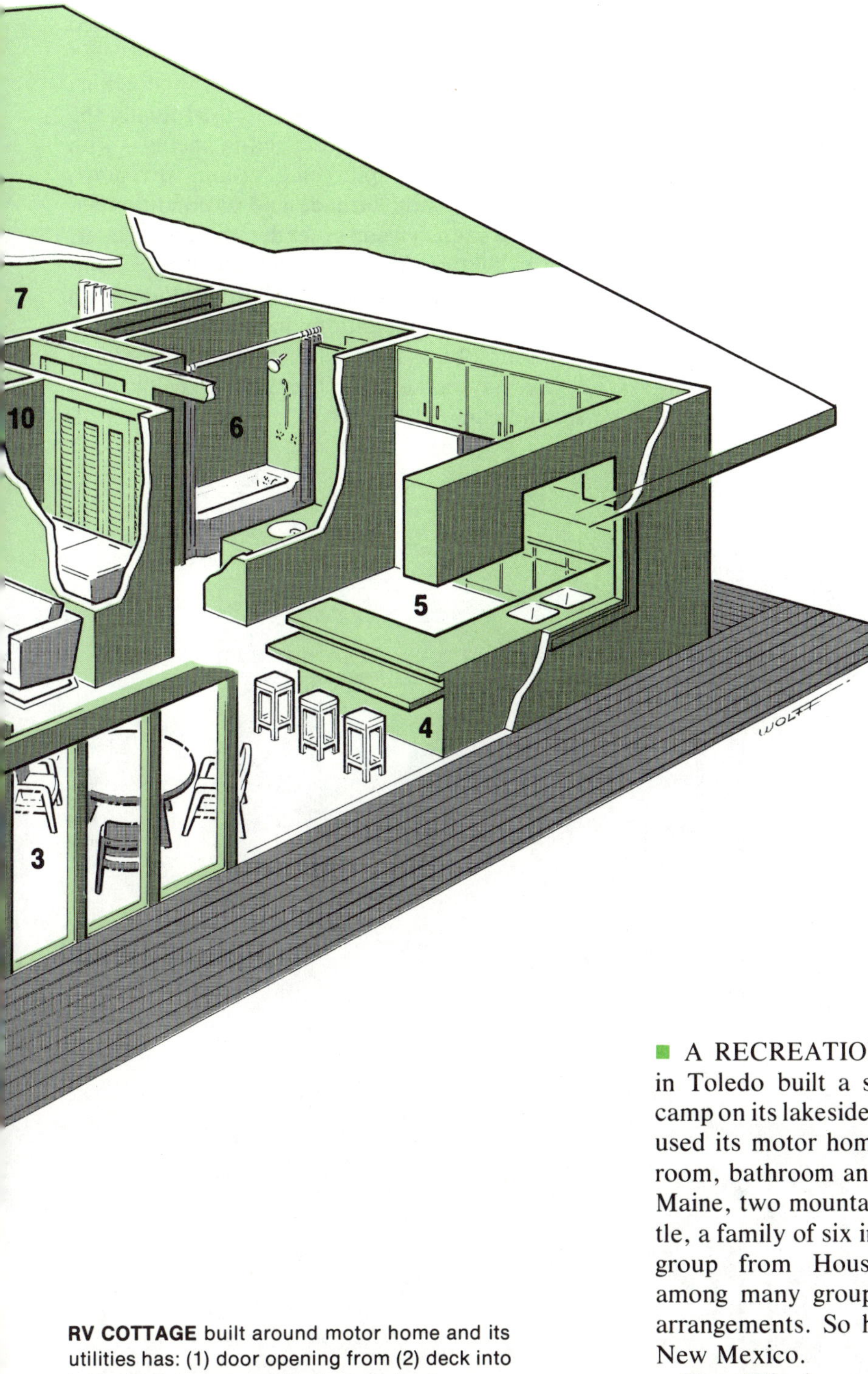


**RV COTTAGE** built around motor home and its utilities has: (1) door opening from (2) deck into basic (3) living area. Added room divisions can include (4) bar/breakfast counter with pass-through space to (5) kitchen. The plumbing and sewer connections allow addition of (6) bathroom. Shutting off back of two-car garage makes (7) bedroom with (8) storage over. (9) Utilities room with furnace and central airconditioner plus (10) laundry room are refinements. (11) Level ramp leads to (12) motor home. (13) Workshop. (14) Garage door. Garage enclosure has louvered (15) front, side ventilation under the roof (16).

A RECREATIONAL VEHICLE FAMILY in Toledo built a spacious one-room summer camp on its lakeside lot in Upper Michigan—and used its motor home parked alongside as bedroom, bathroom and kitchen. A fishing club in Maine, two mountain-climbing couples in Seattle, a family of six in Denver and a water-skiing group from Houston—all RV owners—are among many groups that have set up similar arrangements. So have several RV retirees in New Mexico.

One Winnipeg couple had more specific needs: "We were going to retire in two years," they wrote, "and had bought some land in central Florida. Like many undeveloped spots, it had no gas, electricity or water, but that was no problem since we could live in our motor home. Next to it we put up a simple one-room cottage in which we could store some of our things from our house up North, once we sold it. Eventually we expanded and fixed up the cottage to accommodate our children and grandchildren when they came to visit. Now, part of the year, we shut up the cottage and take to RV touring again.''

The shelter shown here was designed with the needs of such people in mind. The building starts with an enclosure and carport. Check local building codes and restrictions, plus insurance requirements, before getting started. Since some communities don't like the appearance of an RV, we have enclosed the carport with a garage door but louvered the top for ventilation so that the generator, airconditioner or furnace can be employed. For extensive use, exhaust hose extension or chimney connection may be installed.

The floor level of the camp cottage is planned at a height equal to the RV interior with a walkway leading in and accordion walls and ceiling fitting snugly around the RV door. Initially the room can be a simple screened-in shelter—with windows, walls, plumbing, room divisions, kitchen and bath, furnace and airconditioning, separate bedroom and outer decking added later. Storm shutters can close up the house completely when the owners drive off on tour. With sleeping accommodations in the vehicle and a fold-out sofa in the living area, back-bedroom space may be kept as a garage extension for a second car.

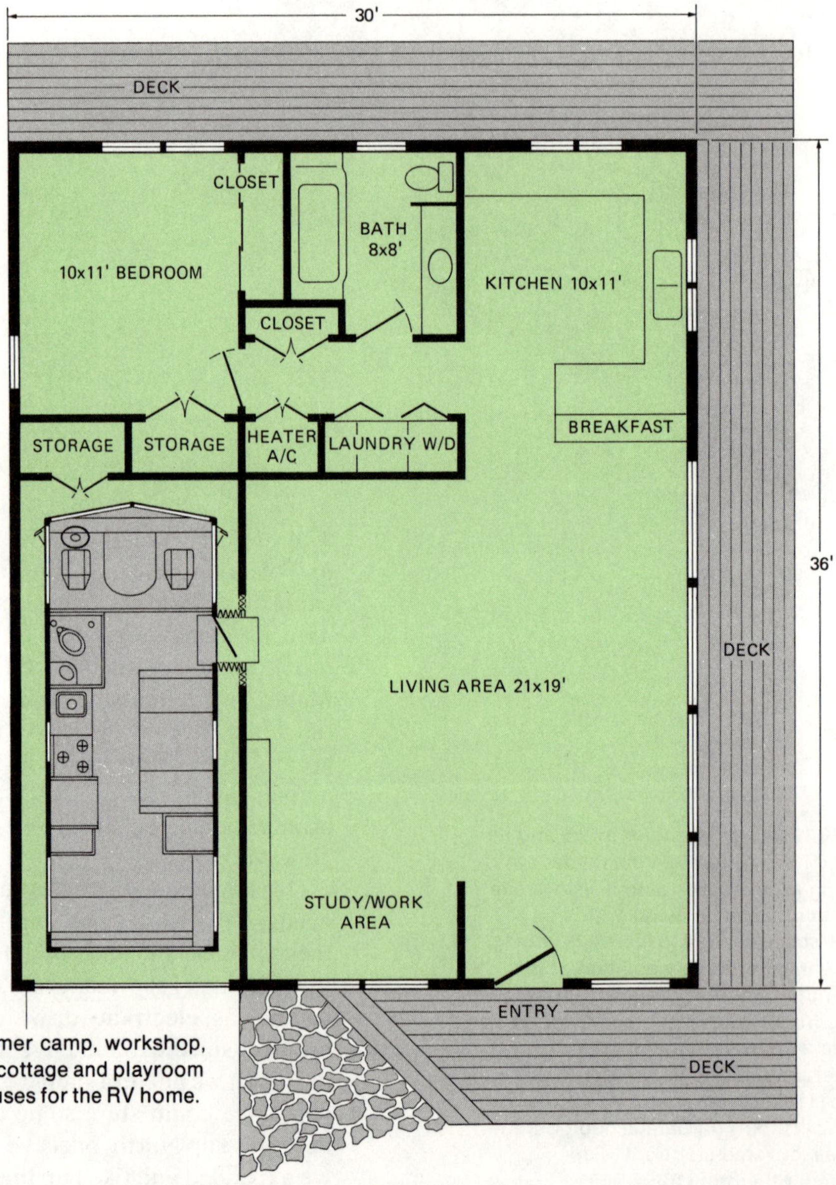


**GUEST HOUSE,** summer camp, workshop, office, mother-in-law cottage and playroom are among the many uses for the RV home.

**Replacing bulb in lighted globe**

*I have a lighted world globe on a pedestal and recently the bulb burned out. Close examination reveals no way to remove the globe from the stand or to reach the socket to replace the dead bulb. Can you enlighten me?—George Meade, Los Angeles.*

Originally, the switch, socket and bulb were installed inside the globe, so there must be a way to remove the fixture. Incidentally, remember these globes are usually of glass so proceed with care! Usually there's a pivot screw at the top—turning this out will release the globe from its peripheral support. At the bottom of the globe you'll likely find a removable flanged disc to which the socket and switch are attached. Remove this disc, replace the bulb and remount the parts in the reverse order.

Work carefully to avoid damaging the gasket between disc and bottom of the globe. When replacing the fixture, be sure to put the gasket back in the same position that you found it.

**Toothpick fillers for nail holes**

*I want to use two finely finished walnut boards in a home-shop project. Because they have a lot of small nail holes, all going clear through the wood, I'll need to stain the boards very lightly. How can I fill these holes so they won't show in the finish?—H.O., Cal.*

You didn't say what kind of walnut—black, California, French, Circassion? All these varieties differ in texture, grain and color. While I think immediately of ordinary fillers or stick shellac, I once solved a similar problem by cutting short lengths from skewer toothpicks and driving them into the holes, just flush. Then I sanded the surface and tinted the lighter ends of the toothpick plugs to match the wood. When finished, the plugs showed only under very close examination.

**Decorating narrow windows**

*How does one decorate those tall, narrow windows in an old home like mine? Two are in pairs, but two others are single. The tops are semicircular.—Mrs. Reginald Kemper, Cincinnati.*

I would think first of either cafe curtains or deep valances with drapery, with the latter being made wider than the windows and attached to the wall. This treatment will have the effect of lowering the height of the windows and at the same time promoting the feeling of width. Of course, there are several other treatments, but it seems to me that the valances would be most effective, especially in a large room.

**Gremlins in the plumbing**

*I have copper plumbing, and when I turn on the hot water there is a curious popping or snapping sound, not rapidly repeated like hammering, but more slowly and at regular intervals. I can't seem to locate it. I've thought it was in the heater, but now I'm not sure. Can you suggest the cause?—E.N., Ark.*

Plumbing noises can have more than one cause. At long range it's not always possible to say definitely what, where, or why. But I think immediately of the hot-water line passing through a partition, possibly a joist, or some other part of the structure with which it is in contact. When you open the hot-water faucet, the copper line warms quickly, expands, and the movement results in a rubbing action against whatever the line may be touching. Investigate this possibility. If my guess is correct, bending the tubing slightly to free it should stop the noise.

Also, there's a possibility that an insulating coupling was not installed at the point where the copper tubing joins the steel pipe. Electrolytic action at this point could build up a coating and gradually restrict the flow of water, although you will more likely notice a lowering of the pressure and possibly hear a hissing sound rather than the noise you describe. Still this remains a possible cause and I'd suggest you have it checked if the other trouble mentioned does not apply.

**When to prune mock orange**

*I have received conflicting opinions on the best time to prune back a large mock orange shrub. Is there any "best" time?—Harry Gray, Peoria, Ill.*

It can be pruned lightly any time, but the best time is soon after flowering, especially if much cutting is needed to reduce it to a desirable shape. Sometimes it's best to prune old or neglected shrubs in two stages: the first, right after flowering and second, wait until the next season to finish the job.

**Log-cabin chinking**

*I'm going to build a small log cabin using straight logs about 4 inches in diameter, with the bark removed and corners notched. What should I use to close the spaces between the logs?—H. Cable, Bismarck, N.D.*

Judging from your description, I assume the spaces will be minimal. If so, I'd force butyl caulking compound between the logs with a caulking gun. Do this inside and out, taking care to apply the material uniformly.

*by W. Clyde Lammey*

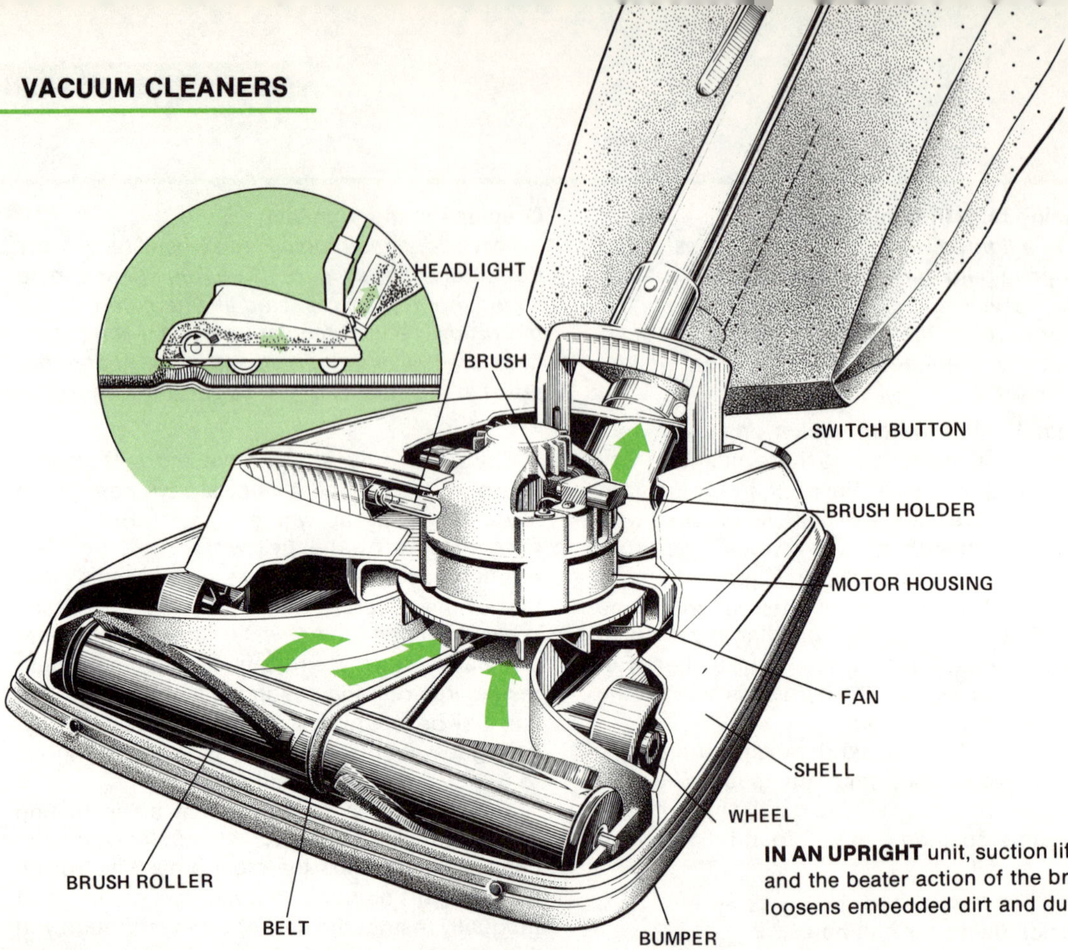


**IN AN UPRIGHT** unit, suction lifts the rug, and the beater action of the brushes loosens embedded dirt and dust.

# How to fix a vacuum cleaner

**By ED FRANZESE**

A VACUUM CLEANER is a simple appliance; with the aid of trouble-shooting charts on the following pages, you should be able to deal with most of its common problems. The machine is basically a motor-driven fan with a nozzle attached, either directly or with a hose, to its low-pressure end. Atmospheric pressure forces air into the nozzle and dirt is carried with it and on through into the bag.

There are two types: the upright and the tank or canister. The upright usually, and the tank sometimes, has a motor-driven brush to loosen embedded dirt.

Nearly all vacuum cleaners use universal motors with replaceable carbon brushes. These bear under spring pressure on the commutator; they are eventually consumed and when worn, can cause problems. Many vacuum-cleaner designs offer direct access to brushes.

SEE ALSO
**Electrical wiring . . . Testers, continuity**

You can test the suction of a hose-equipped cleaner with a vacuum gauge, available through most heating and refrigeration-supply houses; it simply plugs into the hose. Vacuum is expressed in terms of water lift—how many inches above its normal level a column of water is pulled—and between 50 and 70 in. is normal for most cleaners.

When motor armature and fan both turn freely, a malfunctioning vacuum cleaner's trouble is probably electrical. Tests are outlined on the next page. If the ohmmeter reading for the entire circuit is higher than 2-4 ohms, it may indicate poor connections; no reading (infinite resistance) may indicate an open or shorted circuit. You can also check the circuit for grounds by placing one lead of the ohmmeter or continuity tester on one plug prong and the other on any *metal* part of the cleaner, then doing the same with the other prong. There should be no readings. Most cleaners have one or more capacitors across the circuit to eliminate radio interference; if a short or ground is indicated, remove the capacitor and retest. If the short or ground disappears, replace the capacitor with one of exactly the same value.

## Motor will not run

| POSSIBLE CAUSES | WHAT TO TRY |
|---|---|
| 1. Fuse blown or circuit breaker tripped. | Replace fuse or reset circuit breaker. If blowing or tripping is repeated, disconnect power and check for shorts. |
| 2. Line cord defective. | Inspect cord for breaks or fraying. Check for continuity by removing cord at terminals; placing one lead of tester on plug prong, other on corresponding terminal wire, flex cord. There should be an uninterrupted reading. Repeat for other prong, wire. Replace cord if there is no reading or flexing cord interrupts reading. |
| 3. Switch defective. | Place continuity-tester leads on switch terminals; turn switch on. There should be a reading. Turn switch off. There should be no reading. Replace switch if there is variation. |
| 4. Connection loose at terminal block. | Check all terminal-block connections; tighten any found loose. |
| 5. Motor brushes worn or sticking. | Check lengths of brushes. Replace them if ¼ in. or shorter. Check for free brush movement in holder. If tight, sand brushes just enough to make them slide easily. |
| 6. Armature shorted or open. | Place ohmmeter test leads on brush holders, rotate armature manually. Resistance reading should remain fairly constant. Sharp decrease indicates short, infinite reading indicates open. Replace armature in either case; new motor may be required. |
| 7. Fan jammed. | Check for obstructions, clear. Replace fan if bent or damaged. |
| 8. Motor bearings frozen. | Disassemble motor, clean and lubricate bearings. Replace bearings if worn. |
| 9. Motor defective. | Disconnect both motor leads; direct test with 110-v. jumpers. Replace motor if defective. |

## Straight-suction upright

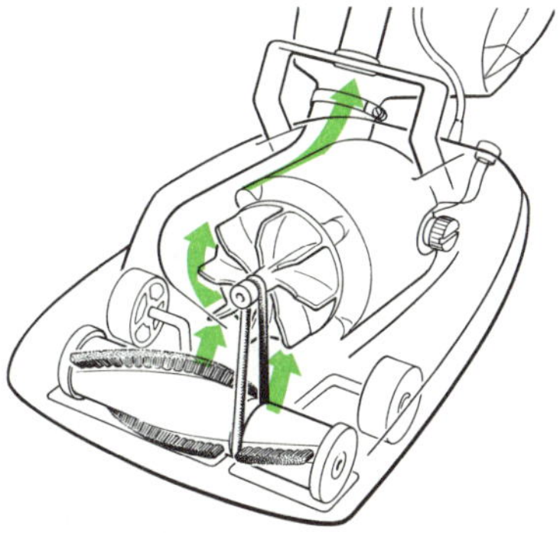

## Typical brush assembly

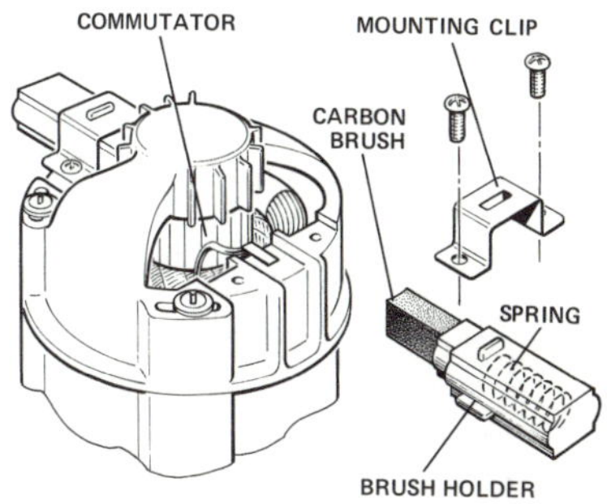


## Motor stops and starts

| POSSIBLE CAUSES | WHAT TO TRY |
|---|---|
| 1. Intermittent break in line cord. | Shake cord while vacuum is running; inspect for wear. Test continuity as explained above. |
| 2. Loose connection. | Check entire circuit; tighten all connections. |
| 3. Switch defective. | Test switch as explained above. |
| 4. Wiring shorted. | Locate short, repair, insulate with electrical tape. |

*please turn the page*

## Motor runs too slowly

| POSSIBLE CAUSES | WHAT TO TRY |
|---|---|
| 1. Bearings tight or misaligned. | Disassemble motor; check, realign and lubricate bearings. Replace bearings if worn. |
| 2. Fan jammed. | See chart, "Motor will not run" (above). |
| 3. Brush contact poor. | Check brush length as in chart, "Motor will not run." If length is okay, stretch brush springs slightly. |

### Typical tank-type cleaner

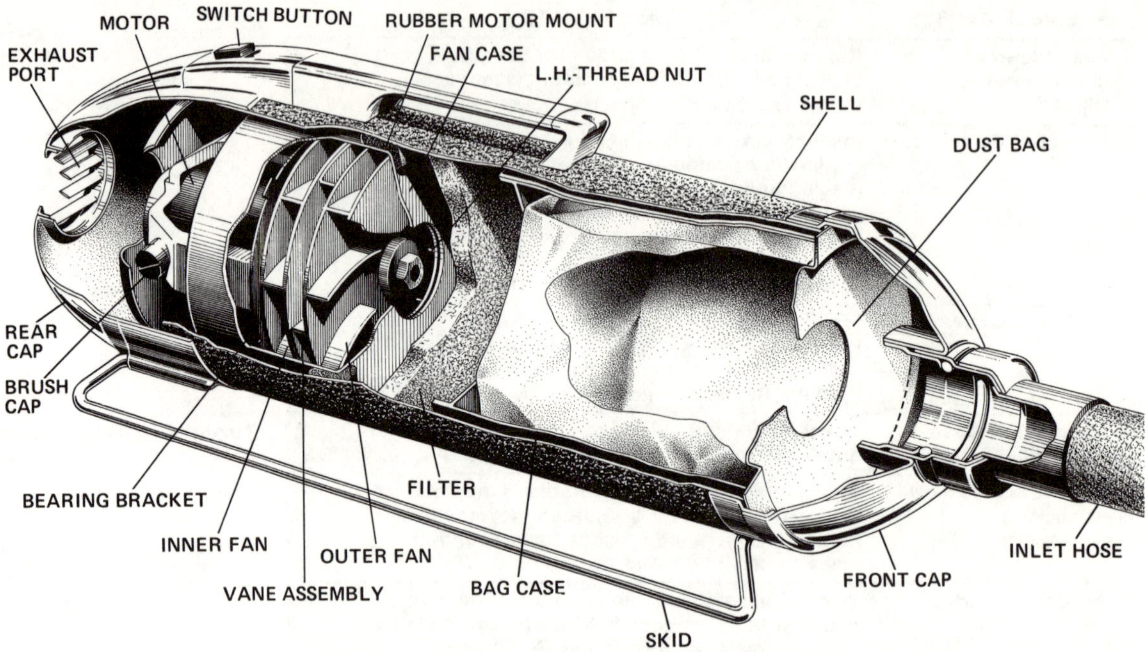


### Motor runs too fast

| POSSIBLE CAUSES | WHAT TO TRY |
|---|---|
| 1. Fan loose. | Check and tighten fan. |
| 2. Armature shorted. | See chart, "Motor will not run." |
| 3. Dust bag overloaded. | Replace or clean bag. |

### Motor sparks

| POSSIBLE CAUSES | WHAT TO TRY |
|---|---|
| 1. Commutator dirty. | Clean thoroughly with trichlorethylene, sand with 2/0 or finer sandcloth. |
| 2. Brushes worn. | See chart, "Motor will not run." |
| 3. Brushes new. | Normal. Sparking will diminish when new brushes wear to shape of armature. |
| 4. Armature wire open. | See chart, "Motor will not run." |

### Motor is noisy

| POSSIBLE CAUSES | WHAT TO TRY |
|---|---|
| 1. Foreign matter. | Clean out motor. |
| 2. Brushes new. | Normal. Noise will diminish when new brushes wear. |
| 3. Armature obstructed. | Check armature bearings for misalignment or wear; realign or replace. |
| 4. Fan bent or loose. | Check fan, tighten on shaft. Replace fan if blades are bent. |

## Suction is weak

| POSSIBLE CAUSES | WHAT TO TRY |
|---|---|
| 1. Attachment or hose connection loose. | Check hose, attachments to make sure connections are tight. |
| 2. Obstruction in hose or attachment. | Check for large pieces of paper, pins, wads of lint, and clear. |
| 3. Cover loose. | Check for correct insertion of bag. Adjust and reclose cover. |
| 4. Bag overloaded. | Replace or clean bag. |
| 5. Hose leaking. | Check entire length of hose for cracks, holes. Replace hose if any are found. Also check for tight connections between hose, tank and attachments. |
| 6. Exhaust port clogged. | Clear exhaust port. |
| 7. Belt broken. | (Upright models.) Replace belt. |
| 8. Agitator brush jammed. | (Upright models.) Clear brush of all foreign matter—brush should turn freely. |
| 9. Nozzle setting wrong. | Check nozzle setting according to manufacturer's instructions for type of cleaning being done. |

## Dust leaks into room

| POSSIBLE CAUSES | WHAT TO TRY |
|---|---|
| 1. Holes in dust bag. | Replace bag. |
| 2. Bag installed incorrectly. | Check manufacturer's instructions for correct installation of bag. |
| 3. Sealing gasket defective or leaking. | Check gasket, replace if worn or broken. Also check gasket alignment where cleaner opens for insertion and removal of bag. |
| 4. Bag overloaded. | Replace or clean bag. |

## Electrical tests

Place test leads across: 1. A and G to test entire circuit (should be 2-4 ohms); 2. A and B, G and H to test line cord (there should be continuity in each leg); 3. C and D to test switch; 4. E and F, I and J to test field coils (there should be continuity in each); 5. I or E and motor case to test for shorts (there should be no continuity); 6. F and J to test armature, turning it by hand (resistance reading should be constant). Tests 1 and 6 require ohmmeter; rest can be done with continuity tester. Power must be disconnected for *all* tests.

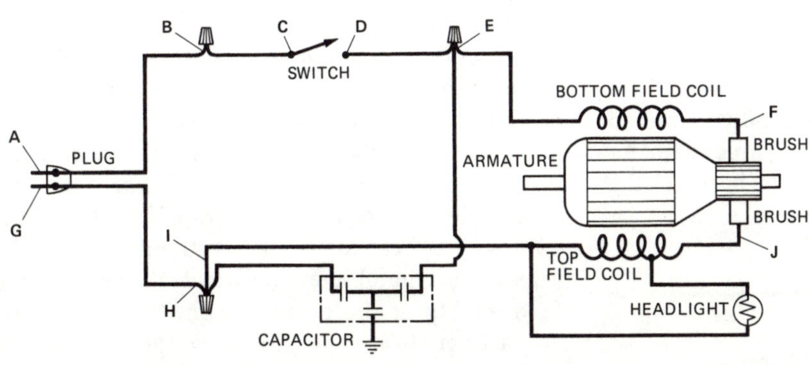


## Canister variations

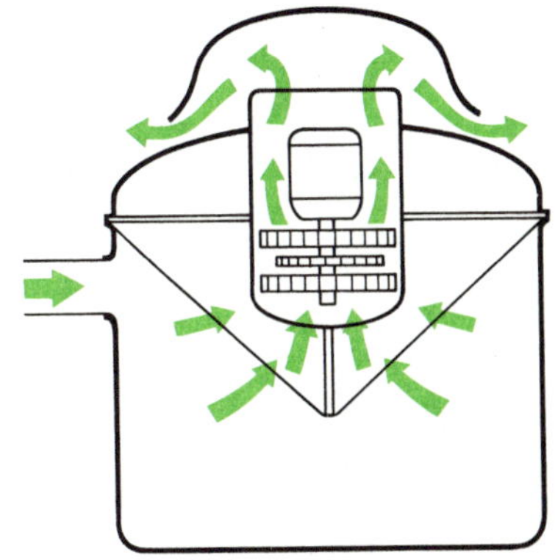

TOP-MOUNTED MOTOR (SHOP VACUUMS)

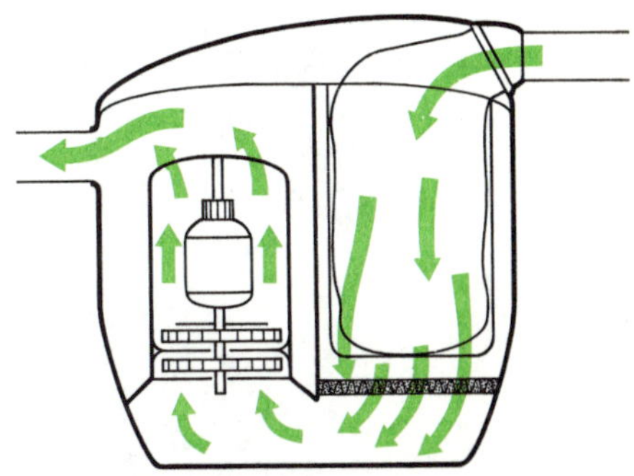

SIDE-MOUNTED MOTOR

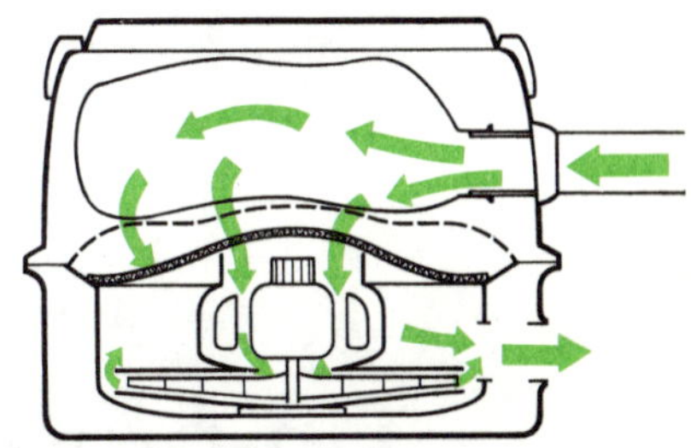

BOTTOM-MOUNTED MOTOR

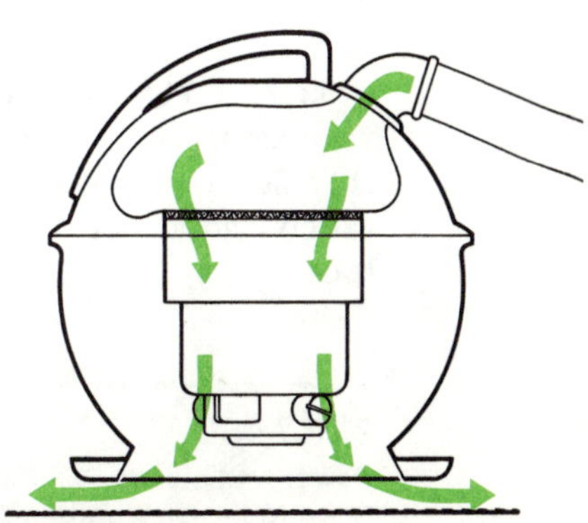

AIR CUSHION

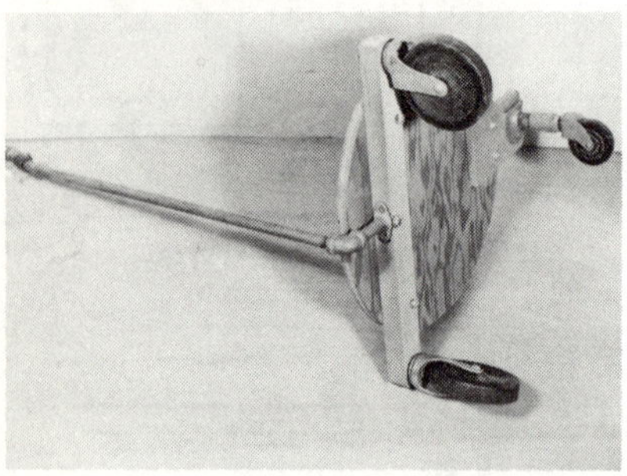

## MATERIALS LIST—VACUUM DOLLY

| Key | No. | Size and description (use) |
|---|---|---|
| A | 1 | ¾ x 17⅝″ dia. plywood (base) |
| B | 1 | ¾ x 4½ x 8″ pine (small caster support) |
| C | 2 | 5/4 x 2 x 20½″ pine** (caster support) |
| D | 1 | ¾″ IPT x 3″ dia. stem-type caster* |
| E | 1 | ¾″ IPT connector* |
| F | 1 | ¾″ IPT nipple* |
| G | 1 | ¾″ IPT floor flange* |
| H | 3 | ¼-20 x 1½″ machine screw, nut, washer* |
| I | 3 | ¼-20 x 2″ machine screw, nut and washer* |
| J | 2 | 5/4 x 2 x 5″ pine** |
| K | 2 | ¼-20 x 3″ fh machine screw, nut and washer** |
| L | 2* or 4** | 6″ dia. plate or stem-type caster |
| M | 3* or 5** | ¼-20 x 2½″ machine screw, nut, washer |
| N | 1 | ½″ IPT waste nut |
| O | 1 | ½″ IPT x 2¾″ nipple |
| P | 1 | ½″ IPT x 90° elbow |
| Q | 1 | ½″ IPT pipe, length to suit |
| R | 1 | ½″ IPT x 45° elbow |
| S | 1 | ½″ IPT x 6″ pipe (thread one end only) |
| T | 1 | ¾″ IPT connector |
| U | 1 | ⅛ x ½ x 2″ strap iron |
| V | 2 | No. 6-32 x ¼″ rh machine screw |
| W | 1 | No. 10-32 thumb screw |
| X | 2 | ¼-20 x 3″ fh machine screw, nut, washer |

*3-wheel dolly only **4-wheel dolly only

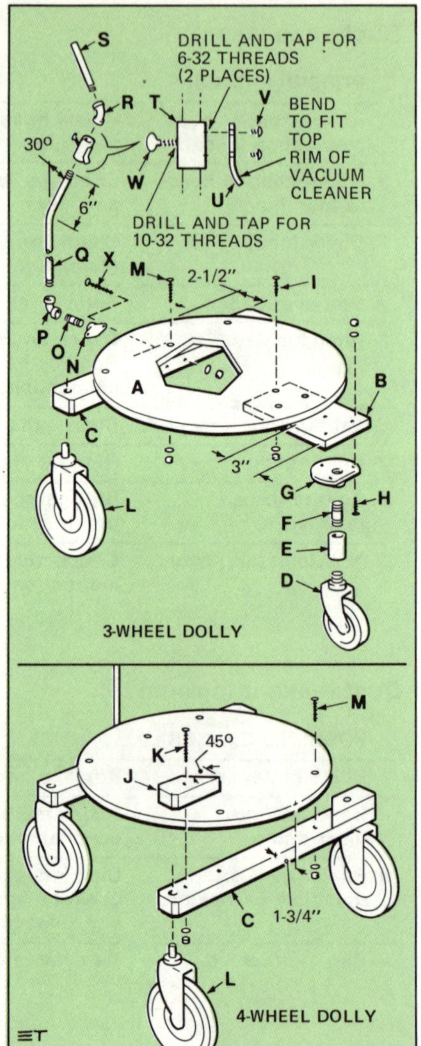


# Tip-proof vacuum dollies

■ THE TWO VACUUM dollies shown here were designed to roll over typically cluttered shop floors without tipping over. Large-diameter casters and a wide span between wheels do the trick.

SEE ALSO
**Power-tool stands . . . Safety, workshop . . . Shop tools . . . Workbenches . . . Workshops**

Construction is basically the same for both versions. First cut the plywood disc to the diameter of the recess in the bottom of your shop vacuum. If your vacuum has no recess or if you desire extra stability, plan to add the retaining blocks (J) shown on the four-wheel dolly.

Cut the caster-support members and bolt them to the plywood disc. Install the casters and check to be sure the dolly platform is level:

To install the rim-clamp assembly, drill and tap connector (T) as shown and *slide* it onto the upright pipe (Q). Attach strap iron (U), which has been bent to suit the vacuum's top rim. Install the thumbscrew (W) to lock the clamping assembly at the proper height. To remove the vacuum from the dolly, simply loosen the thumbscrew and slide the connector and strap clamp off the rim.

# Varnish basics

**CORRECT WAY** to hold a varnish brush—much like you grasp a pencil.

■ FOR SEVERAL reasons I think that varnish is the best finish choice for home craftsmen:

■ Varnish does not dry too quickly, so you have plenty of time for achieving a smooth surface.

■ It gives a durable, tough finish that resists water, alcohol and many other chemicals.

There are some minor drawbacks with varnish, however:

■ Because it takes time to set up, more dust will settle on varnish than on a fast-drying finish like shellac.

■ Though it goes on clear, varnish does have the tendency to darken with age.

For some reason, several veteran craftsmen I know have resisted the newer polyurethane varnishes. They shouldn't. Happily, major varnish manufacturers have introduced a wide selection of finishes in the urethanes ranging from high gloss to an antique-like low luster.

By HARRY WICKS

**SEALER COAT** of shellac should be thinned 50 percent with denatured alcohol. It can then be sprayed on to uniformly seal the surface.

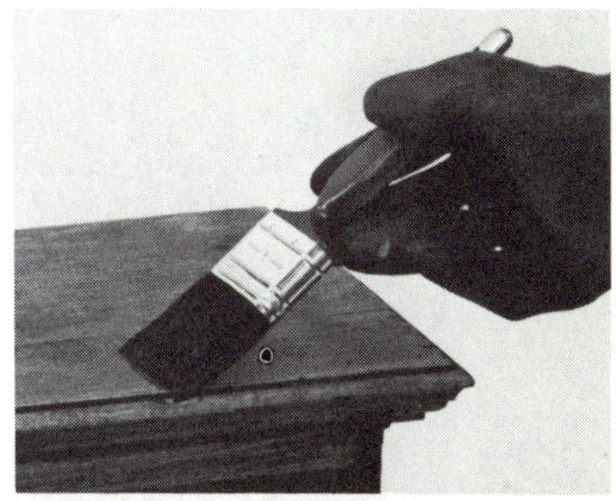

**BRUSH ON** liberal amounts of varnish using with-the-grain strokes.

**THEN LEVEL** the varnish with the brush by using strokes across the grain.

**WHEN DRY,** sealer is rubbed lightly with 00 steel wool.

**PARTICLES** left by steel wool are then brushed off using a clean brush.

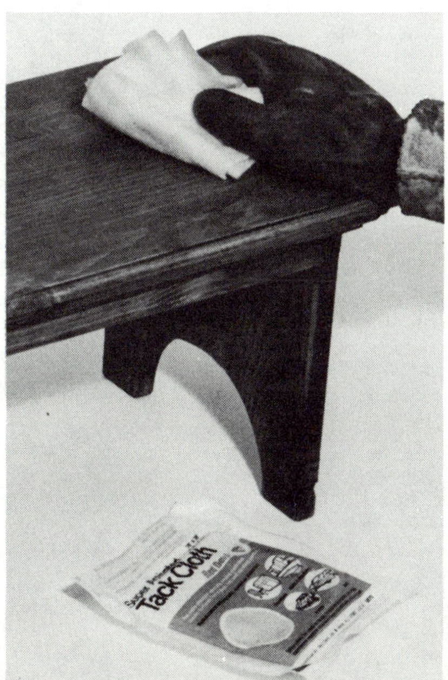


**FINAL** preparation step is to wipe all surfaces with a tack cloth.

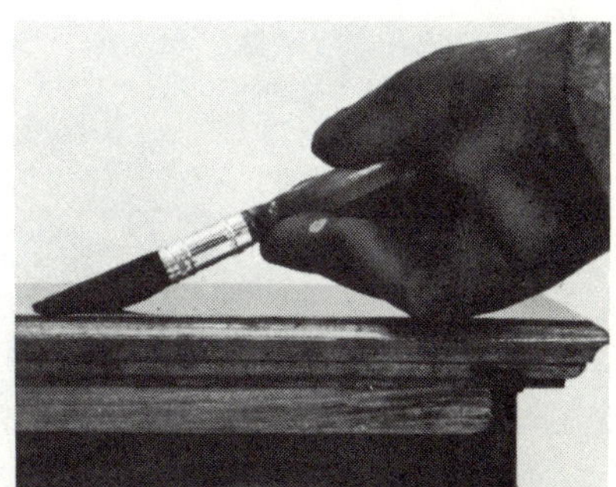

**FINISH BY** "tipping off"—drawing almost-dry brush across surface at 30°.

# Extend your growing season with a hotbed

By JOSEPH R. PROVEY

I LOVE TO RAISE my own vegetables—and I've come up with a way to continue growing them late into the fall. In the spring, I'll have my first garden-grown salad earlier than ever before.

I call the unit which performs these feats a "season-extender," because it extends both ends of the growing season. In the fall, it will protect a patch of vegetables from the sudden killer frost that cuts off much of my garden production in its prime.

Similarly, the unit will enable my plants to tap the early sunshine of March and April without the risk of being stunted by cold nights and the vagaries of spring weather. And it incorporates hardware that even veteran gardeners may want to add to an existing hotbed, cold frame or greenhouse.

The main difference between the season-extender and a conventional cold frame is an automatically controlled lid to assure proper ventilation. The Thermofor vent control eliminates the possibility of forgetting to raise or lower the lid. Ventilation is important because solar radiation, even when the air temperature outside is cool, can quickly raise the air temperature inside the season-extender to a dangerous level for young seedlings. The reverse is also true. A quick drop in air temperature can stunt seedlings.

The unit's walls are insulated with 1-in.-thick rigid Styrofoam panels to help retain heat. The lid is covered with AirCap, a translucent plastic with closed-cell air bubbles that reduce the rate of heat loss through the lid by about 50 percent (over commonly used plastic films and window glass). Vinyl foam weatherstripping tape assures a tight seal between the lid and frame.

Knockdown design permits compact, off-season storage. Interlocking corner joints make the entire frame easy to disassemble.

The season-extender can be used in at least four different ways. You can extend the growing season of a specially-planted, fall-winter crop if

**PROP WITH NOTCH** holds lid open for watering or while you work in the bed. For extensive bed preparation, simply move the unit aside temporarily.

SEE ALSO
**Benches, potting . . . Cold frames . . .
Dryers, food . . . Gardening . . . House plants . . .
Shears, gardening . . . Transplanting . . .
Yard lighting**

**HOTBED OR** "season-extender" holds seedlings for a typical 250-sq.-ft. vegetable garden, with room left over to start several trays of flowers.

**NOTICE THAT IN** this photo the south-facing unit has its lid partially opened. This is accomplished with an automatic vent control.

**AS GROWING NEEDS** change, it's a simple task to move the season-extender and use it in a new location.

**AUTOMATIC** vent control is activated by expansion of heat-sensitive compound inside cylinder.

you build the bed for an August planting. Include rutabaga, bush beans, peas, radishes, lettuce, spinach and any other cool-weather crop that can fit within a 33x76-in. area. Plant the taller varieties in the back where they have more room to climb and will not block the sunlight from low-growing vegetables. When the nights begin to turn cold in October, position the sea-

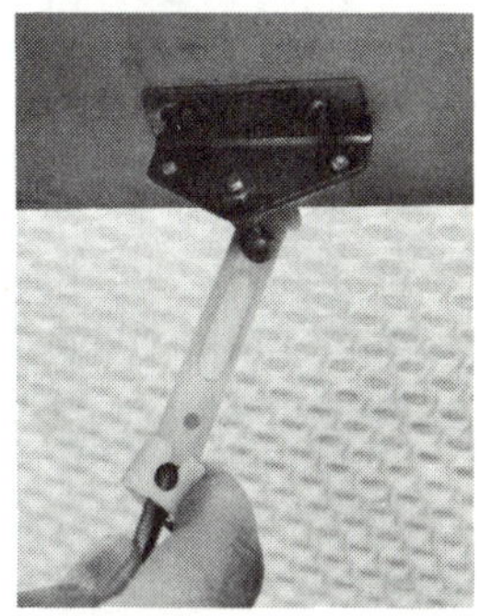

**PUSH ROD** connects arm to lid bracket at ball-and-socket joint. Retaining cuff slides over the joint to secure it.

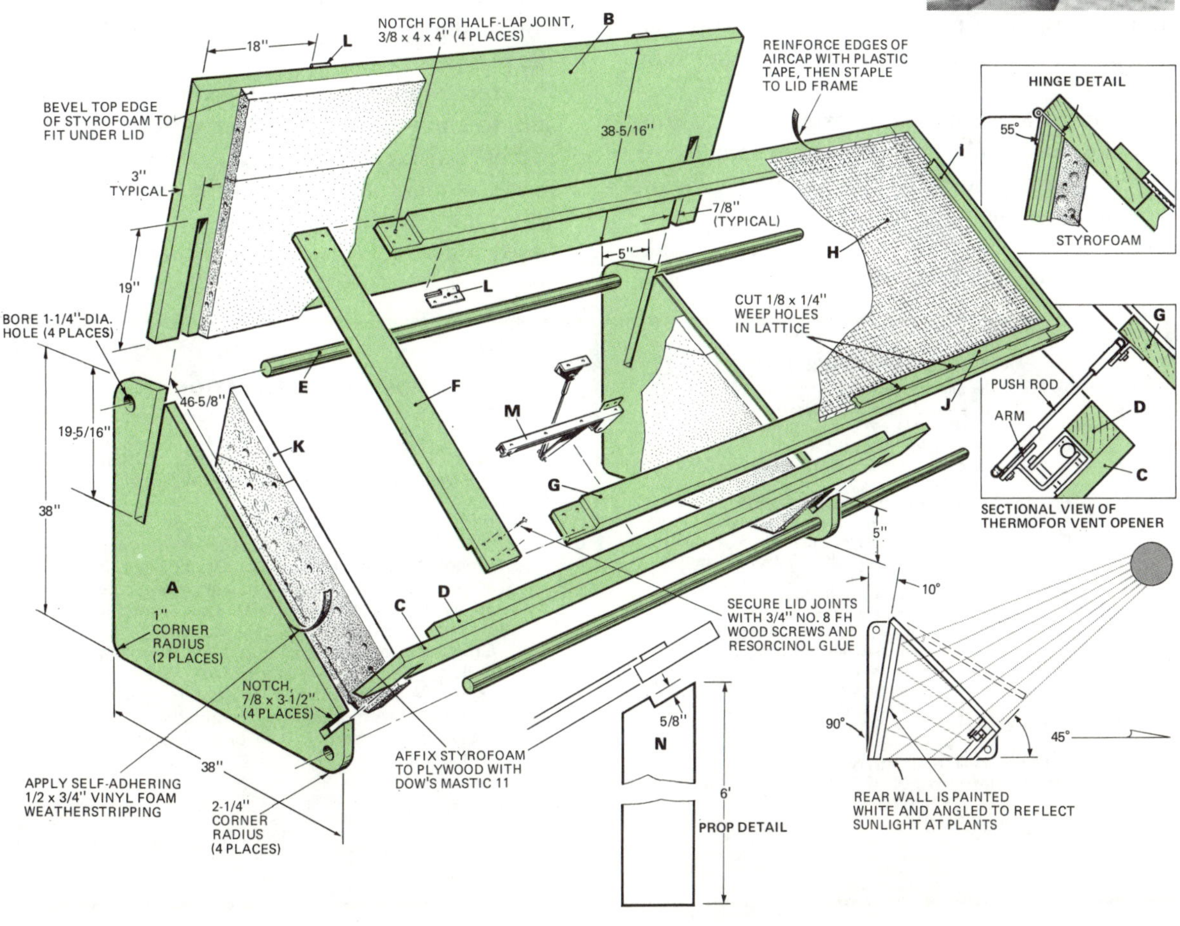

son-extender over the bed and see how much longer this patch will produce.

In the spring, use the unit as a hotbed to start seedlings early. A hotbed requires a heat source other than the sun, such as decomposing manure or soil-heating cables. I chose cables because they last many years and produce even, thermostatically controlled heat.

Instead of a hotbed application, you may choose to make the most of the frame's portability by using it as a "direct-plant" cold frame in the spring. Put it in the garden as soon as the ground can be prepared and sow hardy crops like spinach, lettuce, cabbage, broccoli, cauliflower, Brussels sprouts and radishes. When the patch is well established, move the extender and use it to give a bed of less hardy plants like tomatoes, zucchini, melons or peppers an early start.

Finally, an extender abutted to the south wall of a house and provided with soil-heating cables can be used as a miniature greenhouse to winter over many house, patio and yard plants. If your climate is mild, you may be able to use the season-extender to continue growing vegetables throughout the winter. For cold weather use, disconnect the automatic vent and provide a glass or clear plastic lid in addition to the AirCap material. The rigid lid material is required to protect the plastic bubble film from tearing under snow loads.

Begin building the season-extender by cutting out the four walls and prop from two 4x8-ft. sheets of plywood. Lay out completely before you start cutting. Cut notches as shown in the plans, using a handsaw or circular saw to make parallel cuts and a chisel to knock out waste. Bore holes for the lifters and use a sabre saw to round off the corners. Next, center the Thermofor mounting cleat (D) on the front wall and fasten with 2-in. No. 10 fh wood screws.

To insulate, first transpose the dimensions of the inside wall surfaces onto the Styrofoam. Use the inner edges of the notches as guides. Shorten the length of the back sections by 2 in. in order to form corner butt joints. Use a hollow-ground blade in a sabre saw for cutting the Styrofoam. Insulating the low, front wall is optional—in any case, do not allow it to interfere with the operation of the Thermofor unit.

Next, build the lid frame. I ripped 4-in. boards from one 12-ft. length of 1x10. Cut half-lap joints and assemble as shown.

A protective finish on all wood members is extremely important. Fill all gaps and knotholes with wood putty and exterior paint. I used three coats of Flecto's White Gloss Varathane. Sand and recoat with paint every other year or as needed.

The Styrofoam insulation should also be painted. It deteriorates after prolonged exposure to sunlight. Use *water-based* exterior latex paint only. (Solvent-based coatings will dissolve insulation.) White gloss is best for maximum reflection of sunlight off the back and sides, and onto the plants.

Before slipping the unit together, use a candle stub to apply a coating of wax inside notches to prevent sticking. With walls assembled, affix pieces of rigid insulation to the plywood walls with Dow's Mastic 11 or with a suitable water-based adhesive. *Do not use petroleum-based adhesives.*

**MATERIALS LIST—PM'S HOTBED**

| Key | Pcs. | Size and description (use) |
|---|---|---|
| A | 2 | ¾″ plywood—see plans (sides) |
| B | 1 | ¾ x 38-5/16″ x 7′ plywood (back) |
| C | 1 | ¾ x 7″ x 7′ plywood (front) |
| D | 1 | 1½ x 1½ x 73″ fir (mounting cleat for Thermofor) |
| E | 2 | 1⅛″-dia. x 8′ fir closet pole (lifters) |
| F | 2 | ¾ x 4 x 46⅝″ clear pine (lid framing) |
| G | 2 | ¾ x 4 x 78″ clear pine (lid framing) |
| H | 1 | 4 x 7′ (approx.) heavy duty, C-240, AirCap |
| I | 2 | ¼ x 1⅛ x 41⅜″ pine (lattice) |
| J | 2 | ¼ x 1⅛ x 78½″ pine (lattice) |
| K | 3 | 1″ x 2′ x 8′ Styrofoam (wall insulation) |
| L | 2 | 3½ x 3½″ loose-joint, loose-pin steel hinges |
| M | 1 | Thermofor unit assembly, mounting hardware |
| N | 1 | ¾ x 4″ x 6′ plywood (prop) |

Misc: 6 2″ No. 10 fh wood screws; 16 ¾″ No. 8 fh wood screws; ⅜″ staples; 1¼″ brads; Dow's Mastic 11; resorcinol glue; ½ x ¾″ x 21′ foam tape weatherstripping; ext. white gloss, alkyd or urethane type paint; ext. white gloss latex paint.

Note: All plywood is ¾″ AC or CD exterior grade.

**SHOPPING INFORMATION**

Thermofor unit is available from Bramen Co., Inc., Box 70, Salem, Mass. 01970, or Garden Way, Charlotte, Vt. 05445. It has a five-year warranty and costs $49.50 postpaid.

Write to Sealed Air Corp., Park 80, Plaza East, Saddle Brook, N.J. 07662 for address of nearest AirCap distributor. Or look for it at greenhouse plant supply houses where it's used as a packaging material. Buy extra for replacement as required.

Gro-Quick cables are made by Wrap-On Co., Inc., 341 West Superior St., Chicago, Ill. 60610. Available at garden centers in several lengths with attached thermostat. A 48 ft. cable costs about $10.50 and is replaced free if it fails.

Assemble the lid with screws and resorcinol glue. The AirCap should be installed with bubbles down.

You may substitute a double layer of transparent plastic film for the AirCap. In either case, keep the edges from tearing by lining the inside edges of the lid with plastic tape, stapled in place. Nail lattice strips over the tape and staples, using 1¼-in. brads, 16 in. apart (16 in. on centers). Finish construction by installing hinges, weatherstripping and the Thermofor unit. You might use the leftover plywood to build an inside divider so one section can be used with heating cables, the other without, if desired.

## HOW TO MAKE A PERMANENT HOTBED INSTALLATION

If you don't have an outdoor receptacle, think about installing one for use with your hotbed—and for any other yard tasks requiring electrical power. If you're locating the unit near the house, choose a south-facing wall and mount the outlet on the structure. If installation is away from the house, mount it on a pipe as shown below. Dig a trench and bury UF cable; pass cable through a hole in the basement wall or header joist. Connect circuit to the nearest inside junction box that can handle additional load.

The National Electric Code requires ground-fault circuit interrupter (GFCI) protection for all outdoor installations. GFCIs are available at electrical supply houses and must be installed according to manufacturer's directions. Check with your town electrical inspector before you begin. Call in a licensed electrician if you doubt your wiring ability.

### laying soil-heating cables

Begin by digging a 10-in.-deep pit with the same dimensions as the bottom of your season-extender. Spread a 4-in.-thick layer of pea gravel and sand. Then make an insulated floor with the leftover scraps of Styrofoam. Attach heating cables (see below) with thermostat to insulation and cover with 1 in. of a soil-humus mixture, hardware cloth and more planting medium until the pit is full. Grade the planting surface slightly to slope southward.

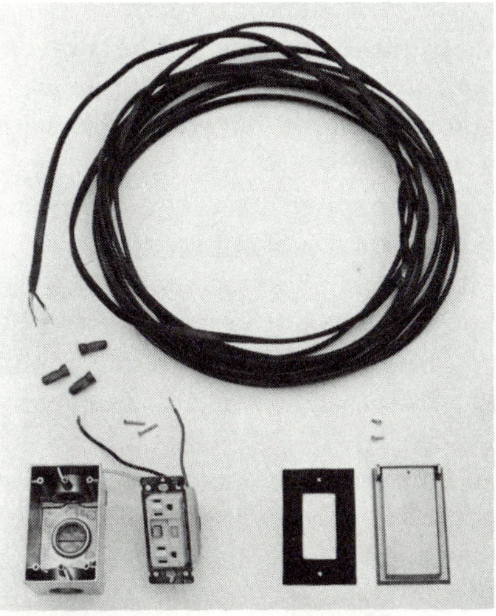

**FOR SAFE** yard/garden outlet you need: a UL-listed outdoor junction box, G.F.C.I. receptacle, weatherproof coverplate with gasket and direct-burial cable.

**USE PLASTIC** tape or insulated tacks to hold soil-heating cables in parallel loops. Maintain 3-in. intervals.

**PVC MAY BE** used for conduit. To join, clean off dust and burrs, pretest fit. Give ¼-in. twist after applying cement.

**COVER HEATING** wires with 1-in. layer of sand or soil: add hardware cloth for protection from misdirected spade.

### OUTDOOR RECEPTACLE INSTALLATION

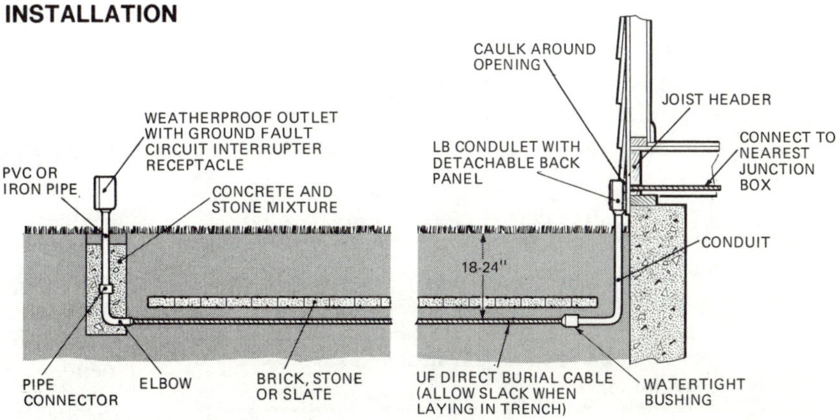

# How to keep varmints out of your vegetable patch

By GLENN HENSLEY

FIRST, LET'S DETERMINE just who your enemies are out on the "garden front." Here's a rundown on 10 of the most common pests and the most effective means you can use to discourage their attacks.

### 1. underground prowlers

Burrowing beneath the surface of the soil, moles create their labyrinths of interconnecting travel tubes. Actually, they aren't after your plants. They want a hearty meal of worms and insects. But in their searching and tunneling, they can dislodge more plant roots in a minute than healthy seed can sprout in a month.

Agricultural and conservation authorities say the best mole control is accomplished by trapping. Choker traps and harpoon traps have proven adequate for the task. The best time to trap is in early spring when the first mole ridges appear.

Find the active mole runways by mashing down the ridges where the runs have entered the edge of your garden. Watch to see which ones the moles will raise again. You can assume that the rebuilt runways are in regular use, so start your trapping there. Install either the harpoon or choker-type trap at those points according to instructions that come with the devices. Such traps are easy to set and are available at hardware stores and garden supply centers.

### 2. the 'friendly' cottontail

And now for another "enemy." He's bouncing along the edge of your garden, flashing a fuzzy white tail, and he's looking for just one thing—a free meal, courtesy of you and your garden.

Rabbits do more damage to the actual plants than do moles, for a cottontail likes to chomp on stems and leaves of vegetables.

So here's your battle plan: Try wire guards around individual plants if you have the room for them. Hardware cloth, also known as chicken wire, works well. Make the guards high enough so that a rabbit can't stand up on his hind legs and reach his lunch.

Repellents can help you cut damage, too. Area or odor repellents, though, are not very effective. These might include mothballs, creosote oil and similar substances. Apparently a rabbit's "taster" is more sensitive than his "smeller," for taste repellents are much more effective in sending him scooting.

During the growing season, you can discourage rabbits by spraying nicotine sulfate on your garden. Add half a teaspoon of 40-percent nicotine sulfate to one quart of water. You may also wish to try one, or several, of the commercially prepared repellents that are available through garden supply stores. Some of these are:

*No Nib'l* can be dusted on or it can be sprayed. The can has a shaker top for dusting. If you want to spray, mix the contents of the 6-ounce can with 2½ gallons of water.

*Improved Z.I.P.* is sprayed on. Use one quart of the material to 7 quarts of water.

*Arasan 75* is another spray-on repellent. Add one quart Rhoplex AG-33 or Latex 512R to 14½ quarts of water. Mix thoroughly with one pound of Arasan 75. Strain and then stir frequently while using.

*Arasan 42-S* sprayed on works well. Add one pint Rhoplex AG-33 or Latex 512R to 7 quarts of water. Mix thoroughly with one pint of Arasan 42-S. Mix only enough repellent for immediate use as the solids settle after standing several days and you'll have trouble getting them to resuspend. It may be necessary to spray frequently in order to cover new growth.

SEE ALSO
Benches, potting . . . Cold frames . . .
Dryers, food . . . Gardening . . . House plants . . .
Strawberry barrels . . . Transplanting . . .
Yard lighting

*Caution:* Do not treat your vegetables after edible portions have started to form on beans, cabbages, lettuce and the like as the repellents may be caught in them and retained. If they are, more than the rabbits will be "repelled."

Make life tough on your rabbit-type moochers. Cleanly cultivate the area around your garden, removing brush piles and heavy wood growth. This takes away a rabbit's natural cover and tends to reduce his desire to hang around for a handout. And don't forget that conservationists recommend intensive hunting (where legal and safe) as a measure to keep rabbit numbers within reasonable limits.

A final weapon in your rabbit arsenal is a good box trap. This is a humane method because you don't kill the animal. You take the trap far away in the woods and release your catch without harm.

### 3. gophers go for food

If you're in gopher country, you know these small ground squirrels "go fer" roots, fruits, seeds and leafy garden vegetation. Their favorite food-hunting sport is digging up recently planted vegetable seeds. They seem to like sweet corn best.

Control measures include the use of poisoned bait. If you expect to use this tricky stuff, you'll be wise to talk to your local agricultural extension service personnel (state college of agriculture people) for advice on handling. When *correctly* distributed, there is little hazard to beneficial wildlife or livestock.

Ground squirrels can be gassed with calcium cyanide, but this, too, is a highly dangerous substance and should be used only with extreme caution. It releases deadly hydrocyanic acid into their burrows (upon contact with air) and that's a powerful gas.

Trapping is your safest method for eliminating ground squirrels. Either No. O steel traps or regular wooden-based rat traps can be placed in shallow pits near burrow entrances. Lure your victim to the traps by sprinkling small amounts of grain on the thin layer of dirt covering the trap trigger.

### 4. the masked villain

Raccoons come, all dressed for the part, as they make like robbers and steal from your growing garden. They like corn, especially when the ears are in the milk stage.

Raccoons are easy to catch with traps that don't kill. However, if you want to go after them with a vengeance you can use No. 2 double-coil-spring fox traps. Several kinds of "sets" are successfully used, but the "dirt hole" is probably the best.

Set the trap about a ½ inch below the ground, one or two feet from the side of a coon trail alongside the garden. Cover lightly with sifted soil. Cover the trap pan with a piece of tissue or canvas to prevent dirt from getting under it and locking it open. Dig a small hole about 6 inches deep and 3 inches across at a slant just behind the trap. Raccoons are attracted to such a set by the use of a gland lure in the dirt hole in winter and early spring and by the use of a food lure the rest of the year. Both lures are available from trapping equipment suppliers.

You can also try using a steel-cage live-trap, baiting it with some freshly cut corn. If your coons are familiar with human scent, you may catch the culprit this way. In his trap, transport him far enough away so that when you release him, unharmed, he'll have to find someone else's garden to plunder.

Ordinary fencing will not keep raccoons from your garden. If they can't go under it or through it, they'll wiggle themselves over it. However, since raccoons prefer late lunches—in the dark—you can sometimes deter them by hanging some lights around the garden. The more movement the lights have, the better, but don't count on this method for 100-percent success.

Oil of mustard is obnoxious to animals—as well as to most gardeners. If you can stand the stuff, you can mix one ounce of oil of mustard and one ounce of household detergent with one gallon of water. Spray applications at three-day intervals may be necessary to stop persistent raccoon raids. Don't spray directly on sweet corn ears, but treat the ground around the stalks late in the evening.

### 5. opossums aren't choosy

Opossums will eat practically anything. If they're plaguing your garden, you'll have to trap them. Repellents seem to have little effect on these night prowlers. No. 1½ or No. 2 steel traps, set in natural or artificial openings in their den areas, will "stop them in their tracks." For bait, use meat scraps, fish or moist dog food.

### 6. pets can be pests, too

Ordinary domestic animals can wreak havoc in your garden when the neighbor's pooch chases your cat through your pumpkin patch. Control? Probably a strong fence, or maybe a permanent leash for both of the villains.

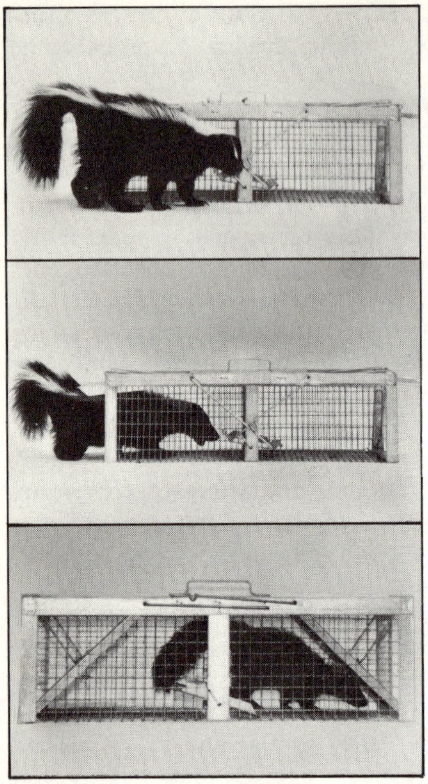

**METAL HAVAHART TRAPS** come in sizes that will accommodate anything from a mouse to a fox. For a free booklet on humane trapping, write: Allcock Manufacturing Co., North Water St., Ossining, NY.

**SIMPLE BOX TRAP** for rabbits and other small animals can be made from scrap wood.

BOX TRAP

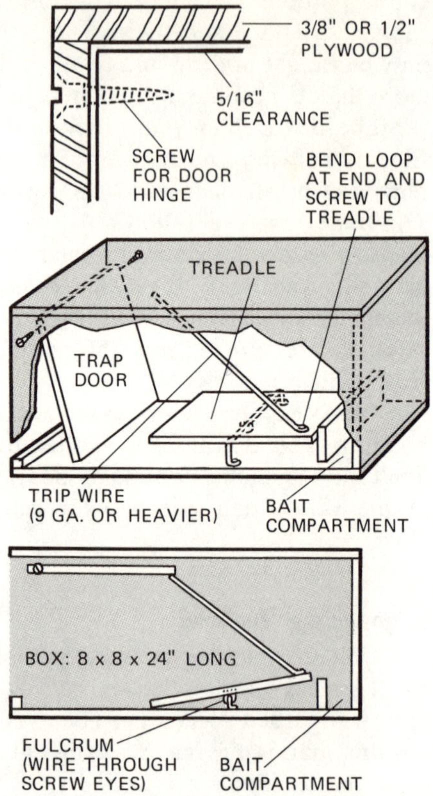


**7. would you believe turtles?**

Box turtles thrive on tomatoes, especially those found lying directly on the ground. You can foil this mobile-homed nomad of nature by driving four or five-foot stakes alongside tomato plants and then carefully tying the plants up to keep the tomatoes off the ground.

**8. scaring away squirrels**

Red and gray squirrels have been known to nibble at garden vegetables, too. Try tying aluminum pie tins to stakes so they flash and clatter in the wind. Only the most persistent, most hungry squirrel will risk his bushy tail amid such a clanking commotion.

**9. dealing with deer**

If deer in your area are proving themselves to be garden pests, you'll find an effective control (probably in conjunction with a tall fence) to be bone tar oil, an odor-producing chemical. It is sold under various trade names. Follow the manufacturer's directions carefully for mixing and application.

It is best to make your first application before deer develop a habit of tasting your garden's offerings. Subsequent applications should be made monthly. If deer are already helping themselves at your smorgasbord, you may have to mix a solution stronger than normal.

**10. airborne attackers**

Not all attacks on your garden will come from enemy forces moving over the ground. You may find your tomatoes the target for airborne action from birds. Scare-type devices will work to keep birds away sometimes, but not always. Sticky repellents have been used along with plastic twirlers, cloth strips and other moving objects and are fairly effective for small areas. The best, most positive protection comes from netting that will completely enclose your crop.

Authorities say, however, that effective bird control depends on three prime factors:

1. Timing: Control measures should be started at the first indication of damage.

2. Persistence: As long as nature's air force attacks (grackles, starlings, blackbirds, cowbirds and sometimes even woodpeckers), your garden is vulnerable, so control measures should be used.

3. Diversification: No single method is always satisfactory: Various devices must be used in combination and their placement frequently shifted.

# METRIC CONVERSION

Conversion factors can be carried so far they become impractical. In cases below where an entry is exact it is followed by an asterisk (*). Where considerable rounding off has taken place, the entry is followed by a + or a - sign.

## CUSTOMARY TO METRIC

### Linear Measure

| inches | millimeters |
|---|---|
| 1/16 | 1.5875* |
| 1/8 | 3.2 |
| 3/16 | 4.8 |
| 1/4 | 6.35* |
| 5/16 | 7.9 |
| 3/8 | 9.5 |
| 7/16 | 11.1 |
| 1/2 | 12.7* |
| 9/16 | 14.3 |
| 5/8 | 15.9 |
| 11/16 | 17.5 |
| 3/4 | 19.05* |
| 13/16 | 20.6 |
| 7/8 | 22.2 |
| 15/16 | 23.8 |
| 1 | 25.4* |

| inches | centimeters |
|---|---|
| 1 | 2.54* |
| 2 | 5.1 |
| 3 | 7.6 |
| 4 | 10.2 |
| 5 | 12.7* |
| 6 | 15.2 |
| 7 | 17.8 |
| 8 | 20.3 |
| 9 | 22.9 |
| 10 | 25.4* |
| 11 | 27.9 |
| 12 | 30.5 |

| feet | centimeters | meters |
|---|---|---|
| 1 | 30.48* | .3048* |
| 2 | 61 | .61 |
| 3 | 91 | .91 |
| 4 | 122 | 1.22 |
| 5 | 152 | 1.52 |
| 6 | 183 | 1.83 |
| 7 | 213 | 2.13 |
| 8 | 244 | 2.44 |
| 9 | 274 | 2.74 |
| 10 | 305 | 3.05 |
| 50 | 1524* | 15.24* |
| 100 | 3048* | 30.48* |

1 yard = .9144* meters
1 rod = 5.0292* meters
1 mile = 1.6 kilometers
1 nautical mile = 1.852* kilometers

### Fluid Measure

(Milliliters [ml] and cubic centimeters [cc or cu cm] are equivalent, but it is customary to use milliliters for liquids.)

1 cu in = 16.39 ml
1 fl oz = 29.6 ml
1 cup = 237 ml
1 pint = 473 ml
1 quart = 946 ml
= .946 liters
1 gallon = 3785 ml
= 3.785 liters
Formula (exact):
fluid ounces × 29.573 529 562 5* = milliliters

### Weights

| ounces | grams |
|---|---|
| 1 | 28.3 |
| 2 | 56.7 |
| 3 | 85 |
| 4 | 113 |
| 5 | 142 |
| 6 | 170 |
| 7 | 198 |
| 8 | 227 |
| 9 | 255 |
| 10 | 283 |
| 11 | 312 |
| 12 | 340 |
| 13 | 369 |
| 14 | 397 |
| 15 | 425 |
| 16 | 454 |

Formula (exact):
ounces × 28.349 523 125* = grams

| pounds | kilograms |
|---|---|
| 1 | .45 |
| 2 | .9 |
| 3 | 1.4 |
| 4 | 1.8 |
| 5 | 2.3 |
| 6 | 2.7 |
| 7 | 3.2 |
| 8 | 3.6 |
| 9 | 4.1 |
| 10 | 4.5 |

1 short ton (2000 lbs) = 907 kilograms (kg)
Formula (exact):
pounds × .453 592 37* = kilograms

### Volume

1 cu in = 16.39 cubic centimeters (cc)
1 cu ft = 28 316.7 cc
1 bushel = 35 239.1 cc
1 peck = 8 809.8 cc

### Area

1 sq in = 6.45 sq cm
1 sq ft = 929 sq cm
= .093 sq meters
1 sq yd = .84 sq meters
1 acre = 4 046.9 sq meters
= .404 7 hectares
1 sq mile = 2 589 988 sq meters
= 259 hectares
= 2.589 9 sq kilometers

### Kitchen Measure

1 teaspoon = 4.93 milliliters (ml)
1 Tablespoon = 14.79 milliliters (ml)

### Miscellaneous

1 British thermal unit (Btu) (mean) = 1 055.9 joules
1 calorie (mean) = 4.19 joules
1 horsepower = 745.7 watts
= .75 kilowatts
caliber (diameter of a firearm's bore in hundredths of an inch) = .254 millimeters (mm)
1 atmosphere pressure = 101 325* pascals (newtons per sq meter)
1 pound per square inch (psi) = 6 895 pascals
1 pound per square foot = 47.9 pascals
1 knot = 1.85 kilometers per hour
25 miles per hour = 40.2 kilometers per hour
50 miles per hour = 80.5 kilometers per hour
75 miles per hour = 120.7 kilometers per hour